Western liberal tradition. To be
free, we must be self-governing;
have rights we must be citizens. Th
argument for strong democracy,
though critical of liberalism, is thus
an argument on behalf of liberty.

Benjamin Barber is Professor of
Political Science at Rutgers Univer-
sity. His books include *Marriage
Voices* (a novel), 1981, *The Artist
and Political Vision* (edited with
M. J. McGrath), 1981, *Liberating
Feminism*, 1975, *The Death of
Communal Liberty*, 1974, *Super-
men and Common Men*, 1971, and
Totalitarianism in Perspective
(with C. J. Friedrich and M. Curtis),
1969.

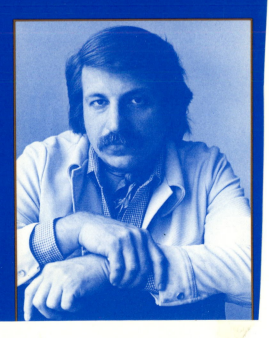

Strong Democracy

STRONG DEMOCRACY

*Participatory Politics
for a New Age*

BENJAMIN R. BARBER

UNIVERSITY OF CALIFORNIA PRESS
BERKELEY   LOS ANGELES   LONDON

University of California Press
Berkeley and Los Angeles, California

University of California Press, Ltd.
London, England

© 1984 by The Regents of the University of California

Library of Congress Cataloging in Publication Data
Barber, Benjamin R., 1939–
    Strong democracy.

    Includes index.
    1. Democracy.   2. Liberalism.   3. Citizenship.
4. Community.   5. Political participation.   I. Title.
JC423.B243 1984   321.8   83–4842
ISBN 0–520–05115–7

Printed in the United States of America
1   2   3   4   5   6   7   8   9

To Jeremy and to Rebecca—
to all the children, soon grown,
for whom democracy is a last, best hope.

Contents

Acknowledgments

This book was begun under a grant from the Council for the International Exchange of Scholars (the Fulbright Council) and completed under a fellowship from the John Simon Guggenheim Foundation; it could not have been completed without the generosity of these two institutions. Essex University provided hospitality for the initial period of research in 1976–77, and the New York Institute for the Humanities offered me a home during the second period in 1980–81. I am particularly grateful to Jean Blondel of Essex, to Gordan Ray of the Guggenheim Foundation, and to Richard Sennett and Ayreh Neier of the New York Institute.

The Rutgers University Research Council made available timely grants that enabled me to attend international congresses where I had a chance to air the themes of the book before a wide critical audience—in Berlin in 1977, Moscow in 1979, and Rio de Janeiro in 1982. I have also presented parts of the project over the years to the Columbia Seminar for Social and Political Thought, to the Philosophy Colloquium of Princeton University, and to colleagues and students at Wesleyan University, Loyola University of Chicago, Kenyon College, Colorado College, the University of Denver, the University of Massachusetts, Johns Hopkins University, Balliol College (Oxford), the London School of Economics and Political Science, Hebrew University of Jerusalem, and Yale Law School. For helping me to arrange these visits, I am grateful to Sheldon Wolin, Donald Moon, James Wiser, Robert Horwitz, Tim Fuller, Alan Gilbert, William Connolly, Richard Flathman, John Pocock, William Weinstein, Fred Rosen, Owen Fiss, and Bruce Ackerman.

I have also benefited from readings of the manuscript, in part or as a whole, by Richard Flathman, Alan Gilbert, Maurice Robin, Michael Greven, Thomas Horne, Andreas Teuber, George Kelly, and—with special care—Judith N. Shklar, who has been a source of supportive criticism since my days in graduate school. These colleagues were unable to deter me from my greater follies, but they argued diligently to save me from my lesser ones.

My graduate students at Rutgers have over the years indulged me in various versions of my argument, and to them I owe a special debt. Jacqueline Bittner undertook bibliographical research and prepared the index; she has my particular thanks. John Samples did extensive and detailed research for Chapter 10, and Richard Battistoni gave me the benefit of his work on voucher education schemes. Along with Jiman Taghavi, Laura Greyson, Bruce Smith, Charles McMillion, Bruce Tuttle, and Edward McLean, Samples and Battistoni wrote dissertations under my direction from which I profited greatly. So it is that students end up teaching teachers.

The faith in human promise that is the guiding prejudice of this book is largely a reflection of the two children to whom it is dedicated: Jeremy and Rebecca. In more ways than they can know, this is their book.

Preface

We suffer, in the face of our era's manifold crises, not from too much but from too little democracy. This Jeffersonian conviction lies at the heart of the argument that unfolds here. From the time of de Tocqueville, it has been said that an excess of democracy can undo liberal institutions. I will try to show that an excess of liberalism has undone democratic institutions: for what little democracy we have had in the West has been repeatedly compromised by the liberal institutions with which it has been undergirded and the liberal philosophy from which its theory and practice have been derived.

In implicating liberalism in the insufficiencies of democracy, I do not mean to attack liberalism. There is little wrong with liberal institutions that a strong dose of political participation and reactivated citizenship cannot cure. In pointing to liberal philosophy as a source of democratic weakness, I do not mean to attack philosophy. I wish only to endorse Saul Bellow's observation that "history and politics are not at all like the notions developed by intelligent, informed people."[1] Liberal philosophy has attracted a great many intelligent, informed people to its ranks; their work has yielded powerful notions of right, freedom, and justice—notions so coherent and well-grounded in philosophy as to be untainted by the political world in which men are condemned to live.[2]

1. Saul Bellow, *To Jerusalem and Back* (New York: Viking, 1976), p. 8.
2. Like every modern writer, I have been torn by the requirements of gender-blind usage and the requirements of style, particularly in a field dominated by the language

Unlike many of the books written by these intelligent metaphysicians of the political, this study does not address problems of truth or justice or the antecedents of politics in nature or science. I begin rather with Graham Greene's belief that in the realm of human relations "Truth . . . has never been of any real value to any human being—it is a symbol for mathematicians and philosophers to pursue."[3] Democratic politics is a form of human relations, and does not answer to the requirements of truth. My task in this book has been to try to find an approach to democracy suitable to human relations rather than to truth. I have been much helped by the tradition of American pragmatism. It is an oddity of American political thinking that it has turned to English and Continental modes of thought to ground a political experience notable for its radical break with the English and Continental ways of doing politics; at the same time it has neglected indigenous sources that have a natural affinity for the American way of doing politics—as anybody who reads Peirce or James or Dewey will recognize.

The English-inflected language of liberalism has left the rhetoric of democracy pallid and unaffecting; I hope to restore and revivify not so much the rhetoric as the practice of democracy—which, however, turns out to be in part a matter of the language and the rhetoric. As will become evident, the crisis of liberal democracy is very much a crisis in language and theory.

That there is a crisis probably does not require demonstration. Crisis has become the tedious cliché with which we flaunt our hard-pressed modernity. From the very inception of the idea of modernity, we have portrayed ourselves in the vivid terms of crisis: the crisis of the modern state, the crisis of liberal institutions, the crisis of leadership, the crisis of party government, and the crisis of democracy. These phrases seem so banal only because the realities to which they point are so familiar.

The crisis in liberal democracy is expressed most pungently in the claim that the world has become "ungovernable," that no leader or party or constitutional system can cope with the welter of problems

---

of "political man," "man's nature," and "mankind." Although I have tried where possible to refer to women and men or to use neutral terms such as "humankind" or "persons," I have frequently reverted to traditional usage and simply written "man" or "men." I hope readers will understand that I intend a generic meaning even where I use masculine terms and that the political equality of women and men is an unstated premise throughout my book.

3. Graham Greene, *The Heart of the Matter* (London: Pelican Books, 1948), p. 58.

that afflict large-scale industrial societies. Like Mary Shelley's good Dr. Frankenstein, modern man has created an artificial world he cannot control. The modern monsters are machines, computers, bureaucracies, corporations, and constitutions; their monstrosity lies less in their wilfullness than in their emancipation from all will and purpose. If the world has become ungovernable, how can men be expected to govern themselves? How can they ask that their representatives govern them well? "Ungovernability" permits presidents who cannot govern to excuse themselves and presidents who will not govern to justify themselves.

If the leaders cannot govern, the people increasingly refuse to be governed. Alienation has become a central indicator of modern political crisis, whether it is measured by plummeting electoral participation figures, widespread distrust of politicians, or pervasive apathy about things public and political. Mean voter turnout in America since World War II hovers around 50 percent for presidential elections—lower than every other noncompulsory democracy in the West. In a country where voting is the primary expression of citizenship, the refusal to vote signals the bankruptcy of democracy.

Political scientists continue to hope that the crisis in participation is a function of party realignment of the kind that occurs in twenty- or thirty-year cycles in most democratic societies. But there is evidence that the party system is breaking down or breaking up, and that representative party democracy may be being replaced by dangerous new variants of neodemocracy—the politics of special interests, the politics of neopopulist fascism, the politics of image (via television and advertising), or the politics of mass society.[4]

As fewer and fewer Americans participate in public affairs, more and more public affairs are being relegated to the private sector. If politics can be redefined as the public airing of private interests, public goods can be redefined as private assets. Thus, soldiers are now "hired" on the private market, public lands are sold off into private hands to be maintained by charging the public for goods and services once deemed to belong to the public, and private "incentive" systems are used to get private corporations to live up to public

4. Political scientists such as Walter Dean Burnham who might once have subscribed to the realignment theory now take a much bleaker view; see Burnham, *The Current Crisis in American Politics* (New York: Oxford University Press, 1983). Others write skeptically about the autonomy of the federal bureaucracy from any form of genuine democratic control; see Eric A. Nordlinger, *On the Autonomy of the Democratic State* (Cambridge, Mass.: Harvard University Press, 1983).

responsibilities. This pervasive privatization of the *res publica* (things public) has deep roots in liberal thinking, although finally it corrupts even the most liberal and indirect forms of democracy. Indeed, it is a major theme of this book that cynicism about voting, political alienation, a preference for things private, and the growing paralysis of public institutions are more than the consequences of modernity. They are symptoms of a malaise that is inseparable from liberal ways of thinking about and doing politics. They are dark mirror images of liberalism's strengths. The major devices by which liberal theory contrives to guarantee liberty while securing democracy—representation, privacy, individualism, and rights, but above all representation—turn out neither to secure democracy nor to guarantee liberty. Representation destroys participation and citizenship even as it serves accountability and private rights. Representative democracy is as paradoxical an oxymoron as our political language has produced; its confused and failing practice make this ever more obvious.

The position I take here asserts that liberalism serves democracy badly if at all, and that the survival of democracy therefore depends on finding for it institutional forms that loosen its connection with liberal theory. Bluntly expressed, my claim is that strong democracy is the only viable form modern democratic politics can take, and that unless it takes a participatory form, democracy will pass from the political scene along with the liberal values it makes possible.

Liberal democracy was, to be sure, an attempt to adapt pure democracy to the realities of governing in a large-scale nation state. Pure democracy suggested a form of government in which all of the people governed themselves in all public matters all of the time; such a form could hardly be expected to function efficiently in a nation of continental proportions with millions of citizens. Representative democracy therefore substituted for the pure principle a definition of democracy as a form of government in which some of the people, chosen by all, govern in all public matters all of the time. This approach purchased efficiency without sacrificing accountability, but it did so at an enormous cost to participation and to citizenship. Strong democracy tries to revitalize citizenship without neglecting the problems of efficient government by defining democracy as a form of government in which all of the people govern themselves in at least some public matters at least some of the time. To legislate and to implement laws at least some of the time is to keep alive the meaning and function of citizenship in all of us all of the time; whereas to delegate the governing power, even if only to representatives who remain bound to us by the vote, is to give away not power but civic activity, not accountability but civic responsibility, not our secondary rights against government but our primary right to govern. If democracy entails the right to govern ourselves rather than to be governed in accordance with our interests, then liberal democratic institutions fall short of being democratic.

In reading Hobbes, Locke, and the American founders and in trying to live as citizens in the institutions fashioned from their ideas, we have persuaded ourselves that democracy is a vital means to other, prior human ends; that liberty, equality, justice, and human rights have a natural existence; and that our governing institutions gain their legitimacy only insofar as they serve these values. But democracy understood as self-government in a social setting is not a terminus for individually held rights and values; it is their starting place. Autonomy is not the condition of democracy, democracy is the condition of autonomy. Without participating in the common life that defines them and in the decision-making that shapes their social habitat, women and men cannot become individuals. Freedom, justice, equality, and autonomy are all products of common thinking and common living; democracy creates them. Jefferson observed that the origin of property from nature was "a moot question" since "stable ownership is the gift of social law, and is given late in the progress of society."[5]

Our most deeply cherished values are all gifts of law and of the politics that make law possible. We are born in chains—slaves of dependency and insufficiency—and acquire autonomy only as we learn the difficult art of governing ourselves in common; we are born inferior or superior as measured by natural endowment or hereditary status; we acquire equality only in the context of socially sanctioned political arrangements that spread across naturally unequal beings a civic mantle of artificial equality. The rights we often affect to hurl impudently into the face of government are rights we enjoy only by virtue of government. The private sphere we guard so jealously from the encroachments of the public sector exists entirely by dint of law, which is the public sector's most significant creation.

The rights we claim title to and the values we live by are, then,

5. Thomas Jefferson, *Writings*, cited in R. Schlatter, *Private Property* (New Brunswick, N.J.: Rugters University Press, 1951), p. 198.

legitimate only as the politics from which they issue is legitimate. My argument here is that strong democracy is the only fully legitimate form of politics; as such, it constitutes the condition for the survival of all that is most dear to us in the Western liberal tradition. To be free we must be self-governing; to have rights we must be citizens. In the end, only citizens can be free. The argument for strong democracy, though at times deeply critical of liberalism, is thus an argument on behalf of liberty.

The problem of human freedom is hardly peculiar to America alone. Yet America has always carried a special responsibility for freedom in the West—a last best hope of our civilization's democratic aspirations. Consequently, I will perhaps be forgiven for dwelling on the American system of government and using its democratic politics as an archetype for the benefits and the ills of the liberal tradition. To restore democracy to America—or to create it where it has never existed—is a cosmopolitan project even if it is constrained by American parochialism. When Langston Hughes pleads for liberty in his impassioned poem "Let America Be America Again," he pleads on behalf of the human race:

> I am the poor white, fooled and pushed apart,
> I am the Negro bearing slavery's scars.
> I am the red man driven from the land.
> I am the immigrant clutching the hope I seek—
> And finding only the same old stupid plan
> Of dog eat dog, of mighty crush the weak.
>
> O, let America be America again—
> The land that never has been yet—
> And yet must be—the land where everyone is free.
> The land that's mine—the poor man's, Indian's
>   Negro's, ME—

There is one road to freedom: it lies through democracy. The last best hope now, as two hundred years ago, is that America can be America: truly self-governing and democratic, thus truly free.

Stockbridge, Massachusetts
August 1983

I know of no safe depository of the ultimate power of the society but the people themselves, and if we think them not enlightened enough to exercise their control with a wholesome discretion, the remedy is not to take it from them, but to inform their discretion.

(Thomas Jefferson)

I

Thin Democracy:
The Argument against Liberalism

Chapter One

Thin Democracy:
Politics as Zookeeping

*[One must not] think that Men are so
foolish that they take care to avoid what
Mischiefs may be done them by Pole-
Cats, or Foxes, but are content, nay think
it Safety, to be devoured by Lions.*

(John Locke)

*. . . democracy has a more compelling
justification and requires a more realistic
vindication than is given it by the liberal
culture with which it has been associated
in modern history.*

(Reinhold Niebuhr)

Liberal democracy has been one of the sturdiest political systems in
the history of the modern West. As the dominant modern form of
democracy, it has informed and guided several of the most successful and enduring governments the world has known, not least
among them that of the United States.

Liberal democracy has in fact become such a powerful model that
sometimes, in the Western world at least, the very future of democracy seems to depend entirely on its fortunes and thus on the American system of government and its supporting liberal culture. This
perceived monopoly not only limits the alternatives apparent to
those seeking other legitimate forms of politics but leaves Americans themselves with no standard against which to measure their
own liberal politics and with no ideal by which to modify them,
should they wish to do so.

Furthermore, successful as it has been, liberal democracy has not
always been able to resist its major twentieth-century adversaries:
the illegitimate politics of fascism and Stalinism or of military dicta-

torship and totalism. Nor has it been able to cope effectively with its own internal weaknesses and contradictions, many of which grow more intractable as the American system ages and as its internal contradictions gradually emerge (a process discussed in Chapter 5).

It is the central argument of the first part of this book that many of these problems stem from the political theory of liberal democracy itself. Liberal democracy is based on premises about human nature, knowledge, and politics that are genuinely liberal but that are not intrinsically democratic. Its conception of the individual and of individual interest undermines the democratic practices upon which both individuals and their interests depend.

Liberal democracy is thus a "thin" theory of democracy, one whose democratic values are prudential and thus provisional, optional, and conditional—means to exclusively individualistic and private ends. From this precarious foundation, no firm theory of citizenship, participation, public goods, or civic virtue can be expected to arise. Liberal democracy, therefore, can never lead too far from Ambrose Bierce's cynical definition of politics as "the conduct of public affairs for private advantage." It can never rise far above the provisional and private prudence expressed in John Locke's explanation that men consent to live under government only for "the mutual preservation of their lives, liberties and estates." And it can never evade the irony of Winston Churchill's portrait of democracy as "the worst form of government in the world, except for all the other forms." A democracy that can be defended only by mordant skepticism may find it difficult to combat the zealotry of nondemocrats.

In fact, Churchill's remark suggests that liberal democracy may not be a theory of political community at all. It does not so much provide a justification for politics as it offers a politics that justifies individual rights. It is concerned more to promote individual liberty than to secure public justice, to advance interests rather than to discover goods, and to keep men safely apart rather than to bring them fruitfully together. As a consequence, it is capable of fiercely resisting every assault on the individual—his privacy, his property, his interests, and his rights—but is far less effective in resisting assaults on community or justice or citizenship or participation. Ultimately, this vulnerability undermines its defense of the individual; for the individual's freedom is not the precondition for political activity but rather the product of it.

This is not to say that there is anything simple about liberal democracy. It is an exotic, complex, and frequently paradoxical form of politics. It comprises at least three dominant *dispositions*, each of which entails a quite distinctive set of attitudes, inclinations, and political values. The three dispositions can be conveniently called *anarchist*, *realist*, and *minimalist*. Although actual democratic regimes usually combine traits of all three dispositions, the individual dispositions are evident in particular theories of liberal democracy. Thus in his *Anarchy, State, and Utopia*, Robert Nozick tries to move from anarchist to minimalist arguments without violating the belief in individual rights that underlies both dispositions. A more complex democratic liberal, Bertrand Russell, managed in the course of his long career to experiment with each of the three dispositions. His early works were tinged with anarchism, his mature works informed by realism, and his late works touched by minimalism. Russell's espousal of classical liberalism and of social-contract theory moved him easily from an anarchist defense of the sanctity of individual rights to the realist conclusion that a sovereign was needed to guarantee those rights to minimalist addenda intended to circumscribe the powers of the sovereign.

The American political system is a remarkable example of the coexistence—sometimes harmonious, more often uncomfortable—of all three dispositions. Americans, we might say, are anarchists in their values (privacy, liberty, individualism, property, and rights); realists in their means (power, law, coercive mediation, and sovereign adjudication); and minimalists in their political temper (tolerance, wariness of government, pluralism, and such institutionalizations of caution as the separation of powers and judicial review).

The anarchist, realist, and minimalist dispositions can all be regarded as political responses to *conflict*, which is the fundamental condition of all liberal democratic politics. Autonomous individuals occupying private and separate spaces are the players in the game of liberal politics; conflict is their characteristic mode of interaction. Whether he perceives conflict as a function of scarce resources (as do Hobbes and Marx), of insatiable appetites (as do Russell and Freud), or of a natural lust for power and glory (as does Machiavelli), the liberal democrat places it at the center of human interaction and makes it the chief concern of politics.

While the three dispositions may share a belief in the primacy of conflict, they suggest radically different approaches to its amelioration. Put very briefly, anarchism is *conflict-denying*, realism is *conflict-repressing*, and minimalism is *conflict-tolerating*. The first approach tries to wish conflict away, the second to extirpate it, and the third to live with it. Liberal democracy, the compound and real American form, is conflict-denying in its free-market assumptions about the private sector and its supposed elasticity and egalitarianism; it is conflict-repressing and also conflict-adjusting in its prudential uses of political power to adjudicate the struggle of individuals and groups; and it is conflict-tolerating in its characteristic liberal-skeptical temper.

In considering these three individual dispositions more closely, then, we must not forget that they are in fact contradictory impulses acting within a single political tradition rather than independent philosophies belonging to distinct political systems.

THE ANARCHIST DISPOSITION IN LIBERAL DEMOCRACY

Anarchism as a disposition may be understood as the nonpolitics or the antipolitics of liberal democracy. It disposes women and men to regard themselves as generically autonomous beings with needs and wants that can (at least in the abstract) be satisfied outside of coercive civil communities. From this viewpoint, conflict is a problem created by political interaction rather than the condition that gives rise to politics. Wedded to an absolutist conception of individual rights, this disposition is implacably hostile to political power—and above all to democratic political power, which because it is more "legitimate" is less resistible.

The anarchist disposition figures most clearly in the liberal democratic account of the ends of politics. These are always circumscribed by the individual and his autonomy. In this view freedom is the absence of external (hence, of political) constraints on individual action; the natural condition of the individual is independence and solitude; and human beings are by definition autonomous, separate, and free agents. The basic classics of the American tradition are rich with this quasi-anarchist individualist imagery. Thomas Hobbes may have become the philosopher of indivisible sovereign power, but he was persuaded that "the final cause, end design of men who naturally love liberty [in entering civil society] is the foresight of their own preservation."[1] John Locke argued with equal force that "the great and chief end therefore of men uniting into commonwealths and putting themselves under government . . . is the mutual preservation of their lives, liberties and estates, which I call by the general name property."[2] And the revolutionary secessionists who founded the American Republic thought it "self-evident" that "all men are created equal, that they are endowed by their Creator with certain unalienable Rights, that among these are Life, Liberty and the pursuit of Happiness." Only after these radically individualist premises, vibrant with the colonial American's distrust of all government, had been laid out and justified could the prudential edifice of government, instituted solely "to secure these rights," be raised.

Thomas Carlyle captured the anarchist disposition of liberal democracy perfectly when he dismissed utilitarian liberalism as "anarchy plus a constable." The liberal democrat may acknowledge the presence and even the possible usefulness of power, but he continues pertinaciously to distrust it. John Stuart Mill's caution that all restraint, qua restraint, is an evil permeates liberal political theory and disposes it to regard politics less as the art of using power than as the art of controlling and containing power. Robert Dahl can thus portray democratic theory as "at a minimum . . . concerned with processes by which ordinary citizens exert a relatively high degree of control over leaders."[3] And David Easton can define democracy itself as "a political system in which power is so distributed that control over the authoritative allocation of values lies in the hands of the mass of people."[4]

It is not surprising that liberals, who regard political community as an instrumental rather than an intrinsic good, should hold the idea of participation in disdain. The aim is not to share in power or to be part of a community but to contain power and community and to judge them by how they affect freedom and private interest. Indeed, as Carole Pateman has noticed, "not only has [participation] a minimal role, but a prominent feature of recent theories of democ-

1. Thomas Hobbes, *The Leviathan*, part 2, chap. 17.
2. John Locke, *The Second Treatise of Civil Government*, chap. 9, par. 124.
3. Robert Dahl, *A Preface to Democratic Theory* (Chicago: University of Chicago Press, 1956), p. 3.
4. David Easton, *The Political System* (New York: Knopf, 1953), p. 222.

racy is the emphasis placed on the dangers inherent in wide popular participation in politics."[5]

Participation, after all, enhances the power of communities and endows them with a moral force that nonparticipatory rulership rarely achieves. Moreover, in enhancing the power of communities, participation enlarges their scope of action. An extensive and relatively ancient literature is devoted to the defense of politics against too much democracy and to the defense of democracy against too much participation. Every critique of majoritarianism, every critique of public opinion, every critique of mass politics conceals a deep distrust of popular participation. Mill, Tocqueville, Ortega y Gassett, and Walter Lippmann are liberals whose commitment to liberty pushes them toward democracy but whose distrust of participation inclines them to favor a government of minimal scope. Their fear of majorities can easily be compared to Proudhon's indictment of universal suffrage as the counterrevolution or to Godwin's warning (in *Political Justice*) that "the Voice of the People is not . . . the voice of Truth and God" and that "consent cannot turn wrong into right."[6]

By the same token, liberal democrats have little sympathy for the civic ideal that treats human beings as inherently political. Citizenship is an artificial role that the natural man prudently adopts in order to safeguard his solitary humanity. That is to say, we are political in order to safeguard ourselves as men, but never men by virtue of being political (as Aristotle and the ancients would have had it).

It is little wonder, then, that liberal democracy is thin democracy. Individualists may find solace in Mill's celebrated caution "that the

5. Carole Pateman, *Participation and Democratic Theory* (Cambridge: Cambridge University Press, 1970), p. 1. An example of this distrust of participation is the question posed by B. R. Berelson, P. F. Lazarsfeld, and W. N. McPhee in their classical study, *Voting* (Chicago: University of Chicago Press, 1954): "How could a mass democracy work if all the people were deeply involved in politics?" (p. 312). Or see the more recent portrait of democracy offered by Thomas R. Dye and L. Harmon Ziegler (*The Irony of Democracy* [North Scituate, Mass.: Duxbury Press, 1975]):

Democracy is government by the people, but the responsibility for the survival of democracy rests on the shoulders of elites. . . . if the survival of the American system depended upon an active, informed, and enlightened citizenry, then democracy in America would have disappeared long ago; for the masses of Americans are apathetic and ill-informed about politics and public policy, and they have a surprisingly weak commitment to democratic values. . . . but fortunately for these values and for American democracy, the American masses do not lead, they follow. (p. 18)

6. William Godwin, *An Enquiry Concerning Political Justice* (Philadelphia, 1796), vol. 2, book 8, chap. 6.

sole end for which mankind are warranted, individually or collectively, in interfering with the liberty of action of any of their number, is self-protection."[7] But caution provides no affirmation of public values, public thinking, or public action, and it makes the democratic forms of public life seem provisional and thus dispensable. If they are only tools of individualism, democratic forms may be supplanted by such competing instrumentalities as benevolent despotism or rational aristocracy—or, for that matter, by the anarchic state of nature whose laws and rights underlie each of liberal democracy's claims to legitimacy and to which social-contract theorists revert as a remedy for illegitimacy.

One can note revealing differences between anarchism as practiced in Europe and the anarchist disposition in America. In Europe, anarchism has most often been espoused by radicals and revolutionaries outside of the political system, by outcasts bent on overthrowing particular governments or the very idea of government. It has been an ideological sanctuary for rebels and aliens, for the driven as well as the desperate.

But in America anarchism has been a disposition of the system itself, a tendency that has in fact guided statesmen and citizens more compulsively than it has motivated dissidents and revolutionaries. It has been incorporated into popular political practice and has become an integral feature of the political heritage. Wherever privacy, freedom, and the absolute rights of the individual are championed, there the anarchist disposition is at work. Wherever free markets are regarded as promoting equality and statist regulation is decried as coercive and illegitimate, there the anarchist disposition can be felt. Libertarian conservatives who denounce big government and right-of-center liberals who denigrate the "democratic distemper" share the anarchist's antipathy to the claims of democratic community.

The political philosophy that issues from such quasi-anarchist ideals as liberty, independence, individual self-sufficiency, the free market, and privacy is encapsulated in the slogan "that government is best which governs least." The government which governs least is of course the government that does not govern at all; the only good state is the state that "withers away" (the liberal Marx also had an anarchist inclination). Given the painful necessity for *some* government, the doctrine of "least is best" finds expression in constitutional safeguards and barriers that limit both the power of rulers

7. John Stuart Mill, *On Liberty* (London: Dent, 1910), p. 73.

and the scope of rulership. Following Hobbes's principle that the greatest liberty is found "where the laws are silent," most liberal constitutions ultimately limit government to specifically delegated powers, reserving all other powers (in the language of the tenth amendment to the American Constitution) to the several states and the people. That the national state bears the burden of proving its right to exercise a power is a crucial indication of liberal democracy's roots in individualist and anarchist thinking.

Liberals of the anarchist disposition are forever trying to solve the classical liberal problem: how can we shape (in Rousseau's model formulation) "a form of association which will defend and protect with the whole common force the person and goods of each associate, and in which each, while uniting himself with all, may still obey himself alone, and remain as free as before"?[8] But for these liberals, the crucial stipulation is that men "remain as free as before," because to them the preservation of their prior freedom is the sole warrant for political association in the first place. Rousseau himself was no anarchist (his romantic reputation notwithstanding), and he chose to resolve the tension by redefining natural freedom as civic and moral freedom and by using obedience to self as the key to solving the puzzle.[9] Liberal democrats, by contrast, are wedded to natural or negative freedom; they can conceive of no solution other than to limit or eliminate all government. Because for them freedom and state power are mutually exclusive, the puzzle is insoluble.

This stance helps to explain why liberal democrats often seem so obtuse about power and conflict in the "natural market." Having stipulated that "nature" means "free" and that "community" means "coercion," they can hardly entertain the possibility that community may support certain kinds of freedom or that nature may nourish forms of coercion and conflict more insidious than those known to democratic politics. The modern liberal railing against big government while holding up the private sector as a model of equal competition and private liberty is doing no more than updating the wishful conceits of early social-contract theory.

Thus it is the anarchist disposition more than any other that leaves

8. Jean-Jacques Rousseau, *The Social Contract*, book 1, chap. 6.
9. Thus Rousseau writes, "what man loses by the social contract is his natural liberty . . . ; what he gains is civil liberty . . . which is limited by the General Will" (ibid., book 1, chap. 8). This formulation actually violates the terms of the problem, since men do not "remain as free as before" but exchange one kind of liberty for another.

liberal democracy so incomplete, so polarized, so thin as political theory and so vulnerable as political practice. Of course realism and minimalism, which we will discuss presently, seek to correct these tendencies. But these influences have not made liberalism very much more sophisticated about power in the private sphere, or more alert to the creative potential of democratic politics, or more sensitive to the social impulses of human nature, or more aware of the capacity of civil community for transformation, emancipation, and justice. The anarchist disposition has stood as a sentinel against public forms of tyranny, and for this we must be grateful. But it has also stood as a stubborn obstacle to the public forms of community and justice, and this recalcitrance must be the occasion of lasting regret.

THE REALIST DISPOSITION IN LIBERAL DEMOCRACY

The disposition that inclines liberal democracy toward individualist ends and the ideal of liberty obviously has competitors. No one would accuse Americans of misunderstanding the importance and the uses of political power in the political arena. After all, it is the use of power in the pursuit of private interests that alone justifies government for the liberal. Realism, in the American context, has entailed a concern for power but also a preoccupation with law (legalism) and with sovereignty understood as will (positivism).

Realism is in its genesis little more than an extension of anarchist premises into the political realm: politics offers a joint guarantee of private interest and a public warrant for the private weal. Yet it introduces a set of attitudes that are quite foreign to the anarchist disposition. Politics for the realist becomes the art of power—to whatever ends it is exercised. And in the wake of power come fear, manipulation, enforcement, deterrence, incentive, sanction, and those other artifacts of the more coercive side of human relations.

To be sure, there is a traditional liberal argument that links anarchism to realism. In Hobbes's account, the natural world of free and equal individuals pursuing their natural interests is self-defeating: among competing individuals, none can be satisfied. One man's freedom is the next man's bondage; man's natural right to power, when exercised by some, can enslave others. Nor is succor to be found in pacts of mutual respect, in contracts promising self-restraint, or in covenants pledging obedience to the prudential rules of enlightened self-interest (Hobbes's "Laws of Nature"). Without collective power and sovereign enforcement—without "the sword"—covenants are but words and guarantee no security at all. And so, ironically, man's love of natural liberty compels him to forsake it and to live by the law, not for its own sake but for its effect on others. What reason and good faith, what charity and altruism cannot achieve, fear and the passions on which fear plays can secure with ease.

Machiavelli is sometimes scorned for the perfidiousness of his morals, but he advanced a perfectly good protoliberal logic when he reasoned "it is better to be feared than loved . . . for love is held by a chain of obligation which, men being selfish, is broken whenever it serves their purpose; but fear is maintained by a dread of punishment that never fails."[10] Men may place themselves under government out of enlightened self-interest (so that others may be constrained), but they themselves obey it solely from fear (the dread of punishment).

What the realists discovered, with Machiavelli, is that fear is self-interest's secret social servant. It is the sole motive that can prompt hedonists to honor the needs and rights of others. Edmund Burke was later to claim that terror was the final redoubt of radical liberalism—the gallows at the end of the groves of Enlightenment philosophy—but it was Hobbes himself who first introduced the imagery of fear: "for the laws of nature, as justice, equity, modesty, mercy . . . of themselves, without the terror of some power, to cause them to be observed, are contrary to our natural passions, that carry us to partiality, pride, revenge, and the like."[11]

In the course of this logical transition from liberty to obedience, a rather more unsettling psychological transformation takes place. The simple-minded impulsiveness of natural need is supplanted by a more complex, artificial calculation that seeks to control the world of necessity by understanding and then by exploiting its laws. The Baconian ideal of knowledge as power pervaded the liberal model of natural man and produced a new species of man and a new form of behavior. It brought forth man the artificer who could create the conditions for his material self's gratification; man the manipulator, relying on fear to preserve liberty; and man the social scientist, playing with the external world of social stimulus the better to govern

10. Machiavelli, *The Prince*, chap. 17 (Modern Library edition, 1950), p. 73.
11. Hobbes, *Leviathan*, book 2, chap. 17.

the internal world of human response. Hedonism is twisted into socially acceptable behavior by political coercion and legal sanctions. The state of nature yields to the sovereign sword; the sovereign sword is wielded as law and judicial sanction; and in the end the logic of liberty is replaced by the felicific calculus, which serves manipulated needs but ignores a freedom that is no longer thought to exist. The road from anarchism to realism, though smooth at every turning, nonetheless leads in this fashion from an extreme idea of abstract freedom to an extreme idea of abstract power.

Western liberal democracy today relies heavily on realist politics. Legislatures and courts alike deploy penal sanctions and juridical incentives aimed at controlling behavior by manipulating—but not altering or transforming—hedonistic self-interest. People are not made to reformulate private interests in public terms but are encouraged to reformulate public goods in terms of private advantage. A president who wishes to induce the public to conserve energy thus proposes a series of dog-biscuit laws, reward-and-punishment sanctions, and carrot-and-stick incentives. These do nothing to create a sense of genuine public interest or to engender affirmative community action in the name of common goals. Quite the contrary, they reaffirm the primacy of privatism by making justice a matter of personal profit. Barry Commoner has elaborated on this inversion of values with devastating insight in *The Politics of Energy*.[12]

Yet although prudence promotes power as a defender of private liberty, the politics and psychology of power place it at an ever greater remove from the liberty whose preservation is its justification. Thus, Hobbes's conception of power as relational, as a prudential "present means to some future ends," becomes in a very short time the much grimmer conception of power as substantive, as an end in itself that leads men to thirst in a vain quest "for power after power . . . that ceaseth only in death." In the same manner, the tolerance with which America's founders greeted power as a tool of national government was soon supplanted by a deep anxiety about power as an essence closely tied to man's basest instincts. "Power," warned John Adams, "naturally grows . . . because human passions are insatiable."[13] Such anxieties were to be exacerbated by the

12. See also Barry Commoner, *The Poverty of Power: Energy and the Economic Crisis* (New York: Bantam, 1976).

13. John Adams, cited in Richard Hofstadter, *The American Political Tradition* (1948; reprint, New York: Vintage, 1973), p. 3.

work of Darwin and Freud and by twentieth-century ideologies of nationalism and "totalitarianism," which, although they were spurned by liberal democrats, nonetheless seemed proof of the dangers of realism as a liberal democratic disposition. So for Bertrand Russell, "the laws of social dynamics are only capable of being stated in terms of power in its various forms."[14] And so for modern social scientists, the study of politics often becomes synonymous with the study of power.

The liberal democrat as realist does not, of course, wish to celebrate power; he means rather to use it in the service of individual purposes and rights, a role that establishes and legitimates it. The polecats and foxes who in brute nature plague one another with their competing lusts must be caged by laws, prodded by penalties, deterred by threats, kept ruly by rules, and made pliable with rewards. Market exchange among them must be regulated, agreements and contracts interpreted and enforced, liberties adjusted and balanced, and privacy delimited and secured. Individuals remain free, to a certain degree; but where their freedom ends, a kind of terror begins. For in the vision of the liberal democratic realist, it is difficult to conceive of any halfway house between absolute authority and absolute freedom, between complete coercion and complete license, between the terrors of government by fear and the anarchy of no government at all.

As a consequence, there is something profoundly schizophrenic about liberal democracy. Failing to acknowledge any middle ground, it often trades in contrasts, in polarities, in radical dichotomies and rigid dualisms: terror or anarchy, force or freedom, fear or love. Torn from within and divided against itself, liberal democracy sets its means against its ends. Its tools of liberation become instruments of subjugation, while its individualist objectives become the agents of social disorder and anomie.

From its beginnings in America, the chief dilemma of liberal democracy has been this war between liberty and power. Because each is defined by the absence of the other, they cannot be disentangled; because each jeopardizes the other, they cannot be made to coexist. How then to discover a form of power that will serve liberty, when power itself is liberty's chief nemesis? America has survived, it has thrived, because power has saved it from the anarchy that lurks in

14. Bertrand Russell, *On Power: A New Social Analysis* (London: Allen and Unwin, 1938), p. 13.

freedom, even as freedom saved it from the tyranny that lives in the heart of power. From the time of the Articles of Confederation, in each era, in each legislative act, in each political program, we see first a struggle against power on behalf of liberty and then a struggle against liberty, against privatism, against radical atomism on behalf of common goals and public goods that only power can obtain.

John Locke limned the dilemma in a brilliant and aptly bestial metaphor when he chastised Filmer and Hobbes for thinking men so foolish as "to avoid what Mischiefs may be done them by Pole-Cats or Foxes, but are content, nay think it Safety, to be devoured by Lions."[15] The liberal impresses into service a sovereign lion and thinks himself secure against his ravenous fellow-creatures, only to discover that the lion has appetites even more insatiable. The helpful Leviathan who is to domesticate the wild men of nature is a skulking monster capable of destroying his wards with the very powers vested in him to protect them. Refusing to share the anarchist's sweet, innocent dream of a natural world without conflict, the realist creates an artificial world of power so efficient in repressing conflict that it threatens to extirpate individuals along with their conflicts and liberty along with its licentious abuses.

THE MINIMALIST DISPOSITION IN LIBERAL DEMOCRACY

From this dilemma is born the justification for liberal democracy's third disposition: minimalism. The problem of minimalism is how to deal with the realist's sovereign power and with the reality of man's endless lust for dominion without having recourse to anarchy; i.e., how to cage the keepers? In the favorite formulation of earlier liberals, *quis custodiet custodes?*—who will guard the guardians? Resting precariously on attitudes of tolerance, skepticism, and wariness and convinced of the need both for power and for stringent limits on power, minimalism is disposed to understand politics neither as free-market relations nor as power relations. Rather, one might say, it sees politics as foreign relations: i.e., as relations among beings too dependent and too naturally competitive to live in peaceful solitude yet too distrustful to live easily in mutuality.

Hence, minimalism promotes a politics of toleration in which every interaction is hedged with temperance, every abdication of personal liberty is circumscribed by reservations, every grant of au-

15. Locke, *Second Treatise of Civil Government*, chap. 7, par. 93.

thority is hemmed in with guaranteed rights, and every surrender of privacy is safeguarded with limits.[16] Because conflict can neither be wished away by anarchist utopianism nor safely disposed of by the coercive authority advocated by the realists, it must be tolerated. The purpose of politics must be to invent or to reshape institutions, customs, and attitudes in a manner that will enable us to live with conflict and dissensus.

Yet because the minimalist distrusts both individuals (anarchy) and the state (power), he finds himself in a bind. He endorses Locke's instrumentalist argument that "power hath no other end but preservation [of life, liberty and estate]" and consequently believes that every coercive intervention by the state must have a justification. But he also understands that liberty contradicts itself, that it usurps the space of one man even as it extends the space of another.

The minimalist thus remonstrates with power in the language of toleration: "If all mankind minus one were of one opinion," he declares with John Stuart Mill, "and only one person were of the contrary opinion, mankind would be no more justified in silencing that one person, than he, if he had the power, would be justified in silencing mankind."[17] And if liberty can be safeguarded only when power is divided, contained, and moderated, the most dangerous power is the most authoritative—namely, the sovereign power of the majority.

It is from minimalism that liberal democracy derives its particular suspicion of majoritarianism, its hostility to the people and to their "impulsive" legislative tyranny. Tocqueville worried that in the United States "the majority . . . exercise a prodigious actual authority, and a power of opinion which is nearly as great; no obstacles exist which can impede or even retard its progress, so as to make it heed the complaints of those whom it crushes upon its path."[18] In a system where power is exercised in the name of the majority, John Stuart Mill asks, to whom can an individual who is wronged apply for redress?

16. Raoul Berger's most recent book restates the minimalist orthodoxy with characteristic force: "Respect for the limits of power is the essence of a democratic society; without it, the entire democratic structure is undermined, and the way is paved from Weimar to Hitler" (*Government by Judiciary* [Cambridge, Mass.: Harvard University Press, 1977], p. 410).

17. John Stuart Mill, *On Liberty*, p. 79.

18. Alexis de Tocqueville, *Democracy in America* (New York: Vintage, 1960), vol. 1, p. 266.

Of course, in reality the American political system places many curbs on majoritarianism, and it is probably correct to say with Louis Hartz that "what must be accounted one of the tamest, mildest, and most unimaginative majorities in modern political history has been bound down by a set of restrictions that betray fanatical terror."[19] Those who despised and feared the American people deployed a panoply of constitutional limits on power and developed a rhetoric to go with them. Gouverneur Morris spoke for many of America's founders when he warned the constitutional convention: "The mob begin to think and reason. Poor reptiles! . . . They bask in the sun, and ere noon they will bite, depend upon it."[20]

Thus the idea that power is a necessary but distasteful and dangerous instrumentality, the more pernicious as the number of its popular advocates grows, is no alien critique of American realism; it is an integral disposition of American liberal democracy itself. Indeed, it is this disposition that contributes many of America's most precious and effective political features: its modesty; its pluralism; its heterogeneity and judiciousness; its toleration for frustration, diversity, and dissent; its self-restraint; and its fairness. Minimalism has sought constantly to reduce the friction that occurs when individual freedom and statist power, when the anarchist and realist dispositions, touch. It calls forth a vision of civil society as an intermediate form of association that ties individuals together noncoercively and that mediates the harsh power relation between atomized individuals and a monolithic government. It envisions in the activities of pluralistic associations and groups and in the noncoercive education of civic men and women alternatives to pure power relations and pure market relations. To a certain degree, it thereby points beyond liberal democracy and offers a starting point for that alternative vision of strong democracy that will be explored in the second half of this book.

Nevertheless, in minimalism such virtues remain largely instrumental: they are valued less in and for themselves than for the sake of the individualist ends they faithfully serve. The individual may be more comfortable acting in a pluralist, group society than in the natural market or in the theater of power politics, but the virtues of

19. Louis Hartz, *The Liberal Tradition in America* (New York: Harcourt, Brace, 1955), p. 129. Hartz concludes, "The American majority has been an amiable shepherd dog kept forever on a lion's leash."
20. Cited by Hofstadter, *American Political Tradition*, p. 6.

the pluralist society are also ultimately to be assessed exclusively by how they promote enlightened self-interest: by how free the individual is and how well his interests are maintained and advanced. There is nothing supererogatory about liberal tolerance, nothing altruistic about mutual respect, nothing other-regarding about self-restraint, nothing communitarian about pluralism. They are all devices by which the individual can assure that others will be restrained. Thus, in revising the golden rule to express what he takes to be a fairer principle of justice, John Rawls never offers any other motive for justice than rational self-interest: inequalities are to be distributed so as to benefit the least advantaged in a society, he argues, because you yourself may end up least advantaged; tolerate others because you wish to be tolerated; and enjoin majorities to which you belong today from rash action because tomorrow you may find yourself in a minority.[21]

This prudential and provisional aspect of minimalism raises serious problems for democracy. To cite one example, racism has been a particularly intractable problem in America because toleration has been circumscribed by self-interest. Since whites have constituted a large and enduring majority, they have not been moved to enfranchise the nonwhite minority by any sense that they might some day be in the minority themselves. Feeling no stronger call to fraternity or community or mutualism, whites have had no "good" (i.e., prudent or self-interested) reason to respect the rights of nonwhites. The limits of liberal democracy are the limits of the self-preoccupied imagination.

Still it is clear that the minimalist disposition does endow liberal democratic politics with a rather less aggressive and a rather more ameliorative mien than realism, without falling into the naïveté about natural power that undoes the anarchist disposition. This softer bearing is evident in Locke's distinction between civil society and government, in Karl Popper's notion of piecemeal social engineering, in Michael Oakeshott's suspicion of radical rationalism and blueprint progressivism, in Robert Nozick's assault on abstract end-pattern reasoning, and in J. S. Mill's cautious sorting out of self-

21. John Rawls, *A Theory of Justice* (Cambridge, Mass.: Harvard University Press, 1971): "[the principles of justice are] the principles that free and rational persons concerned to *further their own interests* would accept in an initial position of equality as defining the fundamental terms of their association" (p. 11, emphasis added).

regarding and other-regarding acts.[22] At its best, the minimalist disposition suspects power without condemning it; it respects freedom without idealizing freedom's conditions; and it recognizes that there are no invisible hands to harmonize natural conflict even as it accepts that the visible hands of political man in quest of power will always be dirty. And though it is caught up in realist-anarchist definitions that make freedom the opposite of community power, its constructs of civil society and group association suggest an intuitive understanding of the need to mediate these oppositions. Consequently, it is less anxious about ambiguity and more willing to live without certainty—the certainty either of perfect freedom or of perfect security—than is anarchism or realism.

In accepting that individuals may err, that needs may be shared, that freedom no more excuses individuals from caring for others than power excuses a collective Other from caring for individuals, the minimalist disposition exhibits a potential for moving beyond liberal democracy. But the direction in which it points remains the road not taken. For minimalism is still tied to the radical individualism that informs liberal democracy in all of its dispositions. It proscribes but rarely prescribes action; it tends to negate rather than to affirm; it discovers in the limits of power not an opening to more creative forms of politics but merely the limits of politics *tout court*. It permits us to tolerate conflict but not to transform it into cooperation. Nor does it show us how to resolve the war of private interests through the creation of public interests or how to discern in man's social condition the potential for a civic and moral liberty that can transcend the natural and negative freedom of solitary beasts.

Because the minimalist disposition is essentially the product of a cautious and critical approach to power and politics, it is subject to John Dewey's striking critique of the liberal imagination: "The instruments of analysis, of criticism, of dissolution, that were employed [by liberalism] were effective for the work of release. But when it came to the problem of organizing the new forces and the

22. Government and civil society were first clearly distinguished by John Locke. Karl Popper discusses "piecemeal social engineering" in his *The Poverty of Historicism* (London: Routledge and Kegan Paul, 1957), chap. 3. Michael Oakeshott states his position most succinctly in his essays in *Rationalism in Politics* (New York: Basic Books, 1962). Robert Nozick attacks end-pattern political thinking in his *Anarchy, State, and Utopia* (New York: Basic Books, 1974). The distinction between self-regarding and other-regarding acts is at the heart of Mill's *On Liberty*.

individuals whose modes of life they radically altered into a coherent social organization, possessed of intellectual and moral directive
power, liberalism was well nigh impotent."[23] Minimalism strays to
the very frontiers of liberalism, but it does not cross them. That
crossing would require a whole new set of coordinates, which no
map in the atlas of liberal politics provides.

POLITICS AS ZOOKEEPING

Liberal democracy's three dispositions, while distinct in their concerns and inclinations, are nevertheless linked in a single circle of
reasoning that begins as it ends in the natural and negative liberty
of men and women as atoms of self-interest, as persons whose every
step into social relations, whose every foray into the world of Others, cries out for an apology, a legitimation, a justification. For all
three dispositions, politics is prudence in the service of *homo econ-
omicus*—the solitary seeker of material happiness and bodily security. The title of Harold Laswell's early classic, *Politics: Who Gets
What, When, How?* could stand as the epigraph of each disposition.
In these stark terms, democracy itself is never more than an artifact
to be used, adjusted, adapted, or discarded as it suits or fails to suit
the liberal ends for which it serves as means.

The uninspired and uninspiring but "realistic" image of man as a
creature of need, living alone by nature but fated to live in the company of his fellows by enlightened self-interest combines with the
cynical image of government as a provisional instrument of power
servicing these creatures to suggest a general view of politics as zookeeping. Liberal democratic imagery seems to have been fashioned
in a menagerie. It teems with beasts and critters of every description:
sovereign lions, princely lions and foxes, bleating sheep and poor
reptiles, ruthless pigs and ruling whales, sly polecats, clever coy-
otes, ornery wolves (often in sheep's clothing), and, finally, in Alexander Hamilton's formidable image, all mankind itself but one great
Beast.

From the perspective of this political zoology, civil society is an
alternative to the "jungle"—to the war of all against all that defines
the state of nature. In that poor and brutish war, the beasts howl in
voices made articulate by reason—for zoos, for cages and trainers,

23. John Dewey, *Liberalism and Social Action* (New York: Capricorn Books, 1963), p.
53.

for rules and regulations, for regular feeding times and prudent custodians. Like captured leopards, men are to be admired for their proud individuality and for their unshackled freedom, but they must be caged for their untrustworthiness and antisocial orneriness all the same. Indeed, if the individual is dangerous, the species is deadly. Liberal democracy's sturdiest cages are reserved for the People. "Democracy is more vindictive than Cabinets," warned Churchill, a prudent custodian if ever there was one: "the wars of peoples will be more terrible than those of kings."

Although they vary in their portraits of human nature, all three dispositions share a belief in the fundamental inability of the human beast to live at close quarters with members of its own species. All three thus seek to structure human relations by keeping men apart rather than by bringing them together. It is their mutual incompatibility that turns men into reluctant citizens and their aggressive solitude that makes them into wary neighbors.

The logic behind the three dispositions tends to lead from one to the other in an ironic circle that contributes to liberal democracy's damaging thinness. The logic progresses by regressing: each problem is solved only at the cost of creating a still more intractable problem. Anarchism posits men in a natural condition of freedom that permits the boundless gratification of unreasoned (unmediated) desires. Such freedom, however, multiplied by the number of those who possess it, is self-defeating. In the words of Richard Tuck (the eighteenth century's antidote to Lockean liberalism), "individuals were invested with rights that they might surrender them absolutely to the sovereign."[24] For Tuck, the freedom that defines the individual itself provides an excuse for its supercession by power.

Liberal democracy thus finds itself in its characteristic dilemma: the natural condition jeopardizes individual man's potential freedom while the state endangers his actual freedom. Liberty cannot survive without political power, but political power extirpates liberty. Sovereign power may be a fit custodian of our liberties, but then *quis custodiet custodes*?

24. Cited by J. G. A. Pocock in "Virtues, Rights and Manners: A Model for Political Theory," *Political Theory* 9, 3 (August 1981), p. 361. Pocock elaborates as follows: "the story of how rights became the precondition, the occasion and the effective cause of sovereignty, so that sovereignty appeared to be a creature of the rights it existed to protect" is in effect the "story of liberalism. . . . because it defined the individual as rightbearer and proprietor, it did not define him as possessing a personality adequate to participation in self-rule." This seems as pithy a summary of the miscarriage of liberalism as we are likely to get.

This dilemma gives liberal democracy its defining ambivalence. It makes Hobbes both a liberal who championed man's natural liberty and the prerogatives with which he is endowed by natural right *and* an authoritarian who felt that liberty could survive only under an indivisible sovereignty. It draws liberal philosophers like Bertrand Russell from anarchism to power realism and then to minimalism in their futile search for a middle ground between liberty and power, for a terrain that scarcely seems to exist within the compass of the liberal imagination. Finally, it gives to the liberal portrait of human nature a perverse and schizophrenic aspect. Man seems at once mean and prudent, base and rational, impulsive and deliberate; man the unsocial beast is nonetheless a calculating machine, at once too driven by desire and too reasonable. A creature of necessity, man is yet blessed somehow with the gift of clairvoyant choice; he is unable to live cooperatively with his fellow humans for a single good reason but he can live with them coercively for a dozen bad ones.

The modern consumer is the most recent incarnation of this small man, the last in a long train of models that depict man as a greedy, self-interested, acquisitive survivor who is capable nonetheless of the most self-denying deferrals of gratification for the sake of ultimate material satisfaction. The consumer is a creature of great reason devoted to small ends. His cherished freedom is chained to the most banal need. He uses the gift of choice to multiply his options in and to transform the material conditions of the world, but never to transform himself or to create a world of mutuality with his fellow humans.

The consumer's world is a world of carrots and sticks. But is human society really held together solely by Hobbes's strange mixture of cold prudence and hot terror? Edmund Burke, who linked the excesses of the French Revolution with the excesses of the French philosophes, remarked with bitterness that their "barbarous philosophy"

is the offspring of cold hearts and muddy understandings. . . . Laws are to be supported only by their own terrors, and by the concern which each individual may find in them from his own private speculations, or can spare to them from his own private interests. In the groves of *their* academy, at the end of every vista, you see nothing but the gallows.[25]

25. Edmund Burke, *Reflections on the Revolution in France* (London: Dent, n.d.), p. 308.

Burke's rhetoric is as extravagant as the revolution he decries. But it remains true that from its inception in early social-contract theory, liberal democracy has considered both man and law as abstractions. It depicts man as a bundle of natural necessity interacting with a legal constitution of artificial necessity: natural desire and artificial fear converge in an arena of stimulus-response to create an artificial polity and a forced tranquility. There is indeed a sense in which the utilitarian calculus, whether explicated by Jeremy Bentham or B. F. Skinner, must necessarily place behind every law the gallows. Artificial incentives—sanctions, penalties, contrived rewards—are the operational morals of legislation: an appropriate inducement is provided for social behavior and an appropriate deterrent for antisocial behavior. The gallows thus becomes a metaphor for the coercion that ultimately underlies those myriad incentives and penalties that supposedly are the only means by which a liberal democracy can inspire men and women to obey the law or to consider the public good. Like some sovereign founder of a universal protection racket, the liberal state manipulates men by first implanting terror in them and then, in return for their socially acceptable behavior and their prudential fealty, protecting them from it.[26]

Burke feared not simply the reign of fear and the government of cold prudence but the corrosive injury that a reliance on self-serving reason and prudent fear could have on the natural bonds that tie men together in society. When fear alone compels compliance (as with Hobbes's sword), when fellowship depends on private interest and civility is a matter of private penalties and private rewards, then "nothing is left which engages the affections on the part of the commonwealth. . . . [Yet] these public affections, combined with manners, are required sometimes as supplements, sometimes as correctives, always as aids to law."[27] Karl Marx offered the same criticism in his *Manifesto*, where he described how the bourgeoisie had "torn asunder" the natural ties of the feudal world and left "no other nexus between man and man than naked self-interest, than callous 'cash-payment.'"

To identify liberal man as governed by need is to portray him as small, static, inflexible, and above all prosiac—as a greedy little var-

---

26. That minimalist and anarchist critics such as Robert Paul Wolff and Robert Nozick perceive states based on extortion as illegitimate is quite understandable. In fact, the anarchist critique of government presumes that political society is coercive.
27. Burke, *Reflections*, p. 318.

mint unable to see, for all his ratiocinating foresight, beyond his appetites. A creature of appetite, or of reason indentured to appetite,
liberal man is seen as incapable of bearing the weight of his ideals.
Freedom becomes indistinguishable from selfishness and is corrupted from within by apathy, alienation, and anomie; equality is
reduced to market exchangeability and divorced from its necessary
familial and social contexts; happiness is measured by material gratification to the detriment of the spirit. Perhaps this is why the miracle of American democracy has produced dropouts as well as beneficiaries, malcontents as well as successes, lost souls as well as
millionaires, terrorism as well as abundance, social conflict as well
as security, and injustice as well as the forms of civility.

These weaknesses are tied to the thinness and provisionality of
the liberal defense of democracy. For that defense is negative rather
than affirmative and can conceive of no form of citizenship other
than the self-interested bargain. But it is not enough for us to be
democrats solely that we might be free; despotism may also offer a
certain freedom, as Voltaire and Frederick the Great tried to prove.
It is not enough for us to be democrats solely to secure our interests
today; tomorrow our interests may be better served by oligarchy or
tyranny or aristocracy or by no government at all. It is not enough
for us to be democrats this year because we do not believe in anything strongly enough to impose our beliefs on others; next year we
may uncover foundations for those beliefs that destroy our self-restraint. Every prudential argument for democracy is an argument
for its thinness; every defense of democracy in lieu of something
better invites one to search for the missing "something better";
every attempt to cut man down to fit the demands of hedonism and
economics makes him too small for civic affiliation and too mean-
spirited for communal participation.

What we have called "thin democracy," then, yields neither the
pleasures of participation nor the fellowship of civic association, neither the autonomy and self-governance of continuous political activity nor the enlarging mutuality of shared public goods—of mutual
deliberation, decision, and work. Oblivious to that essential human
interdependency that underlies all political life, thin democratic politics is at best a politics of static interest, never a politics of transformation; a politics of bargaining and exchange, never a politics of
invention and creation; and a politics that conceives of women and
men at their worst (in order to protect them from themselves), never

at their potential best (to help them become better than they are). Recognizing this, we must continue to believe with Reinhold Niebuhr that "democracy has a more compelling justification and requires a more realistic vindication than is given it by the liberal culture with which it has been associated in modern history."[28]

It is the aim of this book to develop an alternative justification: to associate democracy with a civic culture nearer to the themes of participation, citizenship, and political activity that are democracy's central virtues. We must do so too without falling victim to either the nostalgia for ancient, small-scale republics that has made so many communitarian theories seem irrelevant to modern life or to the taste for monolithic collectivism that can turn large-scale direct democracy into plebiscitary tyranny.

The form of democracy that will emerge in the following analysis—we will call it "strong democracy" to distinguish it from its thin, representative cousin—manages to complement some of liberal democracy's strengths even as it remedies a number of its deficiencies. Before we can explore this alternative, however, we need to know a good deal more about liberal democracy. The rough metaphor worked out above of politics as zookeeping is in fact predicated on certain preconceptual premises ("Newtonian politics"), epistemological convictions ("Cartesian politics"), and a political psychology ("apolitical man"), all of which are intimately associated with the schema they engender and with many of its more visible blemishes.

The next four chapters, which constitute the balance of Part I, are thus devoted to an elaboration of thin democracy and its dilemmas. Part II will offer an alternative form of politics in the participatory mode—strong democracy.

28. Reinhold Niebuhr, *The Children of Light and the Children of Darkness* (New York: Charles Scribner's Sons, 1944), p. xii.

Chapter Two

The Preconceptual Frame:
Newtonian Politics

> *All freedom consists* in radice *in the*
> *preservation of an inner space exempt*
> *from state power.*
>
> (Lord Acton)

> *There may be Laws made, and Rules set*
> *as guards and fences to the properties of*
> *all the Members of the Society, to limit*
> *the Power, and moderate the Dominion of*
> *every Part.*
>
> (John Locke)

> *Individuals have rights. So strong are*
> *these that they raise the question of what,*
> *if anything, the state and its officials may*
> *do. How much room do individual rights*
> *leave for the state?*
>
> (Robert Nozick)

Theories of political life, like theories in general, are contextually nourished. They do not arise out of a vacuum but are constructed from pretheoretical materials that are in one sense or another "givens." Each theory creates its own metaphors, incorporates particular conceptions of space and time, employs special language conventions, introduces new definitions of the terms *fact* and *idea*, and assumes a unique starting point or what I wish to call an "inertial frame of reference." These inertial frames are uniquely important, for they can be understood to embody in summary fashion all of the pretheoretical givens of a particular world view.

An inertial frame is a frame of reference against which a theory's development can be charted, a starting or rest position from which a theorist launches his arguments and to which he can safely return when a given philosophical voyage of discovery fails or is aborted. It is a kind of conceptual grid by whose fixed and permanent coordinates both the location and the velocity of every idea in a theory can be measured.

Perhaps the most obvious example of an inertial frame is the "ether" on which Newtonian physics was once thought to depend. In Newton's mechanical universe, whose governing laws often seemed as simple and certain as the propositions of geometry, there remained a single pretheoretical puzzle: the puzzle of the inertial frame. Position and velocity in Newton's clocklike universe—indeed, the very idea of position and velocity—were stated relativistically; to give them the certitude it required, the deist mind had to imagine them against some fixity. Thus an "ether," materially insubstantial but theoretically necessary, was postulated in order to provide an unmoving and absolute inertial frame for the otherwise well-ordered cosmos.

It is clear that such frames can be vitally important: Newtonian physics collapsed when the extraordinary Michelson-Morley experiment of 1886 proved conclusively that the ether simply was not. Once scientists had the technical ability to measure the supposed physical indicators of the ether, they could find none. Without the ether, Newtonian time and space slipped into a world of relativity whose laws remained mysterious until Einstein devised the special theory of relativity decades later. The new physics operated without an ether or any comparable inertial frame.[1] Yet although it satisfied physicists to a point, it left those with a more commonsensical approach to the physical world in a state of puzzlement from which they have yet to emerge.

Philosophy and political theory are no less dependent than physics on inertial frames, although some kinds of theory are more dependent than others. Plato's theory of forms and Kant's twelve categories contribute to the pretheory as well as to the theory of their respective metaphysics. One cannot "get behind them"; they are not simply a priori but are prior to the very theories they frame. In recent decades, philosophers have taken to scrutinizing inertial

1. The special theory of relativity posits that the speed of light is an invariable constant. Temporal space thus loses its fixity, and objects in motion (relative to one another) appear to contract and expand and to move through time with an erraticism that would alarm even Alice.

frames directly: sociologists and Marxists are probing the relationship between knowledge and interests (see Mannheim or Habermas, for example), while analytic philosophers are examining the relationship between knowledge and language (see Wittgenstein or Ayer, for example).

Yet because of the dialectical interplay of empirical and normative styles of philosophical reasoning, and because of the far less fixed and certain character of humanistic studies, inertial frames in the human sciences have been both more rigid and less subjected to examination than in the natural sciences.[2] Some may even insist that the idea of testing inertial frames is a contradiction in terms, since an inertial frame is intended precisely to provide a test-free pretheoretical substratum over which theory can be laid. John Dewey linked these intentions with the human quest for certainty, which for him explained much of the Western penchant for scientific, "objective" thinking. "Men have longed to find a realm," he writes in *The Quest for Certainty*, "in which there is an activity which is not overt and which has no external consequences."[3] The fixity of an inertial frame comprises just such a realm. This must be where theory begins, rather than where it ends—the sure haven to which metaphysical ships of discovery can always return, however turbulent and unfriendly the high seas.

The use of inertial frames in the human sciences has in fact been closely linked to genetic reasoning in the Western political tradition. Enamored from the outset with geometric and deductive models of thought, the founders of modern moral philosophy and social theory (Descartes, Spinoza, Hobbes) took reasoning to be identical with ideational concatenation. To think was to make logical chains, which had to have both a first and a final link. The inertial frame of refer-

2. In *The Structure of Scientific Revolutions* (Chicago: University of Chicago Press, 1962), Thomas S. Kuhn analyzes scientific theories in terms of paradigms, which are partially pretheoretical. What Carl L. Becker calls "climates of opinion" in *The Heavenly City of the Eighteenth Century Philosophers* (New Haven: Yale University Press, 1962) are pretheoretical modes of interpreting a culture as a whole. And one can certainly find in the work of Richard J. Bernstein, John G. Gunnell, Jürgen Habermas, A. R. Louch, and Peter Winch, among many others, attempts to explore the pretheoretical conditions of political theory and political activity. One of the best recent attempts to capture the pretheoretical essence of a number of current "philosophies of human activity" is Richard J. Bernstein's *Praxis and Action* (Philadelphia: University of Pennsylvania Press, 1971).

3. John Dewey, *The Quest for Certainty* (New York: Capricorn, 1960), p. 7. Inertial frames not only overcome the uncertainty of practical activity, they go beyond theory and so are certain beyond all epistemological doubt as well.

ence is the foundry in which the first link is forged, the unwritten book in which the principles of metallurgy are given.

The connections among inertial frames, genetic reasoning, and deductive models of theory are profoundly important for the development of liberal democratic theory. They have given liberal thought its characteristic resistance to activity, to uncertainty, and to spontaneity; they have endowed it with its stubborn intolerance of complexity, ambiguity, experience, and process; and they have burdened it with pretensions to objectivity and philosophical certainty that have often proved inimical to practical reason and to participatory political activity. It was John Dewey who first noticed that empiricism no less than rationalism "is conceived as tied up to what has been, or is 'given.' But experience in its vital form is experimental, an effort to change the given; it is characterized by projection, by reading forward into the unknown; connection with a future is its salient trait."[4]

In liberal political thought, theory has too often been a function of the past rather than of the future, moving reductively backward through time and argument to starting points, forging chains of reasoning that lead back to first links and thence to inertial frames. There is perhaps no better practitioner of concatenational reasoning than Hobbes, who pioneered what is often called the "resolutive-compositive method":

Everything is best understood by its constitutive causes. For as in a watch, or some such small engine, the matter, figures, and the motion of the wheels cannot well be known, except it be taken asunder and viewed in its parts; so to make a curious search in the rights of states and the duties of subjects it is necessary, I say, not to take them asunder, but yet that they be so considered as if they were dissolved.[5]

For if reason is, as Hobbes argues, "nothing but reckoning," then the "use and end of reason is . . . to begin at [first definitions] and proceed from one consequence to another. For there can be no certainty of the last conclusion, without a certainty of all those affirmations and negations, on which it was grounded and inferred."[6]

---

4. Cited in Bernstein, *Praxis and Action*, pp. 205–207. In a similar vein, Jean-Paul Sartre writes: "Man is, before all else, something which propels itself towards a future and is aware that it is doing so; . . . man is the future of man" (*Existentialism and Humanism* [London: Methuen, 1975], p. 28).

5. Thomas Hobbes, *Man and Citizen*, ed. B. Gert (New York: Anchor, 1949), pp. 25–26.

6. Thomas Hobbes, *Leviathan*, part 1, chap. 5.

Reason as reckoning is reasoning as concatenation, and it leads in the fashion of geometry ineluctably back to starting propositions.

Modern philosophers such as Robert Nozick and John Rawls argue from inertial frames that are more or less explicit. Thus Rawls posits an "original position" where abstract persons—denuded of special psychologies and particular lives—reason from certain essential rational premises they supposedly share by virtue of their being human.[7] The "original position" thus turns out to be the condition for reasoning about justice rather than an element in the theory of justice.

Robert Nozick does not acknowledge his inertial frame as explicitly as does Rawls, but he posits it with even more pretheoretical certitude. "Individuals have rights," Nozick asseverates, "and there are things no person or group may do to them." Hence, he concludes, "the fundamental question of political philosophy" is "why not anarchy?"[8] The inherent givenness of individuality, the absolute sacrosanctity of autonomy and of the rights associated with autonomy, constitutes Nozick's inertial frame. As he allows, this constellation comprises his "rest position . . . deviation from which may be caused only by moral forces."[9] Nozick thereby endows his preference for anarchism with the givenness of a rest position or starting point. Politics is put on the defensive from the outset: always in need of legitimation, insupportable until proven otherwise, it is a "deviation" from an inviolate individualism that can be justified only by "moral forces."

The rhetorical force of a rest position depends of course on its universality. As Nozick rightly admits, "it would not increase understanding to reach the state from an arbitrary and otherwise unimportant starting point."[10] Logic requires that a starting point's fea-

7. John Rawls, *A Theory of Justice* (Cambridge, Mass.: Harvard University Press, 1971), writes:

> The guiding idea is that the principles of justice for the basic structure of society are the object of *original agreement*. They are the principles that free and rational persons concerned to further their own interests would accept in an *initial position* of equality as defining the fundamental terms of their association. These principles are to regulate all further agreements; they specify the kinds of social cooperation that can be entered into and the forms of government that can be established. (p. 11; emphasis added)

8. Robert Nozick, *Anarchy, State, and Utopia* (New York: Basic Books, 1974), pp. ix, 4.

9. Ibid., p. 223. Nozick is here describing what he takes to be Rawls's rest position, but of course he is also depicting a crucial feature of his own frame.

10. Ibid., p. 7.

tures be salient, that the point itself be filtered of its political and moral characteristics (which are to be inferred from the rest position, not read out of it) but that the point nevertheless be "far from non-moral." Nozick, Rawls, and their predecessors in social-contract and rights philosophy have sought a foundation for theory that is pre-moral (pretheoretical) without being nonmoral (arbitrary). If the consensus never achieved by the debate over intuitions and applied theories could be established for starting points, then controversies and moral and political differences could be redefined as due merely to erroneous reasoning—to mistaken inference, invalid syllogism, specious reckoning, and sloppy concatenation.

In this way, the inertial frame becomes rationality itself properly understood—what Arthur Lovejoy called "uniformitarian rationality." With one starting point and one model of reasoning, there can only be one true (logically consequential) outcome and thus only one true notion of politics, rights, obligation, and so forth. Spinoza, Descartes, Hobbes, Locke, Hume, Bentham, Rawls, Nozick, and countless others who have employed analytic-dissective or resolutive-compositive or genetic-reductionist methods in the search for a viable political theory have hoped to seduce their antagonists and overwhelm the skeptics by demonstrating that if only they accept A (which as rational persons they are bound to do), they will be able to swallow B (which after all follows necessarily from A), and so on to C and D, until they reach N. And however unpalatable N may seem, and however at variance it is with their original political convictions, it too must be accepted because it is the final link in a chain of reasoning that leads without a break from that first link—the one that, as rational persons, they felt bound to accept in the first place.

Typically, Nozick and Rawls are anxious to show that their arguments are vulnerable not at the point of inception (where all rational persons are counted upon to concur) but only along their progression from premise to conclusion. Thus they marshall their most formidable philosophical forces in defense of their reasoning from A to N, while they leave A unprotected because it is putatively prior to all argument and thus indefeasible.

The central argument of this chapter is that this model of the reasoning process is grossly deficient as a model of political thinking and that a number of the insufficiencies of liberal democracy can be traced to this deficiency. "Delusive geometrical accuracy in moral arguments [is] the most fallacious of all sophistry," wrote Edmund

Burke.[11] Liberal democrats have proved themselves sophists not by their convictions but by the mode of reasoning they have used to support these convictions. I shall argue in the appropriate place that the proper metaphor for political reasoning is not concatenation but weaving—the interlacing of strands in a cable (to use Peirce's brilliant metaphor) rather than the forging of links in a chain. Liberal theorists have thought otherwise, however, and we can now bring into sharp focus the effects their choice has had on the political practice of liberal democracy.

THE INERTIAL FRAME OF LIBERAL DEMOCRACY

The inertial frame of liberal democracy has several interconnected features, a number of which figure in the actual elaboration of the theory but most of which remain implicit in the pretheory. We can portray these features in terms of a major axiom and several corollaries. The axiom sets up materialism as a pretheoretical base, while the corollaries deal with atomism, indivisibility, commensurability, mutual exclusivity, and sensationalism (as a psychology).

The axiom of materialism posits that humans are material beings in all they are and in all they do—that their social and political time and space are literally material or physical time and space. Within these beings, motivation, agency, and interaction are necessarily physical motivation, physical agency, and physical interaction. Humans are therefore governed by laws that correspond to the laws of physical mechanics. It is hardly a wonder that the early eighteenth century produced an abundance of popular political works with titles such as J. T. Desaguliers's "The Newtonian System of the World, the Best Model of Government, an Allegorical Poem" (1728). Nowhere is materialist imagery more striking than in the introduction to Hobbes's *Leviathan*:

Life is but a motion of limbs, the beginning whereof is in some principal part within; why may we not say, that all *automata* (engines that move themselves by springs and wheels as doth a watch) have an artificial life? For

11. "The excellence of mathematics and metaphysics is to have but one thing before you; he forms the best judgment in all moral disquisitions who has the greatest number and variety of considerations in one view before him" (Edmund Burke in R. J. S. Hoffman and P. Levack, eds., *Burke's Politics* [New York: Knopf, 1949], p. 218).

what is the *heart*, but a *spring*? and the nerves but so many *strings*; and the *joints*, but so many *wheels*, giving motion to the whole body.[12]

The corollary of atomism posits that as physical beings, humans are separate, integral, self-contained, unitary particles or atoms; that, moreover, the human perspective is first of all the perspective of, as well as the perspective from, the isolated individual One. The world is a world of physical Ones.

The corollary of indivisibility posits that as physical beings, humans are unitary wholes acting in consonance with unitary motives (needs, drives, wants, desires, impulses, instincts, etc.). Whatever disharmony may reign among human atoms, their inner condition is unfragmented and tranquil and their motion is as precise and unequivocal as a vector sum.

The corollary of commensurability posits that as physical beings, humans are roughly commensurable one with the other: each is governed by the same laws of behavior and is thus interchangeable with any other.

The corollary of mutual exclusivity posits that as physical beings, humans cannot occupy the same space at the same time, not merely as bodies but in any relevant political, social, or psychological sense. As a consequence, the characteristic mode of human interaction is conflict and the typical human posture is either aggressive or defensive.

The corollary of sensationalism posits that as physical beings, humans feel, think, and imagine only in response to physical causes—namely, sense impressions or sensations. These sensations are thus causally complicit in every mode of human thought and behavior.

Now it should be immediately evident that the axiom of materialism and its several corollaries disclose many of the central features of liberal democratic theory in its fully articulated political form. Atomism can be regarded as the pretheoretical ground for individualism, as is indivisibility for hedonistic psychology, commensurability for equality, mutual exclusivity for the theory of power and

---

12. Hobbes, *Leviathan*, part I, Introduction. Compare this to Hobbes's Epistle Dedicatory to *The Elements of Law, Natural and Politic*, where he writes:

> They that have written of justice and policy in general, do all invade each other, and themselves, with contradiction. To reduce this doctrine to the rules and infallibility of reason, there is no way, but first to put such principles down for a foundation, as passion not mistrusting, may not seek to displace; and afterward to build thereon the truth of cases in the law of nature by degrees, till the whole be unexpungable. (*The Elements of Law*, ed. F. Tönnies [London: Cass, 1969], p. xv)

conflict, and sensationalism for emotivism, utilitarianism, and the predominance of interest theory. These connections, and their impact on the fully developed theory of liberal democracy, are explored in subsequent chapters. Here the focus remains on pretheory itself.

The most striking feature of the liberal inertial frame is the physicality of its language and imagery. There was a "thingness" about Hobbesian and post-Hobbesian liberal thought that seems to have been both new and extraordinary in the history of political discourse. Mimicking the newly revealed physical cosmos of the scientists, political theorists suddenly began to depict the human world as inhabited by units, particles, and atoms, things with a solidity and externality quite at odds with the traditional teleological, psychic, and spiritual understandings of the human essence. Because they move in physical time and space, these things are governed by the laws of physical mechanics. Even the subjective "I" and its imaginative and ratiocinative faculties have a concrete, objective "thingness" that allows them to be depicted (reductively) in the language of physical motion (as in the first five chapters of Hobbes's *Leviathan*). Physicality suffuses the language of early and recent liberal theory. Locke can thus meditate in the *Second Treatise of Civil Government* on how laws and rules act as "guards and fences" to limit the power of other individuals and of society as a whole, while Robert Nozick can ask in his *Anarchy, State, and Utopia* "How much room do individual rights and liberty leave for the state?"[13]

Consider the following characteristic liberal concepts in light of the axiom of materialism and its corollaries: *property* as an extension of the physical self and of physical self-ownership (the labor theory of value); *territory* as the defining embodiment of modern sovereignty and statehood; *boundaries* as the crucial metaphor in conflicts of rights, autonomies, and jurisdictions; *sanctions* as an extension of physical penalties, designed to control behavior through the mechanics of hedonism; *freedom* as the absence of external impediments to motion, as liberty from "chains, from imprisonment, from enslavement by others" (Isaiah Berlin); and *power* as brute force, physical coercion, the absence of freedom.

With a vocabulary of such materiality, liberal theory cannot be expected to give an adequate account of human interdependency, mutualism, cooperation, fellowship, fraternity, community, and citi-

13. Nozick, *Anarchy*, p. 4.

zenship. To take but a few examples, we contravene the corollary of mutual exclusivity daily, in every human interaction that engages us in friendship, partnership, community, or love. The corollary of indivisibility is contradicted every time an individual sets his reason against his passion, every time an actor assumes the identity of a stranger or a spectator is lost in empathy, every time a reveler is submerged in Dionysian communion or a pilgrim is swept away in religious fervor—every time, in short, the single self is fractured into warring splinters or engaged in a relationship or made to transcend itself.

Perhaps the most palpable example of the impact of materialism is the liberal conception of freedom and power. Although there are far-reaching differences among them, Hobbes, Locke, Hume, Godwin, Bentham, Mill, Hobhouse, and modern theorists such as Sir Isaiah Berlin, Robert Dahl, and Harold Laswell have each understood freedom and power as antonyms, each defined (analytically) by the absence of the other. If the political world is to obey the constraints of materialism and its corollaries, then freedom can never be anything other than *"nihil obstat"* (John Laird), than liberty from "chains" (Isaiah Berlin); it can be nothing other than "the preservation of an inner space exempt from state power" (Lord Acton).[14]

It is largely through this polarization that liberalism acquires its characteristic suspicion of politics and its corresponding inclination toward anarchism. If physical constraint and external coercion are the principal adversaries of freedom, then the state, as the principal locus of physical coercion, becomes freedom's most implacable enemy. Politics becomes the art of power and freedom becomes the art of antipolitics. The liberal anarchist who lurks in every Marxist thus emerges in Lenin to proclaim: "While the state exists there is no freedom. When there is freedom, there will be no state."[15]

Robert Nozick echoes the liberal Lenin when he asks, "How much

14. See John Laird, *On Human Freedom* (London: Allen and Unwin, 1947), p. 13; Sir Isaiah Berlin, *Two Concepts of Liberty* (Oxford: Clarendon Press, 1958), pp. 6–8; and Lord Acton, cited in Robert A. Nisbet, *The Quest for Community* (1953; reprint, New York: Oxford University Press, 1969), p. 246. I have distinguished this "abstract physical-mechanist model" of freedom from the "psychological-intentionalist model" in my *Superman and Common Men: Freedom, Anarchy, and the Revolution* (New York: Praeger, 1971), chap. 2. For a discussion of freedom that does justice to its complexity, see Christian Bay, *The Structure of Freedom* (New York: Atheneum, 1965).

15. Lenin, *State and Revolution* (New York: International Publishers, 1932), p. 79. In the same vein, Bernard Bosanquet asserts that "perfect liberty is equivalent to total absence of government" (*The Philosophical Theory of the State* [London: Macmillan, 1951], p. 125).

room do individual rights leave for the state?" He calls up an image of the state as a veritable Leviathan, a whale loitering in a small fish tank, crushing the minnows simply by virtue of its presence. Yet individuals and states are not bicycles and trailer-trucks jockeying for space in a parking lot. The spatial imagery distorts the actual character of social relations. Could we ask, "How much room does friendship leave for self-realization?" without exploring whether friendship is a condition for self-realization? Could we ask, "How much room does education leave for autonomous thinking?" without raising the question whether education is a premise of autonomous thinking? Social and political constructs such as "legal person" and "citizen" suggest that relations may be mutual as well as adversarial, cooperative as well as antagonistic, and overlapping as well as mutually exclusive. Political relations tend to be dialectic, dialogical, symbiotic, and ambivalent. To represent them with material and physical metaphors quite misconceives them. Rousseau's phrase "forced to be free," which liberals have found so loathsome, is in fact an attempt to capture the ambiguous symbiosis that links coercion and liberty in both psychology and politics.[16]

Rendering freedom and power in physical terms not only misconstrues them, it produces a conception of political liberty as entirely passive. Freedom is associated with the unperturbedness of the inertial body, with the motionlessness of the inertial frame itself.[17] It stands in stark opposition to the idea of politics as activity, motion, will, choice, self-determination, and self-realization. Montesquieu regarded tranquility as a symptom of the corruption of liberty—the end of the free Republic. The modern liberal appears to regard it as a republican ideal: man at rest, inactive, nonparticipating, isolated, uninterfered with, privatized, and thus free.

The ideal of freedom as stasis has persisted despite the long tradition of republican thinking that equated political life with the *vita activa* and despite the overwhelming psychological, sociological,

16. Jean-Jacques Rousseau, *The Social Contract*, book 1, chap. 8. Rousseau states his meaning more clearly in book 2, chap. 6 (on Law). There he argues that those who "see" good but reject it "must be compelled to bring their wills into conformity with their reason." Since only men who act in consonance with their reason can be free, this is to "force men to be free." For a discussion, see John Plamenatz, "Ce qui ne signifie autre chose sinon qu'on le forcera d'être libre," *Annales de philosophie politique, V: Rousseau et la philosophie politique* (Paris, 1965).

17. As John Sommerville writes, "Thus freedom is, in an inescapable sense, negative, involving always an indication that something is absent" ("Towards a Consistent Definition of Freedom," in C. J. Friedrich, ed., *Nomos IV: Liberty* [New York: Atheneum, 1962], p. 295).

and historical evidence that freedom and power are not opposites. This fact argues powerfully for the pervasiveness of the material inertial frame in liberal democratic thinking. Yet while physical materialism characterizes all of the three dispositions elaborated in the last chapter, each interprets it in a distinctive manner.

DISPOSITIONAL VARIATIONS IN THE LIBERAL INERTIAL FRAME

To liberal-anarchists, the physical space that liberal politics occupies is an *infinite* space in which modest numbers of human particles move cautiously within circumscribed, nonintersecting territories. Interaction among particles is thus minimal and collision and conflict are correspondingly improbable. The anarchist political cosmos approximates an infinitely expanding cloud chamber maintained at a temperature near absolute zero, where there is almost no significant molecular movement and thus no friction or heat.

The anarchist in fact conceives of human desires as moderate, of human aggression as unlikely, of human conflict as improbable, and of human relations as relatively contact-free and consequently harmonious; for the anarchist perspective is the perspective of the radically isolated self for whom the world is only what it can see with its own eyes. Political space is infinite space because it seems to be occupied only by the single self. The anarchist reads the world as a realm of the One, where the existence of other Ones is scarcely perceived and never felt.

Like the artist separated from the world by his self-consciousness and able to experience it only by reworking it with his imagination, so the anarchist can depict the world only as a projection of his own subjective selfhood. The Others that are present only confirm, by their elusiveness, his own separateness. The great empty spaces between Self and Other promote a definition of consciousness as self-consciousness only and thereby shackle the liberal imagination to the narcissistic ideals of self-preservation, self-interest, and self-determination.

The pretheoretical conviction that the human world is a realm of the One where individual particles are defined in isolation, destined neither for interaction nor for interdependence, imparts to the anarchist the courage of a rights dogmatist. Robert Nozick can thus assert, with a self-assurance that makes scrutiny seem insulting, that "individuals have rights and there are things no person or

group may do to them."[18] Or Hobbes can report, as if he were Newton disclosing the newly discovered laws of mechanics, that "the
right of nature . . . is the liberty each man hath, to use his own
power . . . for the preservation of his own nature; that is to say, his
own life."[19] Or the authors of the American Declaration of Independence can assume the absolute "self-evidence" of all such traditional liberal rights. Rights are absolute because the version of human nature in which they are rooted is indefeasible: an inertial point
of departure behind which it is impossible to go.

The anarchist image of the world as a realm of the One clarifies
the corollary conviction that government—the State—causes rather
than mitigates the evils of coercion and tyranny. If borders are en-
croached upon, it is not because human particles collide by nature
but because artificial Leviathans disrespect the natural separateness
of those particles. Nature has provided sufficient space for each and
every One. It is only the wayward attempt to improve upon nature
by introducing artificial restraints (sovereignty and law) that endangers liberty and creates the illusion of crowds stampeding in close
quarters. Politics, in this perspective, is not how men define and
possess their social natures and guarantee their political selves
against the natural depredations of their fellows; it is the archetypical form of depredation from which natural men need to be
protected.

The liberal-realist and liberal-minimalist images of political space
share with liberal anarchism the defining trait of physicality. Unlike
anarchist space, however, liberal-realist space is distinctively *finite*.
It suggests a densely populated, confined territory within which
myriad particles moving at frenetic velocities intersect and collide.
The temperature of this space is much higher, the interaction of particles far more volatile. Consequently, the realist's world is one of
force and counterforce rather than one of autonomy and independence. Irresistible forces constantly confront immovable objects,
rights collide self-destructively with competing rights, the freedom
of each particle becomes a limit on the freedom of every other particle. Generally speaking, the tranquil anarchy of solitary inertial bodies at rest is supplanted by an anomic tumult in which high-velocity
particles can be detected only in the traces of their endless collisions.

18. Nozick, *Anarchy*, p. ix.
19. Hobbes, *Leviathan*, book 1, chap. 14.

The individual human particle remains paramount—still indivisible, still incapable of coexistence—but its world is now perceived as an overpopulated prison in which the inmates are cut off from escape without being protected from one another. Boundaries are permanently in jeopardy, movement is always constrained, the freedom of each is bound by the movement of every other, and autonomy is subjected to perpetual negotiation and compromise—when it is not simply destroyed.

This stark world ceases to be the realm of One and becomes the realm of Many Ones. Without the comfort of cooperation or the consolation of fraternity, individuals are nonetheless compelled to interaction—which must always appear to them in the first instance as intrusion, encroachment, and interdiction. Encroachment becomes a recurring feature of all existence and is soon associated with the finitude of social space and with the plenitude of men occupying it. Coercion and conflict cease to be the byproducts of wayward human contrivance; they are an ineluctable problem—*the* problem of the human condition. It is not a matter of keeping people apart but of actively *pulling* them apart; not a question of preserving autonomy against the artificial crossing of boundaries but of having in the absence of natural boundaries to deliberately create artificial boundaries in order to restrain natural conflict and coercion.

When translated into psychological language (see Chapter 4), this confined Newtonian vision portrays human life as "poor, nasty, brutish, and short" and pits individuals against one another in a war of all against all. The aggressive restlessness of particles in perpetual motion manifests itself as endless lust and the "perpetual quest for power after power unto death" (Hobbes), while space itself is contracted by the liveliness and motility of its teeming occupants. Whereas we may feel comfortable, even solitary, in a room with twenty-five dozing octogenarians, the same space will seem cramped and confining when peopled by a mere half-dozen hyperactive six-year-olds. As human desires expand, our sense of the world's spaciousness contracts, and so power becomes the salient issue. For the greater our desires, the more we need a way to attain them. Power is *the* means to all possible ends.

The realist world is thus above all a world of power: of force, coercion, and influence. It is a Newtonian cosmos in the conventional sense—containing particles in collision, bodies in motion, forces in contention, worlds in interaction. In such crowded spaces, traffic rules become essential and policemen are mandated by prudence. As Newton's world is kept orderly by physical laws, so the realist's world must be governed by positive laws—by commands and sanctions capable of subduing the unruly souls of relentless aggressors. Out of these social and political mechanics emerges the liberal-realist state in its rudimentary form: the *Rechtsstaat* or Watchman's State, where the object of politics is to deal with conflict, through resolution or toleration when possible, through repression when necessary. The benefits of liberty do not escape the realist, but the art of power is seen as liberty's sole guarantor. In a contracting physical world, intersecting autonomies cancel one another out. Freedom multiplied by great numbers produces anarchic conflict that destroys freedom. The powerful case Hobbes makes for absolute authority is in fact the only case he thinks can be made for absolute freedom.

Newtonian metaphors are perfectly consonant with the previous chapter's portrayal of liberal politics as a kind of human zookeeping. Zoos are defined by their physical externalities—the bars, cages, ditches, fences, closed-in spaces, and sharp-eyed keepers. Governments are likewise defined by their externalities: penal codes, prisons, policemen, laws, artificial boundaries establishing rights and privacy, institutional conventions establishing duties and obligations.

The minimalist does not differ greatly from the realist in his Newtonian bias. Like the realist, the minimalist conceptualizes human relations as molecular interaction at close quarters. However, although collisions remain unavoidable, their volatility is diminished by what the minimalist believes is the lesser momentum of human appetites and the more sluggish velocity of passions and desires. This greater optimism about human nature figuratively lowers the temperature of the test chamber. At times, the minimalist seems ready to go further still—beyond the borders of physical materialism altogether. Concepts such as tolerance, mutual respect, self-restraint, and moderation conjure up images of forms of political interaction in which materialism and its corollaries no longer obtain. The minimalist knows something that opens a door: he knows that conflict does not exhaust the potential of human concourse. The open door leads out toward strong democracy.

Unfortunately, minimalists rarely venture out beyond the threshold of the materialist confines in which their inertial frame imprisons them. Indeed, because the three dispositions are complementary facets of a single form of democracy, minimalism cannot really free itself from that form's materialist pretheory. Anarchist liberals may think that little is required to sustain natural freedom in its prepolitical *status quo ante*, whereas realist liberals may feel that a great deal is required—sovereign leviathans, indivisible powers, unlimited authority, irresistible sanctions. But both recognize that every political argument must begin and end with the radically individuated human particle and its defining autonomy, its privacy and solitude, and its absolute rights and absolute autonomy. His moderation notwithstanding, the minimalist starts perforce from the same position.

This is not to say that liberal democracy is without strengths. The physical materialism of its inertial frame is responsible for a great many of liberalism's unimpeachable virtues. Understanding all political argument as a matter of autonomous individuals seeking to preserve their physical space gives to politics a straightforward (simple if not simple-minded) tractability. The political project can be judged at each step by reference to the universal "ether" of individuals and their rights. Its instrumentalities can be conceived in palpable physical terms—freedom as the absence of impediments on motion, rights as territorial boundaries, conflict as the collision of bodies, legitimate authority as the justifiable crossing of borders, sanctions as external vector forces acting on the inherent momentum of human behavior—and thus subjected to effective control in the name of freedom. The apparent consensual legitimacy of its starting point and the vividness of its material images have helped to make liberal democracy an attractive, accessible, and historically successful theory of political life. Liberty if not equality, individuals if not justice, rights if not common goods have been served with an adroitness rare in any political tradition. Such virtues are not to be dismissed and may even go a long way toward compensating for the insufficiencies of liberalism's inertial frame. Those insufficiencies remain all too real, however.

INADEQUACIES OF THE NEWTONIAN INERTIAL FRAME

The Newtonian inertial frame can be faulted in two ways. First, there are other possible frames for a political theory of democracy that are more convincingly rooted in psychology, sociology, and history and that are certainly no less self-evident than Newtonianism. Second, there is one model for political theory that eschews inertial frames altogether, attempting instead to develop an autonomous theory of political democracy that does not depend on chain reasoning or on the inertial position to which chain reasoning inevitably returns. This theory, briefly noted below, is developed in detail in Part II as "strong democracy."

It is not difficult to conceive of alternative inertial frames. Imagine for a moment that in place of the materialist's understanding of humans as physical beings, we posit the idea of humans as psychic or spiritual beings and that in place of the corollaries of indivisibility, commensurability, mutual exclusivity, and sensationalism, we derive corollaries of divisibility, incommensurability, mutualism, and intentionalism. In so doing we would be treating the human animal as a being with contradictory, diversified, and ambivalent interests—as a person who may have conflicts within himself as well as with other people. We would understand individuals' desires, intentions, talents, and projects as incommensurable, thus making equality a problem for politics to solve rather than the condition for all politics. We would be able to conceive of occupying common space with our friends and fellows without having to surrender our distinctive identities and felt freedoms. And we would be able to see our behavior as determined not merely by external stimuli but also by rationally conceived ends, mutually willed goods, and ideals created out of common discourse and action.

Following the train of these imaginings, we might very well counter Robert Nozick's query "why not anarchy?" with the equally self-evident queries "why not mutualism?" or "why not democracy?", shifting the burden of proof back to those who are disposed toward radical individualism. There is no more reason to think we begin our human journey with absolute rights than that we begin it with absolute obligations. Serious Christians, for example, might presume that obligations are paramount. And the Greeks were at pains to show that individualism and revolution were deviations from the natural condition of free men as citizens of the polis. The Greek term for the noncitizen, or private person—the odd, uprooted, homeless one—was *idiot*, and the word then as now carried the pejorative sense of "ignoramus." The burden of proof, for the Greeks, rested with the man who would celebrate individuality; not even Socrates would take on that burden in the *Crito* or in the *Apology* (where he preferred death to exile).[20]

Change, too, may be viewed as a deviation from a natural and desirable stasis or as itself the norm (as in modern progressive theories of history from Condorcet through Marx, Spencer, and the recent developmental theorists). Burke insisted that revolution, *prima fronte*, always requires an apology, whereas dialecticians such as Hegel regard stasis as a sign of the breakdown of normal historical dynamics.

Robert Paul Wolff once wrote that his "failure to find any theoretical justification for the authority of the state" had led him, reluctantly, to adopt the posture of a "philosophical anarchist."[21] But he might as well have announced that his failure to find any ultimate theoretical justification for natural rights or for radical autonomy had made him a philosophical statist. In fact, as I shall try to demonstrate in Part II, legitimate politics does not have any authoritative starting point in pretheory but is self-generating and self-justifying. Philosophical anarchism and philosophical statism are equally absurd inferences from the same error—namely, that political positions rest on philosophical foundations that are somehow both self-evident and incorrigible. To rest politics on a pretheoretical foundation is to base it on sand. Far from justifying the structures that arise from politics, the practice makes all justification and thus all legitimation impossible. The Mandate of Heaven and the Divine Right of Kings are no less (and no more) secure starting points for political reasoning than the Sanctity of the Individual and the Priority of Natural Rights. The contract theory of Hobbes and Locke was an attempt to use naturalism, with its elegant conflation of the descriptive and prescriptive dimensions of the "natural world" and of

20. In the *Crito*, Socrates places the duty to obey the laws of Athens—even when they are administered by unjust men—far above the desire "to cling greedily to life" and associates his own humanity with his citizenship in the polis. See Plato, *Crito*, 50A–54B.
21. Robert Paul Wolff, *In Defense of Anarchism* (New York: Anchor Books, 1970), p. viii. Wolff's anarchism remained at an appropriately metaphysical level. Wolff condemned actual anarchist acts of violence, which he calls "vicious acts of murder and destruction" that arise out of the "wild fantasies of those deranged young men and women whose frustration and rage have driven them to useless, malicious adventures" (Letter to the *New York Times*, 13 September 1970). This heartfelt rejection suggests something of the abyss that separated and continues to separate philosophical positions from their practical consequences. Robert Nozick thus worries about adopting positions similar to those held by people who are "narrow and rigid"—"bad company" all in all—but reassures himself that his work is only a "philosophical exploration" not a "political tract" (*Anarchy*, pp. x, xii).

"natural men," to undergird and legitimate the consensual state against traditional authoritarianism. But their pretheory was set in a naturalism no less metaphysical than the natural theories of king-ship it supplanted. Kant's and, recently, Rawls's more formalistic moral theories tried to devise a consensual starting point for substantive theories of political and ethical justice; but again the consensual character of the starting point turned out to be resting on sand. Agreement depended on the incorrigibility rather than the theoretical potency of the starting point. In both cases, the politics that emerged offered a poor model for practical citizenship and for the pursuit of common goods; in both cases, syllogistic coherence was won at the price of misrepresenting the conditions of human interdependence. All liberal theories seem finally to reduce to premises that are "essentially contestable"—rooted in irreducible, pretheoretical grounds about which there is no agreement and can be no argument.[22]

Liberal democratic reasoning has, then, been chain reasoning, leading back ineluctably to elementary pretheoretical beginnings that themselves have no beginnings. As deism posited a primeval First Cause for its otherwise orderly and intelligible cosmos, liberal democracy has pushed its theory back into a dawn where there are only shadows and where inscrutable premises appear *ex nihilo* as the justification for all the scrutables that follow.

There are, of course, other philosophical methods. Dialectical philosophy sustains itself while in motion, as it were, looking for conviction in the process of an unfolding logic rather than in its genesis. Pragmatic philosophy looks to ends rather than beginnings to establish its legitimacy, thereby shifting the burden of justification from the invisible to the visible world. I will argue in Part II that the theory of strong democracy is both dialectical and pragmatic. The democratic politics it envisions is autonomous of independently grounded metaphysics, achieving its legitimacy through self-generating, self-sustaining, and self-transforming modes of reasoning and from the kinds of political interaction that incarnate that reasoning. But what is perhaps already obvious here is that the problem of the thin democratic inertial frame is, in its most problematic and disturbing manifestations, the problem of thin democratic epistemology. Certainty about starting points and rest positions is an aspect

22. For an account of the uses of this phrase in politics, see William Connolly, *The Terms of Political Discourse* (Lexington, Mass.: Heath, 1974).

of the problem of "objective" or "certain" knowledge. As it turns out, there is a strong if unremarkable correspondence between the Newtonian inertial frame, as portrayed here, and the Cartesian epistemological frame upon which—as I hope to show in the next chapter—liberal democratic theory has also come to rely.

Chapter Three

The Epistemological Frame: Cartesian Politics

America is one of the countries where the precepts of Descartes are least studied and are best applied.

(de Tocqueville)

For over two thousand years the weight of the most influential and authoritatively orthodox tradition of thought has been devoted to the problem of a purely cognitive certification of the antecedent immutable reality of truth, beauty and goodness.

(John Dewey)

Delusive geometrical accuracy in moral arguments is the most fallacious of all sophistries.

(Edmund Burke)

Liberal democratic theory, like all political theory, depends on particular assumptions about the character of political knowledge. These epistemological assumptions account for many of that theory's strengths and not a few of its weaknesses. The paramount assumption is Cartesian: that there exists a knowable independent ground—an incorrigible first premise or "antecedent immutable reality"—from which the concepts, values, standards, and ends of political life can be derived by simple deduction. It is this sort of inferential certainty that Pufendorf evinces when he claims that it is possible to "reduce moral science to a system as well connected as those of geometry and mechanics and founded upon principles that are equally certain."[1]

1. Samuel Pufendorf, *Droit de la nature et de gens*, sect. 2, n. 6.

John Dewey, as noted in the previous chapter, felt that man's "quest for certainty," rooted in "man's distrust of himself," produced a "desire to get beyond and above himself" through the "transcendence of pure knowledge."[2] Similarly, A. R. Louch speaks of man's "search for ultimate observables" and for a supporting "doctrine of incorrigibility."[3] This futile search seeks a basis for social knowledge secure beyond all challenge, one that will endow political practice with the absolute certainty of generic truth.

Louch and Dewey's analyses of the futility of the quest for certain political knowledge reveal their debt to Charles Sanders Peirce. In his essay on method, which he disguised as an autobiography, Peirce characterized as "irresistibly comical" the need of philosophers for "infallibility in scientific matters."[4] He preferred to think that the true scientist could force himself to live with the "irritation of doubt" despite the inclination to "fix belief" that doubt invariably arouses.

Peirce sympathized with the need for certainty but regretted the consequences. We should perhaps do the same, for the quest for certainty in political thinking seems more likely to breed orthodoxy than to nurture truth and in practice tends to promote the domination of method over substance. Ironically, this procedure produces a fundamentally unscientific inversion of the "judicious method of the ancients," who, as Dewey remarked, were content to base "their conclusions about knowledge on the nature of the universe in which knowledge occurs."[5] The obsession of recent social-science empiricists with methodology has, by contrast, led them to place epistemology before ontology. In an attempt to mimic the hard sciences, of which they rarely have a true understanding, these social scientists have tried to subordinate every understanding of reality to some orthodox construction of understanding. For a brief period, now happily passed, metatheoretical analysis threatened to become the only legitimate form of political theorizing.

The claim advanced here is that this relentless quest for certainty has been a particular feature of liberal political philosophy from its inception. By rooting the political in a prepolitical realm of the im-

2. John Dewey, *The Quest for Certainty* (New York: Capricorn, 1960), pp. 6–7.

3. A. R. Louch, *Explanation and Human Action* (Berkeley: University of California Press, 1969), p. 44.

4. Charles Sanders Peirce, *Philosophical Writings of Peirce*, ed. J. Buchler (New York: Dover, 1955), p. 3. See also Peirce's "The Fixation of Belief" in the same volume.

5. Dewey, *Quest*, p. 41.

mutable, that quest has worked mischief on both the theory and the practice of politics. Politics, the liberal epistemology insisted, could not be portrayed or understood in political terms but required antiseptic categories untainted by the subject matter that was to be their object. In this insistence, liberals were more Cartesian than Descartes. Descartes wrote, "I was convinced that I must once for all seriously undertake to rid myself of all the opinions which I had formerly accepted, and commence to build anew from the foundation, if I wanted to establish any firm and permanent structure in the sciences."[6] But as we shall see below (in Chapter 8), Descartes fortified himself with conventional beliefs before embarking on his journey of discovery, whereas Hobbes and his successors persuaded themselves that theories of political life had truly to be erected *de novo* on wholly nonpolitical foundations. Political obligation had to rest on the prepolitics of human interaction in a hypothetical state of nature; political freedom had to derive from natural liberty and stand without reference to politics; political rights had to issue from natural rights established without reference to social or political conditions; and the whole subtle complex of social and political relations, which the Greeks thought defined the individual human being from the outset, had to be reduced to a physics-based psychology of individual atoms defined in radical isolation from one another.

This pseudo-Cartesian conviction permeates the entire social-contract and state-of-nature tradition: it is no less evident in recent liberal theorists such as Ackerman, Rawls, and Nozick than in Hobbes. There is little to choose between Hobbes and Nozick, for example, when Nozick posits—he does not argue the point, he promulgates it—that among the "possible ways of understanding the political realm," the "most desirable theoretical alternative, to be abandoned only if known to be impossible," is to "fully explain it in terms of the nonpolitical."[7] The very title of John H. Hallowell's much earlier book, *The Moral Foundations of Democracy*, discloses its commitment to a reductive epistemology and to the assumption (in Isaiah Berlin's words) that "political theory is a branch of moral philosophy, which starts from the discovery or application of moral notions in the sphere of political relations."[8]

6. René Descartes, *Meditations*, ed. E. S. Haldane and G. R. T. Ross (Cambridge: Cambridge University Press, 1970), vol. 2, p. 144.
7. Robert Nozick, *Anarchy, State, and Utopia* (New York: Basic Books, 1974), p. 6.
8. Sir Isaiah Berlin, *Two Concepts of Liberty* (Oxford: Clarendon Press, 1958), p. 5.

In each of these cases, the quest for certainty appears to draw the theorist's attention away from the need to render political life intelligible and political practice just and to divert it instead toward the need to render intelligibility absolute and justice incorrigible—even at the high cost of distorting or abandoning the subject matter under study. T. L. Thorson thus finds political aptness in Bertrand Russell's question, "Is there any knowledge in the world which is so certain that no reasonable man can doubt it?" To Thorson, "this is just the kind of 'knowledge' we want about democracy."[9]

At first glance, the quest for certainty appears to be metaphysically impartial. It will accept either side of the great metaphysical controversies about the nature of antecedent being so long as it can base itself on *some* form of antecedent being. Hence, it is open to and has been associated with both idealistic and materialistic conceptions of the independent ground. It has drawn on both rationalist and empiricist epistemology as two tactics in a single strategy: the grounding of the political world in certain, prepolitical truth—in absolute fact or absolute idea. Liberal theorists such as Karl Popper and Isaiah Berlin have recognized the absolutism of the Idea that certain forms of rationalist idealism bring to political thinking, but they have failed to detect similar tendencies in their own empiricism.[10] It is again left to John Dewey to expose the underlying logic:

In spite of the polar oppositions between the two schools, they depend upon a common premise. According to both . . . reflective thought . . . is not originative. It has its test in antecedent reality as that is disclosed in some non-reflective immediate knowledge. The controversy between the two schools is simply as to the origin and nature of previous direct knowledge. To both schools, reflection, though involving inference, is reproductive; the 'proof' of its results is found in comparison with what is known without any inference.[11]

In Dewey's interpretation, the quest for knowledge seems to have two very distinct motives: a desire for intelligibility or for illumination, which is a purely mental condition that may permit (or demand) considerable inexactitude or even fuzziness; and a desire for certainty, which is a psychological condition that, as Peirce noted, may be established only at the cost of illumination. Now these two

9. T. L. Thorson, *The Logic of Democracy* (New York: Holt, Rinehart, and Winston, 1962).

10. Compare Sir Isaiah Berlin, *Two Concepts*, and Sir Karl Popper, *The Open Society and Its Enemies*, 2 vols. (London: Routledge and Kegan Paul, 1945).

11. Dewey, *Quest*, p. 109.

motives are often at cross purposes, despite the fact that complete illumination might in an ideal world nurture a restful state of mind by easing or even erasing the "irritation of doubt." In practice, however, the motives are usually at war. And when that war erupts, both empiricism and rationalism become alternate strategies to achieve a single objective—the extinction of doubt, even at the cost of extinguishing intelligibility as well. T. H. Huxley often treated what he called "materialism" and "spiritualism" as opposite sides of the same absurdity: the idea that we can know anything whatsoever of either spirit or matter.

The liberal imagines that to understand politics, we must know something very definite about either spirit or matter. Since the certainty matters more than the subject, however, liberal theorists may use both empiricist and rationalist arguments freely, often by turns throughout a single line of reasoning. Are Hobbes's psychological hedonism and his associational psychology empiricist in character? Or does his commitment to reason and natural law make him a rationalist? It may be that these are the wrong questions. For what Hobbes himself confesses is that he wishes to "reduce" the doctrines of justice and policy in general to the "rules and infallibility of reason," his objective being to root his new science of politics in certainty rather than to confirm some particular metaphysic.[12] The point in liberal political theory has been to reconstruct the house of politics, fashioned by the history of human dependency from strange and difficult materials, in a simpler and more familiar medium. If stone presents a smoother facade, then the house of politics must be rebuilt in stone, whatever materials it might have been made of in its original state.

To understand politics is therefore always, necessarily, to deconstruct and depoliticize it: that is to say, to decontaminate it of those exotic and unmanageable elements that resist assimilation by the mind in quest of certainty. This is precisely the program of Hobbes's *Leviathan*: politics is to be refashioned as morals, morals remade as psychology, psychology recast as mechanics, and mechanics recreated as particle physics. From such elemental (and elementary) building blocks as these can be constructed the entire political cosmos: the ends of political action and the norms of political decision as well as the standards of political understanding and the measures

12. Thomas Hobbes, *Elements of Law*, ed. F. Tönnies (London: Cass, 1969), from the Epistle Dedicatory.

of political science. Not even Descartes could have dreamed of so complete a recomposition of the world by minds set on certainty.

CARTESIAN CHARACTERISTICS OF LIBERAL THEORY

The method of inquiry associated with the bold epistemological presumptions of early liberalism can be characterized as Cartesian in a broad metaphoric sense, but it is also Cartesian in a number of quite specific ways: it tends to be reductionist, genetic, dualistic, speculative, and solipsistic. Liberal political thought—under which heading we have now included theorizing about the social contract, the state of nature, natural rights, and original positions—can be shown to be correspondingly reductionist, genetic, dualistic, speculative, and solipsistic in specifiably political ways.

To Hobbes, reductionism is self-evidently a desirable method of inquiry. In the "Epistle Dedicatory" to his *Elements of Law*, he insists that to "reduce" the doctrines of justice and of policy in general "to the rules and infallibility of reason, there is no way, but first to put such principles down for a foundation, as passion not mistrusting, may not seek to displace; and afterward to build thereon the truth of cases in the law of nature (which hitherto have been built in the air) by degrees, till the whole be inexpungable."[13] A sturdy house of politics can only arise on an inexpungable and infallible foundation, set deep in prepolitical granite.

John Rawls's "original position" involves a similar reduction. Individual men are decontaminated of the special psychologies and particular interests by which we understand them to be men, so that a political theory of justice can develop from an antiseptic starting place.[14] The theory's success in addressing the political ambiguities

13. Ibid.
14. John Rawls, *A Theory of Justice* (Cambridge, Mass.: Harvard University Press, 1971), part 1. Rawls has expressed some striking reservations about this approach in his recent Dewey lectures on Kantian constructivism. He acknowledges that "justifying a conception of justice is not primarily an epistemological problem. The search for reasonable grounds for reaching agreement rooted in our conception of ourselves and in our relation to society replaces the search for moral truth interpreted as fixed by a prior and independent order of objects and relations" ("Kantian Constructivism in Moral Theory," *Journal of Philosophy* 77, 9 [September 1980], p. 519).
This view is obviously more hospitable to the position developed here, but it raises fundamental questions about the notion of rational self-interest on which *A Theory of Justice* seems to be based. For a discussion, see William A. Galston, "Moral Personality and Liberal Theory: Rawls' 'Dewey Lectures'," *Political Theory* 10, 4 (November 1982).

and uncertainties of the real world is measured by its remoteness from that world.

Robert Nozick's gloss on Hobbesian method is an even more startling example of reductionist decontamination at play. In *Anarchy, State, and Utopia*, he wants to persuade us that

The more fundamental the starting point (the more it picks out basic, important, and inescapable features of the human situation) and the less close it is or seems to its result (the less political or statelike it looks) the better. . . . Discovering that political features and relations were reducible to, or identical with, ostensibly very different nonpolitical ones would be an exciting result. Were these features fundamental, the political realm would be firmly and deeply based.[15]

Now it is evident that all knowledge, all modes of knowing, involve a crucial element of reduction. But the liberal penchant for decontamination leads to reductive abstractions that void politics of its essential meaning altogether. A pure physics of biology that lost track of the concept of life in an attempt at simplification and deductive rigor would hardly count as a science: life *is* the distinction between inorganic molecules and living cells. Yet liberal theorists think they are winning a great victory for social science when they reduce human interaction to physical mechanics and the dynamics of community to the statics of hedonistic individualism—losing track by intent of the very phenomena they purport to illuminate. They have of course been reinforced in their rather odd view of the scientific enterprise by the positivistic and behavioristic tendency to portray reality in monolithic, one-dimensional terms and, as a consequence, to adopt a monolithic, inflexible approach to method.

The pitfalls of methodologism are by now so familiar that a single passage from Dewey may serve to recall them. The essence of human affairs, Dewey explains with the patience of a schoolmaster, "is that we cannot indulge in the selective abstractions that are the secret of the success of physical knowing. When we introduce a like simplification into social and moral subjects we eliminate the distinctively human factors: reduction to the physical ensues."[16] Reduction to the physical is a way to circumvent contingency and the

15. Nozick, *Anarchy*, p. 7 (italics added). I have tried to explore the consequences of Nozick's position for political theory in my "Deconstituting Politics: Robert Nozick and Philosophical Reductionism," *Journal of Politics* 39, 1 (February 1977).

16. Dewey, *Quest*, p. 216.

uncertainties of accident and fortune that seem indigenous to the world of politics. But, as Karl Marx notes in *The Poverty of Philosophy*, "If we abstract from every subject all the alleged accidents, animate or inanimate, men or things, we are right in saying that in the final abstraction, the only substance left is the logical categories."[17]

Marx is excoriating the idealists here, but they are little better than the positivists, who distort reality in the name of science when they declare themselves enemies of all accident and madness in the world. As Jürgen Habermas has noticed, "When the sciences seek to wrest from contingency that which is empirically uniform, they are positivistically purged of insanity; and therefore insanity must remain ungoverned and uncontrolled."[18] To the degree that politics flirts with the anarchic, the ungovernable, and the insane in man's spirit, positivistic social science will be unable to penetrate politics and make it intelligible.

John Dewey makes the same point: "Empiricism," he says, "is conceived of as tied up with what has been, or is 'given,' " whereas "experience in its vital form is experimental, an effort to change the given; it is characterized by projection, by reading forward into the unknown; connection with a future is its salient trait."[19]

Politics is archetypically experiential and thus experimental in Dewey's sense. It is the art of planning, coordinating, and executing the collective futures of human communities. It is the art of inventing a common destiny for women and men in conflict. To create such a destiny is to be autonomous of necessity and its givens and to be capable of meaningful choice. Reductionism ultimately links the future to a past governed by necessity and leaves freedom without a home in the human scheme of things.

If the Cartesian epistemology of liberal democracy is reductionist in its passion for certainty, it is also genetic in its affection for deductivism. In taking the syllogism as the chief instrument of its logic, the reductive method insists on the priority in political reasoning of the axiom or premise. As in a well-conceived geometry, it excavates starting principles the logical priority of which becomes a warrant

17. Karl Marx, *The Poverty of Philosophy* (New York: International Publishers, 1963), pp. 105–106.
18. Jürgen Habermas, *Knowledge and Human Interests* (Boston: Beacon, 1971), p. 282.
19. Cited in Richard J. Bernstein, *Praxis and Action* (Philadelphia: University of Pennsylvania Press, 1971), p. 206.

for their moral and political priority; the house of politics is then built on foundations laid deep within the excavation.[20]

When reasoning is subsumed to geometry and political understanding is made to depend on syllogistic chains no less apolitical in their conclusions than in their necessarily apolitical premises, then political theory becomes apolitical theory and Burke's charge that geometrical accuracy in moral arguments is the most fallacious of all sophistries seems vindicated. The problem is compounded when the starting points turn out to be pretheoretical as well as prepolitical (see Chapter 2) and thus beyond justification or falsification—beyond all rational discussion. The paradox of First Cause (what is the cause of the First Cause?) is particularly troublesome in a method that moves from genetic origins and that rests the entire weight of its argumentative edifice on such remote and abstract "uncaused causes" as abstract rights and absolute liberties.

The abyss that separates actual politics from its starting point in reductionist chain reasoning gives liberal democratic epistemology a propensity toward philosophical dualism as well. The knower is cut off from the known, epistemology is isolated from ontology, thought is radically differentiated from action, and fact and value are identified as residents of hostile universes—polarizations that in every case are contrary to experience and political reality. Once knowing and doing have been pulled apart and given nearly opposite meanings, doing is inevitably subordinated to knowing—particularly in a Cartesian world where the perceptor is prior to the perceived and thinking is prior both to being and to doing ("I think, therefore I am").

This explains why liberal theory often appears to operate in a speculative mode that discomfits Marxists (*The Eleventh Thesis on Feuerbach*), sociologists, conservatives, pragmatists, and other dialectical thinkers with their eyes on history and the concrete social forces that shape it. Genetic reasoning will clearly prefer speculative foundations to concrete realities, and dualism will assure that the two are kept in antiseptic isolation. Theory will be regarded as an autonomous realm that illuminates, guides, and otherwise serves the world of action but remains untainted by it. Where the realm of

20. Robert Paul Wolff precisely captures Rawls's preoccupation with axiomatic starting points: "The claim is simply that in our reasoning about moral and social questions, we can choose to perform the same abstractions from particularities that we have learned to perform in our mathematical reasoning" (*Understanding Rawls* [Princeton: Princeton University Press, 1977], p. 121).

action is dynamic, purposive, and always in process, theory will deliberately attempt to remain static, mechanistic, and causal—precisely in order to capture and subdue the active notions that define politics. The orderliness of epistemology is not merely imposed on but is substituted for the inchoate messiness of the political. Here, deconstruction means control. William James has called this speculative reductionism "vicious abstractionism," which he describes in a fashion that fairly resonates with the Cartesian overtones of liberal theory:

> Let me give the name of "vicious abstractionism" to a way of using concepts which may be thus described: we conceive of a concrete situation by singling out some salient or important feature in it, and classing it under that; then, instead of adding to its previous characters all the positive consequences which that way of conceiving it may bring, we proceed to use our concept privately; reducing the originally rich phenomenon to the naked suggestions of that name abstractly taken, treating it as a case of "nothing but" the concept, and acting as if all the other characters from out of which the concept is abstracted were expunged. Abstraction, functioning in this way, becomes a means of arrest far more than a means of advance in thought. It mutilates things; it creates difficulties and finds impossibilities. . . . The viciously privative employment of abstract characters and class names is . . . one of the great original sins of the rationalistic mind.[21]

Tolstoy teaches the same lesson in an aphorism: "As soon as man applies his intelligence and only his intelligence to any object at all," he chides, "he unfailingly destroys the object."

Underlying the several Cartesian features of liberal political theory is a powerful tradition of philosophical solipsism that can be traced back to Spinoza and Hobbes as well as to Descartes. Bergson remarks that "when man first begins to think, he thinks of himself first." Cartesian liberalism prompts man to think of himself first, second, and last. The tradition understands all knowledge either as a reconstruction of impressions imprinted on the individual subject or as a product of ideas directly apprehended by rational individuals. In both cases—simple empiricism and simple idealism—the mode is radically reflexive. To think is to be conscious of thinking, to reflect on oneself as thinker and on one's mode of thought. Whether it is grounded in a theory of the sense impression or percept as a quasi-physical entity (empiricism) or in a theory of the ideal or the concept as that entity's rational construction (idealism), the

21. William James, "The Meaning of Truth," in *Pragmatism* (Cambridge, Mass.: Harvard University Press, 1978), pp. 301–302.

process is subjective, individual, and reflexive, and thus thoroughly solipsistic. A premium is placed on the radically isolated consciousness, whether it is perceived as sense perceptor or as rational apprehender.

Yet solipsism would seem to be a rather curious outcome for a method devoted to the pursuit of certainty and objectivity. Reflexivity may seem a self-evident starting point for the Cartesian; but, ironically, it is a point of subjectivity that is immune by definition to common judgment and to communal corroboration. Reflexive thinking quickly becomes a cage separating individual consciousness from the very world that consciousness is intended to mediate and confirm. In the language of metaphysics, "things-in-themselves" vanish, leaving sense percepts or rational reconstructions of sense percepts as their sole ciphers.

Empiricist psychology, acknowledging the difficulty, tries to circumvent subjectivism by displaying an aggressive self-confidence. It proclaims its humility ("all knowledge is subjective") in the language of hubris ("subjective knowledge is *all* the knowledge there is"). The trap of private sensory experience may close us off from the world of "things-in-themselves," but by placing the perceiving self at the center of knowing, it gives the self-evidence of direct sensation to the narrowed range of experience that perception certifies as "real." Certainty is won by denaturing experience: by substituting subject for object, percept for thing, idea for concrete construct. Liberal epistemology does just this when it abstracts human beings from the social settings in which their humanity is manifested and then tries to reconstruct them in such hypotheticals as the "state of nature" or "natural rights" or the "absolute and autonomous individual."

There may be a social or a communal dimension to political knowledge, but the solipsistic imagination cannot conceive it. In Charles Taylor's wise words, "The exclusion of this possibility of the communal comes once again from the baleful influence of the epistemological tradition for which all knowledge has to be reconstructed from the impressions imprinted on the individual subject."[22]

22. Charles Taylor, "Interpretation and the Sciences of Man," *Review of Metaphysics* 25, 1 (September 1971), pp. 31–32. Taylor concludes, "If we free ourselves from the hold of these objects, this seems a wildly implausible view about the development of human consciousness."

Like empiricism, rationalism seeks to escape the subjectivism of reflexivity. The naturalistic strategy that treats nature as the locus of the principles and laws apprehended by reason presents itself as one rationalist escape. For rationalist naturalism is impervious to the critique that Hume and his successors leveled at naturalism. The apprehending, rational mind asserts that it is not trapped within itself and separated from the real world because it *is* the real world.[23] If minds in collision cannot agree on what is real, it is because one or the other is in error, not because rational knowledge is subjective.

Yet though it associates reason with nature and thus with the real world, this strategy is oblivious to the social character of knowledge and to the ultimate dependence of private reason (however universal its claims) on public corroboration in the setting of human community. Rationalists and empiricists alike lose touch with the reality that is their common object. Thus does the solipsism of Cartesian epistemology serve to reinforce the radical individualism of liberal democratic political theory; thus is created the social analogue of the rational mind or of the sense perceptor—the private, asocial individual defined by absolute liberty, distinguished by utter isolation, and imbued with a sense that he is circumscribed by total solitude.

Yet the epistemological frame involves more than a broad Cartesian preoccupation with subjective consciousness. Although there is no neat correspondence between the several dispositions of liberal democracy and the variations in the Cartesian frame sketched above, there are interesting linkages that serve to elaborate the liberal model of democratic government.

Cartesian Epistemology and the Dispositions of Liberal Democracy

There is a suggestive though hardly decisive similarity between the anarchist disposition in liberal democracy and rationalist or cogni-

23. I have in mind here not pure philosophical idealism on the model of Kant or Hegel, but rather the Cartesian conviction that subjective consciousness and objective reality cannot effectively be kept separate. A. R. Louch offers this pertinent comment:

The villain of the piece turns out to be the doctrine of incorrigibility. In their search for ultimate observables, classical empiricists were led by the question: have I now got something which would provide the uncontestable basis for any knowledge claim? So they were driven to the equally incompatible extremes of unanalysibility or a mental location of the objects of immediate experience. (*Explanation and Human Action*, p. 44)

At his "mental location," idealism and empiricism collide.

tivist variations of the quest for certainty, where Idea or Concept is construed as the independent ground or antecedent reality of political knowledge and political judgment; between the realist disposition and empiricist or noncognitivist variations of the quest, where fact or datum or sense percept serves as the independent ground; and between the minimalist disposition and skepticist variations on the quest, where certainty is regarded, ironically, as both indispensable and impossible.

In each case, it is presumed that politics is conditioned by the quest, whether successful or unsuccessful, for an independent ground. In each case, since politics is thought to apply knowledge derived from prepolitical grounds—to put stationary truths into motion, as it were—epistemological differences can be detected in the dispositional differences. Thus the linkage between anarchism and idealism takes the form of this implicit definition: "Politics (or, rather, antipolitics) is the application of individual reason to human relations; liberty is reason's chief concomitant." The linkage between realism and empiricism has this formulation: "Politics is the application of science—sense perception organized as systemic, nomological principles—to human relations; power is the chief concomitant of scientific politics." And the linkage between minimalism and skepticism is expressed in this typical formulation: "Politics is the application of doubt to human relations; tolerance is its defining norm."

The first linkage yields a politics of radical individualism, natural rights, and private property (the anarchist disposition). The second yields a politics of power, law, and control (the realist disposition). The third yields a politics of toleration, pluralism, and noninterference (the minimalist disposition). In each case, the political world of action derives both its intelligibility and its guiding praxis from notions about truth, reality, and being that are themselves established independently of politics. In each case, the linkage is more than merely incidental although, as closer inspection makes evident, it remains something less than necessary.

Rationalism is a useful partner to the anarchist disposition because it provides a philosophical framework for absolute freedom and unassailable individual rights. Reason paired with right nurtured the growth of liberal individualist principles in naturalists such as Spinoza, Hobbes and Locke; in utopians such as Godwin and Fourier; and in recent liberal democrats such as John Rawls and

Bruce Ackerman (on the liberal left) and Robert Nozick (on the libertarian right).

If the individual is the source of morals that, while individual, are neither arbitrary nor subjective, some form of objective or universal reason must presumably condition the formation of these morals. The individual must know moral truth in and for himself but also universally. Reason is the vital link—the common process that gives to individual discovery the legitimacy of mutuality. There are individualist irrationalists such as Max Stirner or Nietzsche, but their millennial, antisocial anarchism is alien to the anarchistic element in liberal democracy—which is asocial rather than antisocial, diffident rather than assertive, and laissez-faire rather than Darwinian. Indeed, even where the tradition defines private individuals as deficient in reason, it attributes rationality to mediating structures such as the market or the natural world at large.

Whatever its form, autonomous reason has been liberal democracy's chief weapon in its rebellion against traditional authority. One may even say that modern constitutionalism would not have emerged if men had not believed that legitimate authority can be established consensually through the agreement of rational individuals who, although motivated by desire and private interest, can nevertheless act prudentially in the name of rationality. Reason saved individualism from arbitrariness and made contractual authority competitive with more ancient forms of legitimate authority.[24]

The Protestant Reformation had demonstrated that individuals' capacity to know might supersede institutionalized authority and divine revelation without loosing anarchy upon the world. Reason proclaimed a new faith in the universality of individual knowledge, suggesting that authority could be created as well as given and that what men knew could make them free. The derivation of freedom from knowledge was direct, not oblique: to know was to be free of all heteronomy. In its earliest phase, then, liberal democracy reflected not the Baconian dictum that Knowledge is Power but the rationalist dictum that Knowledge is Freedom.

Yet knowledge was also power. Realism as the Hobbesian disposition within liberal democracy forged early links to empiricism that were no less strong than the links of the anarchist disposition to

24. For a relevant discussion, see Otto Hirschman, *The Passions and the Interests* (Princeton: Princeton University Press, 1977).

rationalism. Empiricism offered a world view in which power realities could be rooted and legitimate coercion explained and justified.
In the doctrine of circumstances (environmentalism), the realist discovered a language well suited to express conflict and control, force
and reaction, law and will. The language of interests typical of realism was a language of necessity. Vector physics and interpersonal,
associational psychology met in Hobbes's mechanistic hedonism.

And so, where the radical individualist (the anarchist liberal) saw
in every interest a possible right and in every action a possible
choice, the realist saw in every right a determining interest and in
every choice an ineluctable necessity. "Will" itself was only the last
"cause" in a long chain of necessity. Natural science displaced natural reason, just as realist politics, organized around the technology
of power, displaced anarchist politics organized around the maintenance of freedom. Thus the two dispositions of liberal democracy
vie with one another as they complement one another, each reducing the key constructs of the other to its own currency: the realist
reifies ideals as wants, free choices as foregone consequences, and
philosophy as ideology: the anarchist imbues cold interest with prudential good and makes of every determinate human interaction a
drama of autonomous will.

The modern heirs to these complementary rivals are modern social science (realism updated) and normative political philosophy
(idealism toned down). The new realists construe politics as power
and deploy power science to conceptualize politics and to guide politicians. The new idealists continue to chase freedom and to deploy
rationalist metaphysics to legitimize politics and rein in politicians.
In the old and the new world of liberal democracy, the two styles
coexist very well, despite their apparently antithetical qualities.
Both depend on external epistemological principles in their construction of the political world, and both concur in regarding politics
as applied knowledge.

The linkage between skepticism and minimalism—our third disposition—is less easy to assimilate to this neat scheme. Uncertainty
and fallibilism hardly seem consonant with the quest for certainty.
Indeed, skepticist-liberals such as Sir Karl Popper have suggested
that liberalism's paramount defense against "totalitarian" variations of mass democracy is doubt (see Chapter 5). Yet fallibilism im-
itates rationalism and empiricism in its claim that political knowledge and action are functions of what we know. The difference is

that the fallibilist is persuaded by neither rationalist nor empiricist solutions to the problem of antecedent reality and concludes regretfully that "there is no body of knowledge such that from it can be derived infallible or even fallible decisions about ultimate political objectives."[25]

Conditional or tentative knowledge means conditional or tentative politics. That is, far from seeking political alternatives to the futile quest for certainty, the fallibilist necessarily concludes that politics is equally futile and so denies altogether the possibility of a philosophically legitimate political community. If the kind of knowledge on which politics must depend cannot be shown to exist, then the political imposition of truth or the application of prior knowledge to social relations can never be justified. Minimalism, tolerance, and strict curbs on governmental activity must follow. Neither the private individual nor the state possesses a warrant for action of a public kind. If we cannot know anything for certain, we should never do anything for certain. This is the lesson of Mill's anticategorical imperative, which declares that a community of all men minus one has no more right to compel that one man to act according to its unfounded prejudices than he has to compel the community to act according to his unfounded prejudices. The one and the many share a mutual ignorance—we may call it "cognitive diffidence"— that can only justify doing nothing at all, or as little as possible.

Now this fallibilist skepticism has unquestionably provided liberal democracy with many of its most valuable safeguards. It has served to counterbalance the Cartesian politics of certainty typical of the anarchist and realist dispositions. Doubting equally the claims of absolute freedom and absolute power, it confronts epistemological dogmatism with diffidence and moderation, arguing that the individual can be better served by tolerance than by certainty. Moreover, although fallibilism begins by endorsing the linkage between knowing and doing, its discovery that knowing can never be certain leads it to question the linkage itself and then to reject the reductionism of liberal democracy, in a sequence that holds out the promise of setting politics free (in the manner elaborated below in Part II).

For the most part, however, fallibilist varieties of liberal democracy have drawn from the failure of the quest for certainty lessons whose impact on community, public purpose, and action can only

25. Renford Brambaugh, "Plato's Political Analogies," in P. Laslett et al., eds., *Politics, Philosophy, and Society*, 1st ser. (Oxford: Blackwell, 1956), p. 67.

be called paralyzing. Political life has been enervated rather than liberated. In the end, wary minimalists have been anemic democrats, proffering a politics as thin as the thinnest gruel. Privacy and passivity are celebrated not because they maximize individual liberty (that is the anarchist's argument) but because privacy and passivity alone guarantee that no delusive certainty will come to dominate a world in which truth has no warrant. Pluralism is advocated not in the name of the intrinsic merits of diversity but because there can be no common or public ends, no common or public goods, no common or public will. Commonality itself is transformed into an enemy of doubt and thus into the nemesis of freedom. The impossibility of certain knowledge becomes the impossibility of affirmative politics; without an agreement on common principle and common thought, there can be no common life.

Thus minimalists have spent much of their time and not a little of their ingenuity trying to dismantle institutions that promote community life and active political citizenship. A vigorous citizen, they feel, is a man who thinks he knows what there is no warrant for knowing: unmask him and send him back to the private sector where his activity will have no public effects. A public good is a prejudice masquerading as a common end: expose it and put in its place pseudopublic interests that are mere aggregations of private interests. Communal politics is a certain path to totalitarianism: reduce it to interest brokerage, and safety will be assured.

Of course there is no such thing as an exclusively minimalist politics or a purely fallibilist political theory. We have seen how effectively the three dispositions of liberal democracy complement one another. In the same manner, the fallibilist argument for limiting government in the name of relativism mixes with and reinforces the idealist argument for limiting government in the name of absolute freedom. The work of John Stuart Mill suggests something of the power that the two dispositions can attain when they operate in combination. Minimalism and idealism soften the realist disposition and are in turn toughened by its politics of power.

The complementarity of the epistemological features of our three dispositions is also evident in liberal democracy's most successful incarnation: the American system of government—where, as de Tocqueville wrote, the precepts of Descartes are least studied and best applied. For America has been a nation in quest of certainty but willing to live with uncertainty. The American people have been deeply ambivalent: both pluralistically tolerant and monolithically zealous. Who, finally, are we Americans? We who are driven by a profound moral fervor that we constantly circumscribe with pragmatic relativism? We who believe in the power of fact and causal necessity at the same time that we bear witness to the power of ideas and creative imagination to alter facts and modify necessity? We who wrought a constitution of high idealism in which one can still detect the odor of pessimistic realism? We are at once proud and humble, imperialistic and restrained. We invade foreign lands, make war in the name of moral absolutes, proclaim ourselves God's own guardians against the depredations of atheistic communism, but then we pull our punches, scrutinize our motives, and limit our vengeance with the modesty of an improbable but genuine innocence.

We admire powerful presidents even as we move to cripple them; we long for the effective use of power even as we impede it. We wish our politics to be consonant with truth and justice, and we puzzle or appall Europeans with our intolerance for the realities of power and compromise (Watergate, for example). Yet at the same time we distrust the moralizers and despise the intellectuals for their affected certainties. We conduct a politics of passion in the name of moderation and use the extremes of the party system (Goldwater and McGovern, for example) to identify and buttress the center—into which we coerce partisans of both liberalism and conservatism (Carter and Reagan, for example).

We crave a politics that is the moral equivalent of war, but we become pacifists when such a war begins. We lace our laws with moral strictures that affect to enforce morality by fiat (Prohibition once, the school-prayer and anti-abortion movements today), yet we eviscerate the public institutions and neglect the public services (parks, schools, libraries, cultural institutions) that promote public morality and civic pride.

As individuals we are Calvinist enough, but as a community we eschew all common cause. (Only in America could Common Cause be the name of a private political lobby.) The frontiersman remains an American archetype, his rugged individuality and benign cynicism a model for our behavior in business and politics alike. Our convictions, powerful and persuasive, are finally all personal and private; only our doubt is deeply social, so that despite our private moral authoritarianism, we are reluctant to pursue the legislative enactment of our private views to the end.[26] We know what we want as individuals and are active in pursuing our private interests, but we deny that the community can know what it wants and do not permit it to have needs other than our own needs aggregated.

My argument is that a good deal of this moral ambivalence, and much of the confusion of character that derives from it, arises out of the attempt to apply ambiguous epistemological lessons about the nature of knowledge to the practical problems of determining the community will and the public good. The philosopher Santayana had a different and more promising formulation of the epistemological problem of democracy:

> The problem of knowledge which it most concerns man to solve is not that artificial and retrospective one about the primordial articulation of our dream, but the practical progressive problem of applying that dream to its own betterment and of transforming it into the instrument and seat of a stable happiness.[27]

Yet even Santayana speaks in the language of application—of dreams dreamed first and only then applied to a world of action. But politics presumes the autonomy of practice. Antecedent reality, whether sensed, intuited, or dreamed, is always beyond politics, is always utopian in the sense of being nowhere with respect to its realities. For politics is defined by its *somewhereness*, its concrete historicity in the real world of human beings. Knowledge grounded in nowhere, even where it has a philosophical warranty of truth and certainty, cannot serve politics. Instead, it generates the kinds of confusion we have associated here with American political consciousness.

The alternative, hinted at in Santayana's counsel, is dreams that belong to and are engendered by politics, relative truths that emerge from common life. Politics does not rest on justice and freedom; it is what makes them possible. The object of democracy is not to apply independently grounded abstractions to concrete situations but rather to extrapolate working abstractions from concrete situations. In a word, politics is not the application of Truth to the problem of human relations but the application of human relations to the prob-

26. The Reverend Jerry Falwell thus meets with distrust not only among liberals but also among his own conservative townspeople in Virginia. For a thoughtful discussion, see Frances Fitzgerald, "A Reporter at Large: The Reverend Jerry Falwell," *The New Yorker*, May 18, 1981.

27. George Santayana, *Obiter Scripta* (New York: Charles Scribner's Sons, 1936): p. 15.

lem of truth. Justice then appears as an approximation of principle in a world of action where absolute principles are irrelevant.

What we would in any case seem to require in the real political world are not reflexive truths garnered in reflective equilibrium but enabling norms developed amidst concrete common problems; not absolute certainty but relative conviction; not philosophical incorrigibility but practical agreement; not ultimate knowledge but shared ends, common values, community standards, and public goods in a world where ultimate knowledge may be unattainable. Indeed, democracy may exist entirely without moral foundations; it may be the political answer to the question of moral uncertainty—the form of interaction for people who cannot agree on absolutes. Because democracy generates roots—different roots in different soils—it knows no single environment, no one unchanging soil, no perfect agriculture. Truth in politics seems, as William James said of truth in general, to be something which is "made in the course of experience" rather than something discovered or disclosed and then acted upon.

The Cartesian epistemology of liberal democracy operates from what we may call the fallacy of the independent ground, and its reliance on this fallacy contributes to its thinness as theory. Determined to develop a politics of applied truth (or a politics of passivity reflecting the elusiveness of truth), the liberal must find impossible routes from nowhere (antecedent reality) to somewhere (concrete human relations). He must put down foundations for a ship at sea and try to root moving caravans. He yearns for the stationary in a world that is forever in motion and is all too willing to set a hypothetical sun in motion if only he can make the real earth stand still.

There are epistemological alternatives far more suitable to democracy and to politics in general. An epistemology of process, which could understand truth to be a product of certain modes of common living rather than the foundation of common life, would be free of the metaphysical problems posed by rationalism and empiricism. Men and women would cease to regard themselves as citizens because they once consented to certain abstract truths. Rather, they would see themselves as capable of creating pertinent practical truths because they had become citizens. Citizenship is the root rather than the product of common value; consequently, there must be citizens before there can be common truth.

To the liberal democrat, the citizen is an individual who applies a personal truth to human relations. To another sort of democrat, the citizen is one who contrives common truths in the absence of knowable individual truth. The necessity for common choice and common action in the face of individual uncertainty and collective conflict defines his political world. He knows he must act even while he knows how little he knows. He knows that action can afford neither the agnosticism of skeptical philosophy nor the dogmatism of the quest for reflective certainty.

The vision of strong democracy elaborated in Part II of this book tries to give this kind of democrat a voice and in doing so to shield democracy against the pseudodemocratic and antidemocratic ideologies to which the thin theory of liberal democracy has been vulnerable.

It is perhaps apparent by now that the epistemological frame developed here, along with the pretheoretical frame sketched in the previous chapter, bears directly on the psychological frame of liberal democracy. The view of human nature implicit in reflexive consciousness and in the image of the solipsistic sense perceptor is closely allied with the general psychology of radical individualism. Indeed, methodological individualism may be said to represent individualist psychology stretched to encompass an epistemological terrain. To complete our portrait of liberal democracy, then, we now turn to the psychology of radical individualism.

Chapter Four

The Psychological Frame:
Apolitical Man

> . . . *for the world, which seems*
> *To lie before us like a land of dreams,*
> *So various, so beautiful, so new,*
> *Hath really neither joy, nor love, nor*
> *light,*
> *Nor certitude, nor peace, nor help of*
> *pain;*
> *And we are here as on a darkling plain*
> *Swept with confused alarms of struggle*
> *and flight,*
> *Where ignorant armies clash by night.*
> (Matthew Arnold)

> *In such condition [the state of nature]*
> *there is . . . continual fear, and danger of*
> *violent death; and the life of man, soli-*
> *tary, poor, nasty, brutish and short.*
> (Thomas Hobbes)

It is a commonplace of political theory that particular understandings of political life are intimately associated with particular views of human nature—with views of the "nature of man" and of the hypothetical "state of nature" sometimes used to define the human essence. "What is government itself," remarks James Madison in *The Federalist* no. 51, "but the greatest of all reflections on human nature?" The liberal democratic view of human nature is in fact bound to politics with a special force by virtue of the peculiar logic of social-contract theory. As purveyed by Spinoza or Hobbes, the instrumentalism of this logic insists that the human condition necessarily entails a certain form of political life. Plato imagined the just polity as the just man writ large. Hobbes counseled that we should "rightly understand what the quality of human nature is, in what matters it is . . . fit to make up civil government."[1]

Liberal democratic politics is thus the logic of a certain form of radical individualism written out to its last political conclusion. It is atomism wearing a social mask. That mask gives to liberal democracy its characteristic dependency on interest theory and rational-choice models and insulates it from more social understandings of human nature in the political setting.

The ties in liberal theory between human nature and politics are neither coincidental nor correlative but intrinsic to the theory itself. To be a liberal democrat is to hold certain views about human nature, and to hold these views is to be a liberal democrat. These relations extend both to the pretheoretical and to the epistemological frames of liberal democracy. The liberal psychology of man is a psychology of how men come to know the political world. The three frames are bound together almost incestuously, each exploiting its family kinship to forge intimate analytic ties with the other two.

Yet of the three, the psychological frame is the most palpable. Unlike the other two, which can be conjured up only by a considerable effort at abstraction, the liberal theory of human nature is limned in poetry, touched by drama, caricatured in utopian literature, exposed by psychoanalytic theory, and directly revealed by radical individualism in modern culture. It is no secret deficiency of liberalism but one of its most formidable strengths.

Man Alone: The Psychology of Individualism

The liberal psychology of human nature is founded on a radical premise no less startling for its familiarity: man is alone. We are born into the world solitary strangers, live our lives as wary aliens, and die in fearful isolation. The dominant reality of human life, in Robert Nozick's phrase, is "the fact of our separate existences."[2] The species is an abstraction; only the individual is real. *We* is thus for the liberal always a suspicious reification of some abstract mean or of some enumeration or aggregation of *me*'s. We are the children of Eden, expelled from the Garden and divested forever of the kinship

1. Thomas Hobbes, *Man and Citizen*, ed. B. Gert (New York: Anchor Books, 1949), p. 99.
2. Robert Nozick, *Anarchy, State, and Utopia* (New York: Basic Books, 1974), p. 33. Nozick uses the word *fact* in a typically naturalistic fashion here, rendering a hypothetical view of human nature in language that seems descriptive.

that might have made us brothers and sisters. We may live together, but we always live together apart.

The paramount feature of human existence in this perspective is alienation: separateness. However, it is an alienation to be celebrated rather than regretted. Human solitude has naturally been a theme in the Western tradition from the beginning, but it has most often been viewed with alarm as an aberration, a pathology, or a curse. To the ancient Greeks it was a threat and a punishment, a hazard of pride and an ineluctable cost of hubris. Oedipus at Colonnus was Oedipus of Thebes disgraced and exiled. Ostracism could seem to the Greek a fate worse than death. Socrates preferred hemlock to flight from Athens.

Christian theology enlarged on the classical theme of exile, placing it at the center of man's spiritual history. Reinhold Niebuhr saw clearly that "the ideal of self-sufficiency, so exalted in our liberal culture, is recognized in Christian thought as one form of the primal sin."[3] Apartness was a terrible form of divine vengeance: cast out of the Garden, man was condemned to the solitude of painful, alienating labor, to spiritual isolation, and to the mortality of a body raised from dust and destined to return to dust. Self-sufficiency, individuality, and autonomy were the futile illusions of pride; each was a denial of God's paternity, of man's fraternity, and of the mutuality of common Creation. The puzzle of Christian freedom—Augustine was perhaps its most vexed student—made it hard to distinguish freedom from willfulness and often associated liberty with a swerving away of the will from God.[4]

It was only with the Renaissance that man's essential aloneness came to be construed as a liberation rather than a purgatory. It has been liberalism's genius to transform the unavoidable into the desirable, the fate worse than death into the ideal life, and the invisible walls keeping us out of the Garden into bulwarks protecting us from its seductive communal intimacies. There is no redemption, only the paradise of solitude. In the new worldly nirvana, the struggle to overcome and to transcend isolation is supplanted by the struggle to fortify it with rights and to undergird it with liberty and power. Communion comes to mean interference, exile becomes privacy.

---

3. Reinhold Niebuhr, *Moral Man and Immoral Society* (New York: Charles Scribner's Sons, 1932), p. 60.

4. St. Augustine, *The City of God* (New York: Random House, 1950), book 14, sects. 11, 12, 13, and 27. Cf. book 6, sect. 17, and book 12, sects. 1, 6, 7, and 8.

The kinship of tribalism and feudal relations and the citizenship of the classical polis are alike identified as bonds, and community itself comes to be understood as slavery. In the Renaissance city, anonymous strangers learned that commerce could take the place of concourse and that market relations could take the place of civic relations.

Indeed, the Renaissance forged an entirely new vocabulary from the ancient lexicon of exile. In one of those extraordinary changes of paradigm through which a whole political world can be transformed, freedom was transvalued: the term used to label the isolation into which men were accidentally or punitively thrown—by rebellion, ostracism, uprooting, exile, noble hubris, or other cataclysms—took on the aspect of liberation. Individuality gave to solitude the glamor and dignity of autonomy and religious conscience. Privacy and individual rights conferred upon deracination—the tearing asunder of bonds that Marx's *Manifesto* portrays with such ambivalence—the legitimacy of legal personhood.

Without this transvaluation, neither liberalism nor democracy would have been possible. Yet with it the possibilities of community shrank, and the hope for a democracy that could be communal as well as egalitarian and participatory as well as consensual withered. "Does not thy spirit thirst for communion, for redemption and salvation in reunion with God?" asked the early Christians. "Does not thy spirit thirst for liberty?" asks Max Stirner, that apotheosis of the modern liberal individualist imagination.[5] Reason and consent removed God from his Providence in order to establish man's will in place of the hegemonic authority of religion. But Providence was linked to communion and thus to community, and so community too became an enemy of liberty. Citizenship could no longer be tied through friendship to particular poleis rooted in common beliefs: it became instead an abstraction of the law. No wonder then, as Alasdair MacIntyre has recently written, that "a modern liberal political society can appear only as a collection of citizens of nowhere who have banded together for their common protection."[6]

5. Max Stirner, *The Ego and His Own*, ed. James J. Martin (New York: Libertarian Book Club, 1967), p. 155. "Nothing is more to me than myself," writes Stirner (p. 5).

6. Alasdair MacIntyre, *After Virtue* (Notre Dame, Ind.: University of Notre Dame Press, 1981), p. 147. Glenn Tinder addresses the relationship between community and religion in his book *Community* (Baton Rouge, La.: Louisiana State University Press, 1980). See chap. 8, "Community and Faith," for a dicussion of the groundlessness of modern morals.

The powerful alchemy of liberalism turned the stranger into the individual, the alien into the entrepreneur, and the deracinated into the free. Citizens were not friends but adversaries. What ancient Athenian, what Christian, what feudal freeman or feudal serf, what Spartan mother or Theban sister, what soldier, what patriot, what clansman or tribesman or townsman could imagine that to be uprooted, unclaimed, and alone was to be free? What Aristotelian citizen, defining himself as human by virtue of his civic friendships, could say with Howard Roark, Ayn Rand's epitome of liberated self-sufficiency: "I came here to say that I do not recognize anyone's right to one minute of my life. Nor to any part of my energy. Nor to an achievement of mine. No matter who makes the claim, how large their number or how great their need. I wish to come here and say that I am a man who does not exist for others."[7]

A self that exists only for itself, without regard to species, to justice, to need, to equality, or to obligation is Man Alone in extremis: man mimicking the self-sufficient God he has rejected.

The self on whom the logic of liberal democracy depends does not of course always meet such stringent standards. It is compromised by democracy, tainted with a creeping mutualism, corrupted by political friendship, undone by human insufficiency. But liberalism's more consistent theoreticians and its more zealous practitioners try to approximate the ideal. Hobbes's natural man—whose life, spent in a "ceaseless search for power after power unto death," can only be solitary, nasty, brutish, and short—is a man who does not exist for others. Robert Nozick's free man, entombed by his rights and owing nothing to the weak, the poor, the disabled, and the disadvantaged, is a man who does not exist for others. The modern privatized client-consumer who demands his rights, sells his services, contracts his relationships, votes his interests, and cost-analyzes his life-plan is a man who does not exist for others.

And so our great modern free world is all too often a world in which men and women do not exist for others; in which, although there are no public censors, there can also be no public goods; in which monolithic social ends are prudently outlawed by imprudently proscribing all social ends; in which altruistic behavior is discouraged in the name of bargaining efficiency and utility accounting. In this world, there can be no fraternal feeling, no general will, no selfless act, no mutuality, no species identity, no gift relation-

7. Ayn Rand, *The Fountainhead* (New York: New American Library, 1943), p. 686.

ship, no disinterested obligation, no social empathy, no love or belief or commitment that is not wholly private. With Kierkegaard, the liberal democrat assures us that as we spin off into a kind of political madness, our vertigo is but "the dizziness of freedom."

Aloneness is the most salient feature of liberal psychology, but it is by no means its only feature. Because man is solitary, says the liberal, he is also hedonistic, aggressive, and acquisitive. Man is defined not simply by liberty (Man the Solitary) but also by needs (Man the Hedonist), power (Man the Aggressor), and property (Man the Acquisitor or Proprietor); that is to say, man is need-driven, power-seeking, and property-acquiring. Since liberals believe, with Herbert Spencer, that everything that is true of the higher animals at large is of course true of man, they begin to draw his portrait by reducing complex human behavior to simple hedonism.[8] Each social characteristic (language, reason, culture, politics, law) can be shown to have derived from animal traits and from the conditions created by the exercise of these traits. Complex social motives can be restated as simple mechanical motives and then, in the final reduction, as a physical mechanics of the passions. Hobbes is justly famous for the virtuosity with which he achieved this reduction, while Bentham is admired for giving it a practical political life in his *Principles of Morals and Legislation*.

As the German materialists liked to say, *Mann ist was er isst*, we are what we eat—material creatures of hunger and thirst. Whether as Caesar or as Faust, as Hamlet or as Guildenstern, we are moved to act in the world by a lust for survival if not for pleasure and by an abiding fear of loss, pain, and death. All human life, all thought and all culture, is but an extension at levels of increasing complexity of these simple motives.

If needs are paramount, it follows that the chief concern of human beings must be to maximize the means by which they can satisfy their needs. Thus for every liberal-contract theorist from Hobbes to Rawls, the central question of politics becomes: How is power acquired and distributed? Power *is* means: to be need-driven we must be power-seeking; to be successful hedonists we must be efficient aggressors. Power is no more than the "present means to some future good" (Hobbes), the "primary social goods" by which the human animal secures the interests arising out of his defining needi-

8. Herbert Spencer, *Man versus the State* (New York: Appleton, 1897), pp. 361–62 et passim.

ness (Rawls). Quite naturally, politics under these conditions can only be the art or science of power—of who gets what, when, and how.

Man the hedonist entails man the aggressor; similarly, man the aggressor entails man the acquisitor or proprietor or expropriator. As C. B. Macpherson has suggested, the concepts of liberal freedom and liberal property are linked. Liberal man in the Hobbesian perspective is understood "neither as a moral whole nor as part of a larger social whole, but as an owner of himself. . . . The human essence is freedom from dependence on the wills of others and freedom is a function of possession."[9]

Power-seeking, like freedom-seeking, finds its natural extension and logical end in property-acquisition. For property is a form of cumulative power, an authoritative variety of institutionalized aggression, by which the claims of individuals to adequate means are given a permanent and legitimate home. Raw power is time-bound; it yields only temporary control, providing a transient security that lasts only as long as the direct mastery of animal over animal can be sustained. Possession lends to coercion a security over time, enhancing the effect of power by diminishing the need for its perpetual exercise. What we merely "need" from the common environment, we must beg, borrow, or take—over and over again and at continual risk. What "belongs" to us, we only have to protect and use, and at much less risk. Better that our adversaries acknowledge our "legitimate authority" as symbolized by property than that they be cowed by brute force, even if it is brute force that establishes our original claim. Carl Sandburg ingeniously exposed how similar the claim of force and the claim of property really are—and how different they seem—in this fiercely radical section from his poem "The People, Yes":

> "Get off my estate."
> "What for?"
> "Because it's mine."
> "Where did you get it?"
> "From my father."
> "Where did he get it?"
> "From his father."
> "And where did he get it?"

9. C. B. Macpherson, *The Political Theory of Possessive Individualism* (New York: Oxford University Press, 1964), p. 3.

"He fought for it."
"Well, I'll fight you for it."

The proprietary claim transforms power into authority, force into right, and mere possession into rightful ownership. But the notion of legitimacy that underlies authority, right, and ownership remains prudential and individualistic, drawing us back to the self-evidence of Man Alone as the true ground of its justification and potency. The legitimacy of man the proprietor is really no more than the legitimacy of man the aggressor—a feature of liberal thinking that a number of mutualist anarchists have perceived quite clearly. Some, such as Proudhon, used the insight to assail property; others, such as Robert Paul Wolff (in his *In Defense of Anarchism*), used it to legitimize aggression. Liberals are of course hoping to capitalize on property's self-evident and conservative status as a successful form of institutionalized power. *Keeping* somehow seems less offensive than *taking*, if only because the present (what one has) is always with us while the past (how one got it) grows more and more remote.

The truth is (*pace* Proudhon) that property is not theft. To be sure, it once was theft, but time has cast the original deed in shadows, and the passing years have consecrated it with the longevity of tradition—"it was my father's, and his father's before him."

Whatever legitimacy original right is given by solitude and self-ownership, time and tradition enhance. The question of right, however, is for the liberal always a question of origin. That is why the labor theory of value occupies so central a place in legitimacy theories from Locke to Marx. The labor theory of value is Locke's attempt to formalize the connection between the natural reality of self-ownership and the legitimacy of property.[10] While Marx contests Locke's essentialism (that each man has an individual, defining essence), he accepts and utilizes the argument for self-ownership as the centerpiece for his theory of exploitation and surplus value.[11]

10. Locke writes: "Though the Earth, and all inferior Creatures be common to all Men, yet every Man has a *Property* in his own *Person*. This no Body has any Right to but himself. The *Labour* of his Body, and the *Work* of his Hands, we may say, are properly his. Whatsoever then he removes out of the State that Nature hath provided, and left in it, he hath mixed his *Labour* with . . . and thereby makes it his *Property*" (*Second Treatise of Civil Government*, chap. 5).

11. Marx writes: "*Rent, Interest, and Industrial Profit* are *only different names for different parts* of the *surplus value* of the commodity, or the *unpaid labour enclosed in it*, and they *are equally derived from this source, and from this source alone*" (*Wages, Price, and Profit*, in Karl Marx and Friedrich Engels, *Selected Works* [Moscow: Foreign Languages Publishing House, 1958], vol. 1., p. 431; emphasis in original).

For Locke, man is as he owns and is because he owns. From this self-ownership issues first liberty, the right to room or space for the owned self; and then labor, the right to the power that belongs to the owned self; and finally property, the right to the product of self and labor as it is mixed with the otherwise commonly held bounty of nature (land and goods alike). Freedom is the self in motion, power is the impetus by which it moves, and property is the self appropriating the medium in which it moves.

Since we do not exist for others, neither does the world exist for others, nor even for "us" in common; the world exists for me alone, and property is the *me*'s claim to it. Naturally, however—and this is the paradox of liberalism—I no more exist for others than do they exist for me. Their claims are thus equally assertive and equally self-evident, if wholly repugnant. The right to expropriation, exercised by others, is a fount of endless transgression against me. My right to property is their right to plunder. The competing Other is always an alien. Fellow creatures are fellow predators. My strength is thus measured by their weakness, my freedom by their servitude, and my power by their impotence; and, of course, vice versa.

What the liberal theory of human nature does, in short, is to define man in ways that deprive him of the potential strength of mutuality, cooperation, and common being. It casts him into permanent exile in a world in which, though he may struggle for survival and wish for security and fight for gratification, there can in reality be "neither joy, nor love, nor light, nor certitude, nor peace, nor help of pain."

A perspective on human nature that was less wary of mutuality and more inclined to integrate social dimensions of human life into the human essence would have less need for such hedonist-individualist concepts as power, property, and rights. And it would use these concepts, when it did use them, to describe complex social interactions. For once the self is conceived as an interactive, socially embedded creature, the idea of absolute self-ownership loses its credibility and the defense of property that is drawn from self-ownership becomes problematic. Properly understood, the war of all against all may be a war we make for ourselves, not out of whole cloth but out of an intentional distortion of our social natures.

It is this consideration that often prompts leftist critics to construe radical individualism less as a premise than as a consequence of certain forms of social organization. If men are seen as solitary, competitive, selfish, and warlike, they contend, it is because the abstraction "natural man" is a crude extrapolation from a particular society. C. B. Macpherson thus reads Hobbesian and Lockean psychologies as variations on the theme of possessive market man that, in their claim to universality, are fraudulent.[12] To Macpherson, "moral and political theory took the wrong turning when it began to interpret the human essence as possession or acquisition."[13] But from the point of view of the logic revealed here, possession followed necessarily from power, just as power followed from necessity and from the demands of self-ownership. For the solitary individual, however independent and self-sufficient liberal theory tried to make him, remained a paltry and inadequate creature. But where Man Alone is feeble, Man Alone armed with power and vested with property is a fortress. State-of-nature hypotheses might constrict his being and imprison his affections, but they endow him with a semblance of freedom and more than a semblance of moving agency in the world.

Indeed, the hedonist, the aggressor, and the proprietor share characteristics vital to democratic man. Radically isolated individuals are autonomous individuals, capable of voluntary choice and thus capable of self-government; they are ratiocinative and thus able to envision and choose among commensurable options; and they are psychologically interchangeable, which trait provides the egalitarian base upon which democracy rests.

Marxism may elucidate the social framework of human development more convincingly than does liberalism but, at least in its classical deterministic incarnation, it does so at the cost of autonomy. It denies both the autonomous will of the individual, by subordinating it to historical forces men cannot govern, and the autonomy of the political realm itself, by subsuming it to a socioeconomic "base" that is determinative. The autonomy posited by liberal psychology is paradoxical and frequently inconsistent with other elements in the

12. Long before C. B. Macpherson elaborated in detail how social-contract theorists seemed to read back into "nature" the proclivities of men living in well-developed, property-holding societies, Jean-Jacques Rousseau wrote of Thomas Hobbes: "He ought to have said that the state of nature . . . was the best calculated to promote peace, and the most suitable for mankind. He does say the exact opposite, in consequence of having improperly admitted, as part of savage man's care for self-preservation, the gratification of a multitude of passions which are the work of society, and have made law necessary" (*A Discourse on Inequality*, in Rousseau, *The Social Contract and Discourses* [London: Dent, 1913], p. 181).

13. C. B. Macpherson, *The Real World of Democracy* (New York: Oxford University Press, 1972), p. 11.

liberal framework, but it does offer a firm foundation for freedom and dignity.

Liberalism also offers a clear-cut and simple (perhaps simplistic) account of human behavior that is conducive to positivistic uses of law and social control. Men not only have the freedom to choose, they have straightforward motives and a capacity for simple reckoning that turns political choice into an exercise in vector physics. Every deliberation involves self-evident needs, desires, and drives that when weighed, interpreted, judged, and evaluated by prudential reason yield unambiguous vector results. Thorstein Veblen has drawn a verbal picture of this vector-physics version of psychology that is worth quoting at length:

The hedonistic conception of man is that of a lightning calculator of pleasures and pains, who oscillates like a homogenous globule of desire of happiness under the impulse of stimuli that shift him about the area, but leave him intact. He has neither antecedent nor consequent. He is an isolated, definitive human datum, in stable equilibrium except for the buffets of the impinging forces that displace him in one direction or another. Self-imposed in elemental space, he spins symmetrically about his own spiritual axis until the parallelogram of forces bears down upon him, whereupon he follows the line of the resultant. When the force of the impact is spent, he comes to rest, a self-contained globule of desire as before.[14]

Not for the liberal is the complexity of such astonishing men as Rameau's nephew, who in Diderot's portrait had "no greater opposite than himself," or Ibsen's fractured poet engaged in "an unending struggle between the hostile forces of the soul."

The classical tripartite division of the soul into the passions, reason, and the will—two horses and a chariot that are not always pulling in the same direction—is superseded by the elementary harmonies of hedonism: pains and pleasures that are commensurable and determinative, prudential reason that is subordinate to them, and will that is but the last cause in hedonism's chain of consequences that runs from first impulse to final action.

This integrality or "givenness" of human nature as defined by simple needs has the virtue of making men roughly interchangeable. Precisely because they are not distinguished by diverse "dominant" functions or by the presence or absence of reason or nobility or will or some other faculty, men cannot be ranked and ordered. In

14. Thorstein Veblen, *The Place of Science in Modern Civilization* (New York: Huebsch, 1919), pp. 73–74.

the new psychology, they have their commonness in common. Complex souls seem to inhabit stratified and often hierarchical social orders; the ancient republic and the medieval corporation bear witness to this truth. Simple souls are capable of democracy, although it may be a democracy of the mean and an equality of the base that they enjoy.

Nonetheless, equality does not possess the normative status of liberty in the liberal psychology of man. It is merely a contingent feature of commensurability and has none of the force that community or fraternity has in more participatory theories of democracy. Indeed, it is more men's common apartness, which is the root of liberty, than their sameness, which is the root of equality, that defines the liberal democratic man. The equality of thin democracy is the equality of boxers placed in common weight classes to ensure fair and equal competition. As Hobbes notes, it is because the weakest man can expect to kill the strongest if he has to that man's natural condition is one of rough equality. Such defensive equality promotes neither fraternity nor justice. It reduces the competitors in the war of all against all to a like size and thus achieves little more than an evening-up of the odds—nodding cynically in the direction of the grim reaper and his equalizing scythe.

The contingent status of equality in liberal democratic theory is perhaps most evident in the priority enjoyed by liberty in every case where values conflict. Since equality involves less what we owe to others than what they owe to us, it is put aside whenever it interferes with liberty. Men, though created equal, are created not *for* equality but for liberty and for the right to secure the safety and pleasure of the self. Thus, as Rawls insists, liberty is always lexically prior to equality and to all other goods.

The general portrait of the liberal psychology of man that I have sketched here has certain practical consequences but, in consonance with its pretheoretical frame and reductionist epistemology, it retains a maddeningly abstract flavor. States of nature, hypothetical history, and original positions are all paths away from the concrete political now to metaphysical abstraction. What Marx observed about Feuerbach seems appropriate to the liberal deconstruction of concrete, historical man: "Because [Feuerbach] still remains in the realm of theory and conceives of men not in their given social connection, not under their existing conditions of life, which have made them what they are, he never arrives at the really existing active men, but stops at the abstraction 'man.' "[15] Man Alone is an abstraction, and while it is a splendid source of certain liberal ideals, it is an impediment to the understanding of political man. Liberty is given a sanctuary but politics is robbed of a home—and of intelligibility. And as the defense of liberty grows rich and powerful, the theory of democracy grows impoverished and thin.

ANARCHIST VARIATIONS ON LIBERAL PSYCHOLOGY

There are optimistic and pessimistic interpretations of radical individualism: Man Alone may be regarded as an aspiring divinity, as a perfidious demon, or simply as an itinerant waif in an indifferent cosmos. Hedonism, aggression, and acquisition can be celebrated or cursed or tolerated.

The anarchist disposition is to celebrate. Man sufficient unto himself is man touched by the divine. Not quite God, man is nonetheless a Promethean figure aspiring to God's luminosity, envying his power, expropriating his fire, stealing his secrets, and yearning to dwell in an omniscient solitude otherwise known only to him. It is Shelley's *Prometheus Unbound* who stalks the anarchist imagination:

> Sceptreless, free, uncircumscribed—but man:
> Equal, unclassed, tribeless, and nationless,
> Exempt from awe, worship, degree, the king
> Over himself . . .

Man's frailty makes him dependent and his weakness is the cause of his sociability; conversely, to be self-sufficient is to be independent and powerful. But these traits (in traditional imagery) belong to the gods and can be acquired by men only at the cost of hubris and only then through an act of theft. The anarchist—Nietzsche is his most ardent spokesman here—is willing enough to pay the Promethean price, if man can reap the Promethean reward and make fire his own.

There is in these epic metaphors a certain nobility that lifts the

15. Karl Marx, *The German Ideology*, ed. C. J. Arthur (New York: International Publishers, 1970), p. 64.

Conservatives mock the deracination of liberal man with the same gusto; thus, for example, Joseph de Maistre: "I have seen in my time Frenchmen, Italians, and Russians; I even know, thanks to Montesquieu, that one may be a Persian; but as for *man*, I declare that I have never met with him in my life; if he exists, it is without my knowledge" (*The Works of Joseph de Maistre*, ed. J. Lively [New York: Macmillan, 1965], p. 80; the passage is from de Maistre's *Considerations on France*).

anarchist disposition above the smallness of most liberal democratic thinking. The scraggy, hungry survivor is also a maker; the aggressive self-gratifier is also an artificer. Liberal man may have a small self, but with it he can do great things. Nature is conquered and its laws mastered even if only in the name of base needs. Science, religion, art, and politics take on the aspect of creations of the human soul, although liberal psychology construes them as instrumentalities of the body meant to facilitate its needs.

The anarchist celebration of man does more than idealize liberty. It conjures up the solitary spectator to truth and beauty apotheosized in poetry and art. The poet is less repelled by the worldliness of his fellow beings than he is drawn out of their world by forces that recognize only his own solitary consciousness. Aristotle distinguished between men as creatures of compromise, fated by their intermediary status between animals and gods to practice politics and moral virtue, and men as aspiring immortals, wishing (if mostly in vain) for that higher form of virtue (intellectual virtue) that Aristotle associated with solitary reflection. Plato's philosophers were loath to return to the "cave" of mundane politics and to exercise in the common interest those higher faculties best enjoyed in solitude.

The artist in the Western tradition has always understood his stance to be solitary and asocial or even antisocial.[16] His kinship with the anarchist has always been obvious. "It is peculiarly difficult," Herbert Read laments, "for the artist in society . . . to stand apart yet to mediate. Society will never understand or love the artist. . . . The artist . . . must accept the contrary experience, and drink, with Socrates, the bitter cup."[17] Emma Goldman portrays Nietzsche admiringly as an "aristocrat of the spirit" because "all true anarchists [are] aristocrats."[18] The anarchist sometimes appears as an artist who wishes to recreate the entire world, to spread and mix the entire human race on his palette and so paint a social world in colors never dreamt of by the politicians or the historians; and the artist sometimes is an anarchist who rejects every human authority save his own, making imagination the twin of solitude and creativity the defining essence of his individuality.

16. I have taken a particular interest in the theme of liberal individualism and the poetic imagination; see my "Poetry and Revolution," *Modern Occasions* (spring 1971), and Benjamin R. Barber and Michael M. G. McGrath, eds., *The Artist and Political Vision* (New Brunswick, N.J.: Transaction Books, 1982).

17. Herbert Read, *To Hell with Culture* (New York: Schocken Books, 1964), p. 9. Read accepted a knighthood all the same.

18. Emma Goldman, *Living My Life* (London, 1932), vol. 1, p. 194.

This kinship, although it suggests why anarchism has been politically inept, ennobles the human image of liberal democracy. The artist, wrenched from his own life experience by the alienating lucidity of his self-consciousness, envisions in his imagination a world more rooted and consoling than the real one his gifts have stolen from him. Rousseau, who opposed the imagination in his political hopes, made it the final consolation of his ravaged personal life.[19] By celebrating independence, the anarchist disposition gives us the courage to live with the solitude that liberal theory and practice claim is our destiny. By cherishing liberty and spontaneity, it provides the indispensable condition for self-realization within the limits of apartness. By apotheosizing individual consciousness and its defining creativity, it lends to our hedonistic impulses the dignity of higher purposes. By conceiving man as maker, it transforms the relentless search for power and for mastery over man and nature into an exercise in artistry and a scientific enterprise. In anarchism, the subhuman and the superhuman are confounded, to the advantage of hope. For in the less-than-human qualities of man the hedonist can be found more-than-human omens of man the divine.

This ambivalence is evident in many liberal democratic societies. Americans often appear to be both cynical and idealistic. How many American archetypes are at once both base and noble? The Pioneer, the Entrepreneur, the Discoverer, the Outlaw, the Inventor, the Vigilante, even the Founder: each is a compromised idealist, a cynical naïf, a noble aggressor, a creative expropriator, an anomaly of nature with a beast's body and a divine head.

Ours is an individualism that idolizes man at the same time as it distrusts him, that exults in privacy as it condemns greediness, that mythologizes the individual while it institutionalizes conformity, that is uncomfortable with a selfishness and a cynicism around which, nevertheless, the entire political and economic system is structured. We repudiated the cynicism of Europe and called for a political order based on the most elevated view of man's capacities, and then we designed a constitution based on the very lowest expectations.

This ambivalence makes it very difficult to be an American. To define humans by traits they must steal, by features they can find

19. Thus the romantic imagination appears as the chief motif of *The Reveries of a Solitary Walker* but as a corrupter of men in *The Discourse on Arts and Sciences* and the *Letter to D'Alembert*.

more easily in animals or gods than in themselves, is to define them in terms that they may be unable to live up to—or down to. The demand for superhuman capacities may permit ample human capacities to atrophy. The tendency of so many anarchists to end their careers of celebrating abstract man by reviling actual men is all but inevitable when the definition of *human* requires much more than most actual men have the strength to be. The cry that Nietzsche placed on Zarathustra's lips—"Man is something to be surpassed!"—leaves common women and men only with the despair of unachievable goals, goals that are not immanent ends that can be realized through growth and through transformation of self or community but transcendental ideals that can be realized only by expropriation or self-abandonment. With arms that are too long, man cannot scratch himself; with eyes that are too far-sighted, he cannot see himself. The anarchist takes man beyond himself and thus beyond both the simple human power conferred by mutuality and commonality and the mundane help of the communities within which we establish ourselves as human—whether they are communities of science, art, religion, fellowship, or political purpose.

REALIST VARIATIONS ON LIBERAL PSYCHOLOGY

The realist disposition inherits and subsequently compounds many of the frustrations that anarchism leaves behind within the liberal tradition. The man who would be a god but cannot must end as an animal. The realist inherits this beast and makes the most of him. If the realist regards women and men with lessened expectations, it is their condition as much as their nature that is to blame. Solitary aggressors who live in a confined world of scarcity offer reason for trepidation. Tell acquisitors and expropriators that prudence requires them to share land and divide booty and agree upon covenants and live peaceably with others, and they will ask, why? in whose interest? with what guarantees? And the war of all against all will go on, even after social contracts have been drawn up and oaths of allegiance sworn.

We might say that the anarchist comes upon Man Alone by day in the shining luminosity of his highest aspirations, whereas the realist stumbles upon Man Alone by night, in the murky shadows of a debilitating alienation. In the darkness, solitude seems more vulnerable than creative, and the separation from others that spurs the spontaneous imagination of the daytime anarchist is grounds by dark only for "continual fear and danger of violent death." It is in that midnight that men live out their lives "as on a darkling plain." Like Hobbes, the realist conceives natural man as the twin of fear, for terror is his constant companion. And if the realist menagerie consists of lions and foxes, whales and sheep, wolves and pigs, it is because we are here as in a jungle, where even our most "human" characteristics—reason, language, culture—are so many teeth and claws in the endless struggle for survival.

Man is, moreover, quite immutable. Man's self-sufficiency, which to the anarchist suggests creativity and spontaneity, is to the realist an expression of rigidity and inflexibility. Resistant to change, realist man is disinclined to accommodation and suspicious of growth. The politics that issues from realism's wariness is thus a politics of limits, of control, of coercion, of sanctions, and of safeguards. Beginning with Machiavelli's attempt to contrive a politics of stability for men who are "ungrateful, voluble dissemblers, anxious to avoid danger and covetous of gain," this kind of politics gains momentum in Hobbes's liberal-authoritarian state, which is rooted in the premise that no civic tyranny can be worse than nature's war of all against all. It culminates in the efficient bureaucracies of later liberalism—in the schemes of Marat, in the penal reforms of Beccaria, and in Bentham's manipulative science of legislation and punishment. All of these liberal institutions take man as he is (a beast with reason) and use his selfishness to make him social. Men are made to obey but not to change or grow.

The toughness of realism in the face of natural man's vulnerability explains why the liberal state can assume so authoritative a face (as in Hobbes) and why the tradition of *raison d'état*, which liberals such as Ernst Cassirer and Carl J. Friedrich have assailed, is nonetheless compatible with the liberal quest for security.[20] *Raison d'état* can also be *raison d'individu*, when the individual consents to authoritarian rule because he feels that a system of order that governs for its own sake is more trustworthy—or less untrustworthy—than the unmediated, natural impulses of his fellow beings. The authoritarian state may compromise my liberty and make its own survival its central

20. See Ernst Cassirer, *The Myth of the State* (New Haven: Yale University Press, 1946), and Friedrich Meinecke, *Machiavellianism: The Doctrine of Raison d'État and Its Place in Modern History* (Cambridge, Mass.: Harvard University Press, 1960).

purpose, but it spares me the depredations of anarchic others and guarantees me what little liberty it leaves me with.

Implicit in the realist's acquiescence to force in the name of security is a distinctive understanding of hedonism. The liberal psychology of hedonism sketched above conceals what can be called the "fallacy of symmetry." This fallacy, evident in hedonist psychology from the time of the Epicureans, is a result of a confusion between the nature of pleasure and the nature of pain—which are conflated on the hedonist spectrum. The presumption (and thus the error or fallacy), which is shared by realists and anarchists alike, is that pleasure and pain are wholly commensurable indicators of a common generic form of sensation, to be differentiated only by degree on a single continuum of happiness. Pain connotes units of negative happiness below a neutral zero point, while pleasure connotes units of positive happiness above the zero point. The units themselves are wholly commensurable and are interchangeable in any conceivable hedonistic calculus. Pleasures and pains can thus be weighed, ranked, and traded off—and the putative symmetry of the continuum will guarantee a rational-choice outcome. This alleged symmetry not only endowed the hedonistic calculus with perfect rationality, it also provided a basis for interpersonal (and thus objective or intersubjective) standards by which the claims of competing individuals might be adjudicated. The prevalence of the fallacy is evident in its wide acceptance in modern economic and ethical theory and in public-choice models of policy-making—for example, in the theory and practice of strategic deterrence.[21]

Most critics of the hedonistic calculus have deplored its reduction of qualities to quantities, its inability to discriminate between kinds as well as degrees of pleasures and pain, and its narrow reading of human motivation. John Stuart Mill elaborates such criticisms incisively in his essays, *Utilitarianism* and *Bentham*. Yet the fallacy of symmetry is no less debilitating to liberal democratic practice, for by confounding pleasure and pain—hopeful expectations and the willingness to take risks and fearful aversions and the avoidance of risk—it confounds anarchist and realist politics.

Realism and anarchism accept hedonism and rationalism in prin-

---

21. Gaming models such as those deployed by Thomas C. Schelling in *The Strategy of Conflict* (Cambridge, Mass.: Harvard University Press, 1960), are central to discussions of strategic deterrence despite the particularly obvious incommensurability of possible losses and "gains" (*sic*) in a nuclear holocaust.

ciple, but the anarchist is drawn to a temperament in which pleasure and gain predominate, whereas the realist is drawn to a disposition in which pain and loss are paramount. The anarchist archetype thus turns out to be the adventurous risk-taker, forever reckoning possible gains and glibly spurning the doubts that such risks arouse in more prudent souls. To him reason says: Take a chance. Nothing risked, nothing gained. The realist archetype is the wary pessimist, more fearful of loss than desirous of gain, willing to sacrifice the possible benefits of the long shot for the security of the sure thing. To him reason says: Stay put. Nothing risked, nothing lost. The one rushes headlong into life, an inveterate gambler; the other stands fast. The one works hard at living, the other at avoiding death.

Michael Oakeshott captures each of these ideal types with remarkable clarity. In his *On Human Conduct*, he sees the gambler's historical persona in "younger sons making their own way in a [Renaissance] world which had little place for them, . . . footloose adventurers who left the land to take to trade, . . . town-dwellers who had emancipated themselves from the communal ties of the country-side, . . . vagabond scholars."[22] In an earlier essay, "On Being Conservative" (1956) Oakeshott portrayed a more prudent mentality with equal acuity. To be conservative, he wrote, "is to prefer the familiar to the unknown, to prefer the tried to the untried, fact to mystery, the actual to the possible, the limited to the unbounded, the near to the distant, the sufficient to the superabundant, the convenient to the perfect."[23]

The anarchist disposition belongs to the adventurer, the man impatient with limits and willing to take his chances with the aggressively defended rights and liberties of his fellow beings if his own "rights" are given free rein. The realist is the conservative, willing to pay almost any price in tyranny for the guarantee of present tranquility and for the certainty that the future will resemble the past. In these terms, it is possible to reevaluate a number of theorists with respect to their attitude to the hedonist asymmetry. John Rawls, for example, despite his reputation as a liberal, is a realist and thus a conservative on these matters. His natural man (in the "original position," which is Rawls's equivalent of the "state of nature") is any-

---

22. Michael Oakeshott, *On Human Conduct* (New York: Oxford University Press, 1975), p. 239.
23. Michael Oakeshott, *Rationalism in Politics and Other Essays* (New York: Basic Books, 1962), pp. 169–70.

thing but a gambler. He is more than ready to surrender his right to extraordinary gains in order to protect himself against extraordinary losses. His fear of being "least-advantaged" in any society he may belong to prompts him to forego the chance to be "most-advantaged."[24] Robert Nozick, on the other hand, is typically anarchist in his adventurous psychology of human nature. He is less interested in life insurance than in a free life. His natural man prefers to have an opportunity to maximize his gains, even if this choice diminishes his capacity to protect against loss. He is an aggressor willing to be aggressed against, a trespasser willing to be trespassed against, and a bargain-hunter willing to be outwitted.[25] Rawlsian man and Nozickian man would have a difficult time conversing, and they would be unable to find common rational grounds for adjudicating their differences. Their notions of the good life are simply incommensurable.

Nor does the appeal to reason overcome their differences. Reason in its prudential guise (its liberal guise) is a means to a good or an end. If hedonism (once the fallacy of symmetry has been exposed) offers two versions of the good life—one associated with hope and pleasure, the other with fear and pain—then there will be two modes of prudence and two courses of rational behavior. Rawls's argument that rational men in the original position will seek a principle of difference that serves the interests of the least advantaged is plausible only if rationality is measured by how it promotes *security*. Likewise, Nozick's argument that rational individuals will not consent to any form of political authority other than one that leaves their natural liberty intact is plausible only if rationality is measured by how it protects the absolute autonomy of isolated individuals. Reason is without an intrinsic character here: it merely disguises the incommensurability of the divergent psychologies it serves.

The asymmetry of pleasure and pain in the hedonist psychology appears in practice as well as in theory. It underlies certain national stereotypes, for example. One might say, to take the American case,

24. Rawls contends that his original position is free of all "special psychologies" and that his choosers in the original position select principles of justice rationally. But this argument depends on the fallacy of hedonism and cannot withstand the separation of pleasure and pain into two distinct categories. For a full discussion, see my "Justifying Justice: Problems of Psychology, Measurement and Politics in Rawls," *American Political Science Review* 69, 2 (June 1976).

25. Nozick ultimately accepts the minimal security offered by a "Dominant Protection Association," but he cedes to it no prerogatives that would permit it to compromise the autonomy of individuals without their explicit, voluntary consent.

that America was for its first century a nation of gain-seeking gamblers who, encouraged perhaps by the boundlessness of the land and its resources, were prepared to hazard risks that today seem awesome. Men in more constricted societies such as England have developed more conservative, realist temperaments, suited to the less promising odds of overpopulation and scarce resources. Hobbes, Hume, Burke, and Bentham, for all of their ideological differences, were to a man cautious. Each regarded change as fraught with danger, each saw in violent revolution the price paid rather than the victory won, and each thought that a little freedom secured was worth more than a great deal unsecured.

Nations, like individuals, may evolve from one psychology into the other over time. As young men who are conservative have no hearts and old men who are radical have no brains (according to Clemenceau), so smart young nations tend to be adventurous while wise old nations tend to be conservative. Even capitalism, though dependent on entrepreneurial risk-taking in its formative stages, becomes conservative and risk-avoiding as it matures.[26] Just as accumulating capital and preserving capital are two different matters, so getting liberty and preserving it are two different matters. The politics of fear and the politics of hope, rooted as they both are in hedonism, are finally two very different politics. For Man Alone as a would-be god and Man Alone as a prudent beast are radically disparate beings, as different from one another as joy is from terror, gladness from sorrow, anticipation from regret, and lust for life from fear of death. These asymmetries finally destroy much of hedonism's unifying power in the liberal theory of human nature. They turn the anarchist and realist dispositions within liberalism into adversaries rather than cousins. And they give to liberal institutions their perplexing ambivalence about freedom and security, rights and social justice, privacy and public goods, and rationality itself.

MINIMALIST VARIATIONS

Minimalism once again appears as a mediating disposition that softens the harsh disparities of anarchism and realism. Neither as optimistic and glowing as the anarchist about solitude nor as pessimistic

---

26. The conservatism of mature capitalism has become a cliché. Theodore Lowi explores it with acuity in *The End of Liberalism*, 2d rev. ed. (New York: Norton, 1979), in terms of what he calls the "socialization of risk."

and wary as the realist about freedom, the minimalist places a special faith in prudential reason. He acknowledges that "covenants without the sword" may be violated out of self-interest, but he also knows that covenants unratified by obligation will—however sharp the sword—be violated whenever the sword is in its scabbard, or whenever its point is directed elsewhere, or whenever its wielder grows distracted, lazy, pusillanimous, or faint-hearted.

If man is indentured to need by his animal nature, the minimalist reminds us, that indenture is attenuated by his capacity to defer gratification. While it serves his passions, his reason also guides and orders them. Man is at least a little changed for being rational. The Golden Rule can be construed as the projection of narrow self-concern (doing well by others so that they will do well by you), but such deference to prudence is nonetheless beyond the hungry lion or the wily fox. In the end, the menagerie with its skulking man-beasts is only a metaphor and, at least for the minimalist, man *is* man.

On this basis, it is possible to conceive of a politics of prudence and accommodation that bears at least a faint resemblance to genuine morals. Through the minimalist back door, ethics, justice, equity, and even religion creep into liberal democracy's otherwise secular and hedonistic conception of the human world. It does not take a very careful reading of Locke to satisfy most readers that his natural man—although he is a soft clay on which experience in the form of sensation works permanent lessons—is more than beast; that the capacity for human association, for piety and reverence, and for civility readily insinuate themselves into his otherwise materialistic individualism.

In the work of John Stuart Mill, the minimalist brush paints in even more vivid colors, creating a human landscape in which the ideals of moral perfectibility and human self-transformation are visible. Yet once again, the promise of richer, more politically rewarding possibilities is never realized. In the end, while the minimalist is at pains to accommodate the polarizing dichotomies of anarchist and realist, he is himself a servant of their founding premises: that man is ultimately alone, that self-interest defined by elementary material needs is his paramount motive in all human interactions, that solitude is a basic state that can be mitigated but not overcome, and that autonomy, equality, and rights are conditions for rather than products of political life.

GODS AND BEASTS, BUT NOWHERE CITIZENS

The illusion of apartness is a common thread that weaves together the distinctive notions of man as beast and man as god held by realist and anarchist. "The man who is isolated," wrote Aristotle, "who is unable to share in the benefits of political association, or has no need to share because he is already self-sufficient, is not part of the polis, and therefore must be either a beast or a god."[27]

God and beast are both self-sufficient manifestations of being. Neither pure reflection nor pure physicality depends on concourse or mutuality. Pure spirit contemplates in utter solitude; pure body survives by appropriating its environment by and for itself. Only at the peculiar confluence of body and spirit that issues in human life does self-sufficiency become problematic. Dispossessed of the sufficiency that might attend pure physical or pure spiritual being, paltry man is thrown onto the mercy of his species. His imagination invests the needs of his body with a force and liveliness that outrun his individual powers. Capable of comparing himself with others, he discovers that he needs them. Unable to transcend his own needs by an act of imaginative will (the dream of Plato's Philosopher), he must turn to others merely to gratify those needs.

Thus it turns out that the freedom of man, which the liberal persuades himself man must enjoy by nature, lies entirely with the human species and with the history man makes in common. Only through association can he live beyond his own flesh: through traditions and institutions, through creations and achievements, through discoveries and conventions, through contracts and promises—all collective tributes to an elusive immortality that Man Alone can never know.

If Man Alone lacks the reality of freedom, he also lacks the facility for change. He may, like Prometheus, be something of a thief, but he is no Proteus. Burdened with unchanging needs and inflexible, determinative impulses, he is made incompetent for politics (the art of change) from the outset. Because human development is generally understood as a function of mutual activity, species behavior, and collective endeavor, it depends on social being. In denying man's sociability, the liberal necessarily denies the possibility of

27. Aristotle, *Politics*, book 1, sect. 14 (1253A).

growth or the hope of change. As Reinhold Niebuhr has noticed, social-contract theory "perpetuates the illusion that communities remain primarily the instruments of atomic individuals, who are forced to create some kind of minimal order for their common life, presumably because the presence of many other such individuals in some limited area makes 'traffic rules' necessary." This illusion, Niebuhr concludes, "completely obscures the primordial character of the human community and the power of historical destiny over human decision."[28]

The author of human language, thought, philosophy, science, and art as well as of law, convention, right, authority, and freedom is not Man but men. It is from common rather than individual consciousness—from generations of communal labor and not the passing whimsies of individuals—that the enduring features of human identity are born. We are above all creatures of time, defined by a history that we make together. The unique capacities that comprise our humanity—memory (the capacity to recall and use the past), rationality (the capacity to analyze and use the present), and imagination (the capacity to link past and future in an act of creation)— merge our singularities into the commonness of time and thus bind us to one another, above all in language and conversation and in the politics that conversation makes possible (see Chapter 8). It is this temporality of human consciousness that led Hegel to conceptualize the essence of consciousness as its history and that prompts certain modern philosophers such as Alasdair MacIntyre to argue that personal identity has significance only when placed in the temporal context of a narrative that has both a social and a historical dimension.[29]

The radical individualism of liberal democracy denies this immersion in time and thus denies the possibility of change or growth in human nature. The world may be mutable, but men are not; the

28. Reinhold Niebuhr, *The Children of Light and the Children of Darkness* (New York: Charles Scribner's Sons, 1944), pp. 53–54.

29. "Empiricists, such as Locke or Hume, tried to give an account of personal identity solely in terms of psychological states or events. Analytical philosophers . . . have wrestled with the connection between those states and events and strict identity. . . . Both have failed to see that a background has been omitted, the lack of which makes the problem insoluble. That background is provided by the concept of a story and of that kind of unity of character which a story requires. . . . The concept of a person is that of a character abstracted from a history. . . . [This is then] the narrative concept of selfhood" (Alasdair MacIntyre, *After Virtue* [Notre Dame: University of Notre Dame Press, 1981], p. 202).

technology that liberates us from nature does so only by demonstrating our continued subjugation to our own animal needs.

There is a profound negativity in this view of human nature that is associated with the thinness of liberal democratic theory. Charles Sanders Peirce has written that "individual man, since his separate existence is manifested only by ignorance and error, so far as he is anything apart from his fellows, and from what he and they are to be, is only a negation."[30] The politics of individual man, Man Alone, cannot help but be a politics of negation—of the repression or toleration of conflict in deference to the immutability of private interests and of the protection of atomic individuals defined by their solitude. Do what must be done, but for the rest, *laissez faire*. Leaving men alone is what liberal democracy does best. When it must interfere or interdict it does so in the name of leaving alone. Protection, preservation, and the security of private interests (including liberty and property as well as life) are the whole of the liberal agenda. It is a difficult and an honorable agenda to be sure. But it is nonetheless a very small agenda tailored to the small men its theories portray.

There is an alternative vision that runs from Aristotle through Rousseau to Marx's *Sixth Thesis on Feuerbach*: "The essence of man is no abstraction inhering in each single individual. In its actuality it is the ensemble of social relationships."[31] In this vision, we see our choice as a choice between being citizens or being slaves. We can be merely dependent, subservient to nature and to one another, or we can through politics transform subservience into interdependence. But we cannot exist as abstract solitaries in a human world that is social to its core. We can learn how to become creative individuals *within* the families, tribes, nations, and communities into which we are born, or we can remain heteronomous pawns of such associations. But we cannot get out of them, either by returning to the primeval forest or by scaling Mount Olympus.

The only question is whether our politics can free us or will further enslave us. It is often said that efforts to supersede liberal democracy and to move it toward greater participation and commonality overcome the negativity of liberalism only by taking on the character of totalism—barbarism with a human face. Before beginning, in the

30. Charles Sanders Peirce, cited in Richard Bernstein, *Praxis and Action* (Philadelphia: University of Pennsylvania Press, 1971), p. 198.

31. Karl Marx, *Theses on Feuerbach*, in Marx and Engels, *Selected Works*, vol. 2, p. 336.

second part of this book, to elucidate the participatory theory of democracy, which I will call "strong" democracy, we must detour to this liberal counterargument. Thus I will devote the last chapter of this part of my book to showing first, that the great aberrations of twentieth-century political culture—majoritarian tyranny, mass society, and totalitarianism—have resulted more from the thinness of liberalism than from the participatory aspirations of strong democracy; and, second, that while the illusions of Man Alone may breed the malignancy of unitary government, strong democracy may offer in the idea of mutuality a genuine remedy.

Chapter Five

Thin Democracy
in the Twentieth Century:
The Potential for Pathology

Liberty is a food easy to eat, but difficult to digest.

(Jean-Jacques Rousseau)

The bourgeoisie . . . has pitilessly torn asunder the motley feudal ties that bound man to his "natural superiors" and has left no other nexus between man and man than naked self-interest, than callous "cash payment."

(Karl Marx)

My conclusion is in direct contradiction to the original idea with which I began. Starting from unlimited freedom, I arrived at unlimited despotism.

(Shigalov, in Dostoevski's *The Possessed*)

It has been the conventional wisdom of Western liberal democratic thought—of what we have called the "thin" theory of democracy— that many of the more invidious pathologies of our grim era have derived from democratic excess: from the revolt of the masses (Ortega y Gassett), or the tyranny of the majority (Walter Lippmann), or the rule of mediocrity and the leveling effects of egalitarianism (Mill, Nietzsche, and de Tocqueville), or the serfdom of the planned society (Fredrick Hayek), or the despotism of the Idea enacted as the General Will (J. L. Talmon and B. Henri-Lévy), or the specter of Big Government (Milton Friedman). In each case, the charge is that democracy untempered by liberalism becomes distempered democracy, that popular government carries within itself a seed of totalitarian despotism that can be prevented from germinating only by the judicious application of a constitutional herbicide made up in equal doses of individual liberty, natural rights, private property, and market capitalism.

From the perspective of liberalism, untempered democracy has in fact been a significant genetic factor in such twentieth-century mutations as Stalinism, Nazism, and mass society—each of which has been portrayed not as an anomaly but as the evolutionary outcome of democratic distemper. This distemper, the argument concludes, is visible today in the hostility to individuals and their rights displayed by planning, welfare systems, regulation, coercive schemes for social justice, and, in general, Big Government.

The distrust of democracy is in fact as old as political thought itself. Philosophers have always approached popular rule with suspicion, preferring to link justice to reason and harmony in the abstract. The Greeks paid democracy no compliment when they associated it with the disorder of the rabble (ochlocracy). Plato, Aristotle, Polybius, and later Cicero and Machiavelli all admitted the demos into government as at best one element in a mixed constitution and at worst as a source of fraction and anarchy to be controlled and repressed at all costs.

This bias persisted into the modern political era when, with the rise of actual democratic regimes, it found its way into the doctrines of the separation of powers, of checks and balances, and of limited government. Madison's *The Federalist* number 51 threw the full force of this distrust into American constitutional thinking.[1] It has been taken up with regularity since then, most recently by neoconservative liberals with roots in Lippmann and Ortega and in de Tocqueville and Mill[2] and by social-choice liberals such as William H. Riker,

---

1. "In order to lay a due foundation for that separate and distinct exercise of the different powers of government, which to a certain extent is admitted on all hands to be essential to the preservation of liberty, it is evident that each department should have a will of its own. . . . [The] policy of supplying, by opposite and rival interests, the defect of better motives, might be traced through the whole system of human affairs, private as well as public. We see it particularly displayed in all the subordinate distributions of power, where the constant aim is to divide and arrange the several offices in such manner as that each may be a check on the other—that the private interest of every individual may be a sentinel over the public rights" (James Madison et al., *The Federalist Papers*, no. 51 [New York: Random House, 1937], pp. 336–37).

2. Typical of the neoconservative critique is Samuel Huntington's attack on what he takes to be the excesses of 1960s-style democracy. In his contribution to the Bicen-

who argued in his *Liberalism against Populism* (1982) that "populists can, on moral grounds, justify tyranny by supposed embodiments of the popular will such as socialist dictators."[3]

One can of course find considerable wisdom in a perspective whose origin is so ancient and whose proponents are so varied and distinguished. It is a perspective that has insulated Western democracy from much possible abuse and that has given to the American political tradition its peculiar balance of exuberance and restraint, of popular government and elitism, of daring and modesty. Yet there are good historical and theoretical reasons for believing that the liberal critique is flawed. Three of these reasons are worth noting here.

First, there is what we must reluctantly recognize as the dispositional elitism of almost all "great political theory." The most democratic of theorists have felt betrayed by their own aristocratic genius, even as they tried to make good their commitment to democracy.[4] The rest have been content to translate genius into theories of natural aristocracy and government by truth or wisdom. This is no less true of the modern social theorists who call themselves legal philosophers (or theorists of rational justice) than of the ancients whom they still, in their own jurisprudential and academic manner, try to emulate.[5] In truth, a people has as much reason to suspect its phil-

---

tennial issue of *The Public Interest*, Huntington wrote: "Problems of governance in the United States today stem from an 'excess of democracy.' . . . [T]he effective operation of a democratic political system usually requires some measure of apathy and non-involvement on the part of some individuals and groups" ("The Democratic Distemper," *The Public Interest* 41 [Fall 1975], pp. 36–37).

3. William H. Riker, *Liberalism against Populism* (San Francisco: Freeman, 1982), p. xii (from the "Analytical Table of Contents"). Riker cites Marcus Raskin's *Notes on the Old System: To Transform American Politics* (New York: McKay, 1974) as his primary example of populist politics. Despite his peculiar use of a rather untheoretical tract from the 1960s as his target (or straw man?), what Riker apparently means by the term *populist democracy* is a Rousseauist conception of the General Will—which, however, he misconstrues as a conception wedded to a substantive moral outcome. Like so many other critics of democracy, Riker explicitly models his argument on Sir Isaiah Berlin's *Two Concepts of Liberty* (Oxford: Clarendon Press, 1958).

4. One thinks again of Jean-Jacques Rousseau, torn between consciousness of his own inner sublimity (expressed in such confessional works as *The Reveries of a Solitary Walker* and the *Confessions* themselves) and his commitment to equality and democracy for ordinary men. The schism accounts for the controversies in interpretation between those who understand Rousseau as an egalitarian collectivist and those who portray him as a romantic individualist. It has led some to reject the democratic interpretation altogether; see, for example, Terence Marshall, "Rousseau and Enlightenment," *Political Theory* 6, 4 (November 1978): 421–56.

5. Thus John Rawls and Robert Nozick each seeks rules or principles of justice that will take the place of public deliberation and choice. A rational state founded on

osophical counselors as the counselors have to suspect the people. The story of Socrates has another side—little publicized because the publicists have all been philosophers—that makes his execution seem a little more deserved, if no less horrendous.[6] Danger lurks in democracy, but danger also lurks in a tradition of philosophizing that has devoted itself to condemning the rabble publics who, one might say, have been waiting for eons to be enlightened by those who have in fact only denigrated and betrayed them. This danger, indigenous to philosophy, cannot be our theme here. But it should be kept constantly in mind as we examine the liberal critique of democracy.

A second vital objection to the liberal critique is that it misapprehends the character and diversity of direct or participatory democracy. The typologies it constructs generally envision only one ideal type of pure democracy, which is then made to embrace such distinct variants as participationism, majoritarian tyranny, consensualism, totalism, communitarianism, and various theories of the General Will.[7] To this nefarious stereotype is then attributed every supposed malady of democratic excess, and this attribution becomes the grounds for indicting and convicting every possible alternative to thin liberal representation. Direct democratic strategies are thus made guilty by association and dismissed as imprudent, risky to freedom, or worse.

This sequence suggests that we need to look closely at the classificatory schemes used to sort out varieties of democracy and to ex-

---

Nozick's conception of entitlement or on Rawls's two rules of justice would have little need for politics, and democracy would be not the condition for but at best the expression of a foreordained equality or of a predetermined set of rights.

6. I realize that this is a provocative charge. Its very radicalism suggests how completely we have accepted the philosophers' account of Socrates' trial and death. However, as M. I. Finley points out in his splendid little book *Democracy, Ancient and Modern* (Princeton: Princeton University Press, 1973), Socrates was associated with the Thirty Tyrants. Moreover, he was tried under the Law of Diopeithes for impiety, and this law not only had its analogue in Plato's *Laws* (which made impiety punishable by death) but was aimed primarily against the Sophists and other adversaries of Athenian participation and democracy. For a related discussion, see Sheldon Wolin, *Politics and Vision* (Boston: Little, Brown, 1960), chap. 2.

7. Thus, even a friend of participation, such as Jane J. Mansbridge, offers only "adversary" and "unitary" democracy in her typology of regime types; this bias forces her to reject unitary democracy on the grounds that it is monolithic and coercive, even though she despises adversary democracy, which she wishes to "get beyond." See Jane J. Mansbridge, *Beyond Adversary Democracy* (New York: Basic Books, 1980).

amine whether the pernicious forms (labeled *unitary democracy* below) can be separated from the healthy forms (labeled *strong democracy*). It is the conclusion of the second part of this book that such distinctions are not only tenable but are indispensable to the theory and practice of modern democracy. Since this line of argument is at the heart of that later discussion, I will not elaborate it here.

The third objection to the liberal arguments against democratic excess—and the central one, for our immediate purposes—is that thin democracy has itself inadvertently nourished some of the pathologies it has attributed to direct democracy and that strong democracy may offer remedies for the very diseases it has been thought to occasion. The balance of this chapter will be devoted to this third line of argument.

History tends to substantiate the claim that the modern era's political pathologies resulted at least in part from the liberal democratic experience and from the thin theory on which it is founded. A thousand contingent factors, of course, were also at work—accidents of time and place, forces generated by cultural attitudes, and events quite unrelated to liberal ideology. But totalism seems to be as much a response to the failures of liberalism as it is a tribute to the success of liberalism's competitors.

At the end of the last century, Emile Durkheim wrote that "what is characteristic of our development is that it has successively destroyed all the established social contexts; one after another they have been banished either by the slow usury of time or by violent revolution, and in such fashion that nothing has been developed to replace them."[8] And well before Durkheim Marx had written, in one of his most celebrated indictments: "the bourgeoisie, wherever it has had the upper hand, has put an end to all feudal, idyllic relations. It has pitilessly torn asunder the motley feudal ties that bound man to his 'natural superiors' and has left no other nexus between man and man than naked self-interest, than callous 'cash payment.' "[9]

Liberal democracy has had an enormously successful history, but it has also contributed to the molding of mass men: individuals de-

8. Emile Durkheim, *Suicide* (Paris, 1897), p. 446.
9. Karl Marx and Friedrich Engels, *The Communist Manifesto*, part 1, in Marx and Engels, *Selected Works* (Moscow: Foreign Languages Publishing House, 1958), vol. 1, p. 36.

fined by their privacy and their property yet unable to determine
who they are, emancipated by rights and freedoms but unable to act
as morally autonomous agents, driven by ambition and lust yet dis-
tanced from their happiness by the very powers that were supposed
to facilitate its achievement. Liberal democratic man, secure in his
rights and governed by impartial laws and accountable representatives, is obviously not mass man, let alone totalistic man. As ideal
types, the one is completely opposite to the others. But liberal democratic man is burdened with a psychology that disposes him toward the very pathologies he most fears. As a philosophical abstraction he is perfectly safe; as a figure encumbered with a real history,
however, he walks a tightrope, forever in danger precisely because
of the abstractness of his safety net. The perfect liberty of theory may
spell anomie in practice; perfect independence may mean defense-
lessness against actual bondage; perfect individuality may produce
actual deracination; perfect privacy may breed an incapacity for fellowship; perfect representation may induce a paralysis of activity
and a torpor of the political will. The model is perfect, but perfection
can be a defect in the real world of history. "History proves," wrote
Franklin Roosevelt, "that dictatorships do not grow out of strong
and successful governments, but out of weak and helpless ones." If
that is so, we should be able to specify our charges against liberal
democracy by examining its several defining dispositions.

THE ANARCHIST DISPOSITION AND THE PATHOLOGIES OF LIBERTY

Because, as Rousseau has written, "liberty is a food easy to eat but
hard to digest," those rare peoples who acquire it are very likely to
lose it again.[10] The experience of abstract individuality with which
the Western idea of freedom has been most often associated seems
to invigorate pioneers and philosophical heroes better than it nourishes ordinary citizens. "Despotism is never more secure of contin-
uance," wrote the wary de Tocqueville, "than when it can keep men

10. Jean-Jacques Rousseau, *The Government of Poland* (Indianapolis: Bobbs-Merrill,
1980), p. 8. Or, as de Tocqueville writes, "there is nothing more arduous than the
apprenticeship of liberty. . . . [I]t is generally established with difficulty in the midst
of storms; it is perfected by civil discord" (Alexis de Tocqueville, *Democracy in America*
[New York: Vintage Books, 1960] vol. 1, p. 256).

asunder."[11] The individualist conception of liberty keeps men free only by keeping them apart and thus, ironically, prepares them for the more tyrannical forms of community by confining them within the more anomic forms of independence.

Robert Nisbet may have spoken as a conservative in his sociological critique of liberal atomism, but his analysis seems accurate. "We may regard totalitarianism," he writes, "as a process of the annihilation of individuality, but, in more fundamental terms, it is the annihilation, first, of those social relationships within which individuality develops."[12] Indeed, no less a liberal than Arthur Schlesinger, Jr., has noticed that "the most important thing for the preservation of civilization is a belief in moral standards." Schlesinger has gone so far as to argue that credible moral standards must rest on "a fervent belief in a supernatural order."[13]

The extensive psychological and sociological literature that attempted after World War II to explain the "authoritarian personality" vividly portrayed the relationship of the darker side of freedom and mobility in a mass society—deracination and anomie—to the pathologies which that war had been fought to overcome.[14] The denizen of the modern metropolis whose life of anonymous hysteria is spent chasing jobs, life-styles, material goods, sexual partners, and fashionable principles is, by the classical Hobbesian definition, as free as ever a subject of sovereignty can be. That such a person may also conform, precisely by virtue of his "freedom," to many modern varieties of psychopathology—that he may well become an

11. De Tocqueville, *Democracy*, vol. 1, p. 256. De Tocqueville warns against "the despotism" to which "an innumerable multitude of men, all equal and alike, incessantly endeavoring to procure the petty and paltry pleasures with which they glut their lives" might be susceptible.

12. Robert A. Nisbet, *The Quest for Community* (New York: Oxford University Press, 1953 and 1969), p. 201. I prefer the term *totalism* to *totalitarianism*, for reasons developed in my essay in C. J. Friedrich, M. Curtis, and B. R. Barber, *Totalitarianism in Perspective: Three Views* (New York: Praeger, 1969). However, the term *totalitarian* retains its currency—helped along by the neoconservative distinction between friendly authoritarianism and unfriendly totalitarianism—and this is not the place to rehearse my objections to it.

13. Arthur Schlesinger, Jr. quoted in *The New Republic*, 25 July 1981. Schlesinger himself quotes Chesterton, who wrote that "the trouble when people stop believing in God is not that they thereafter believe in nothing; it is that they thereafter believe in anything."

14. The classical study is by T. W. Adorno et al., *The Authoritarian Personality*, 2 vols. (New York: Harper and Row, 1950). A contemporary study that applied lessons from Durkheim to the modern political era was Sebastian de Grazia's important book, *The Political Community: A Study in Anomie* (Chicago: University of Chicago Press, 1948).

irrational fundamentalist, a political extremist, a bigot, or even a ter-
rorist—suggests possible flaws in the conception of freedom as "the
absence of external impediments on motion."[15]

Similarly, the idea of natural rights has served a vital political
function by providing an abstract guarantee for individuals against
illegitimate encroachments by the state or by fellow citizens. But it
is at best a fiction (the fiction of the "person") and loses most of its
credibility and all of its utility when it is offered as a real and sufficient psychosociological foundation on which real women and men
can build meaningful, free lives within a community. Not only is the
capacity for democracy impaired, but the possibility of a concretely
satisfying liberty is jeopardized.

The trouble, clearly, is that the liberal notion of freedom was designed to answer a set of philosophical questions but has been put
to work as a starting point for solving practical political questions.
What was a useful fiction in formal argument has become a dangerous illusion in a real world where the rules of formal argument are
beside the point. We need not succumb to Erich Fromm's vision of
liberty as self-realization to understand that freedom is a social construct based on a rare and fragile form of human mutualism that
grants space to individuals who otherwise would have none at all.
Nor need we be Kantians to perceive that the will unimpeded by
external obstacles is not free in any recognizable human sense until
it is informed by purpose, meaning, context, and history. Solitude,
when it is not simply an illusion, is not freedom but misanthropy.
Self-direction brings freedom only when the self is emancipated
from mere impulse and appetite, when it is associated with inten-
tion and purposes that by their nature can only arise within the
guiding limits of a society and a culture. To be unimpeded and infinitely mobile is not freedom but deracination, unless by *free* we
mean only "homeless."

The anarchist disposition, then, is sensitive to public tyrannies
(the state, the majority, even the law in its coercive majesty) but

15. The description is Hobbes's. The several varieties of psychopathology con-
cealed in the psyche of liberal man have been explored by, among others, Erich
Fromm, *Escape from Freedom* (New York: Holt, Rinehart, and Winston, 1941); Christian Bay, *The Structure of Freedom* (Stanford: Stanford University Press, 1958); Viktor
Frankl, *The Will to Meaning: Foundations and Applications of Logotherapy* (New York:
New American Library, 1969); and Hannah Arendt, *The Origins of Totalitarianism*
(New York: World, 1951). It seems noteworthy that this line of inquiry has been pur-
sued almost exclusively by psychologically oriented social scientists with a European
background.

oblivious to private tyrannies, whether of the joint-stock corporation or of the anarchic soul. It guards diligently against that "immense and tutelary power" of the majority, which de Tocqueville feared could reduce a people to a "flock of timid and industrious animals."[16] But it pays scant heed to the tyranny of opinion that de Tocqueville condemned with equal cause.

Historical irony has left its mark here: the defense of the individual against the old tyrannies of hierarchy, tradition, status, superstition, and absolute political power has been sustained by a theory of the radically isolated individual defined by abstract rights and liberties. Yet this theory, as put into practice in the world of actual social relationships, has eroded the nourishing as well as the tyrannical connections and has left individuals cut off not only from the abuses of power but from one another.[17] And without one another, individuals have become easy targets for authoritarian collectivism. The theory that was supposed to defend men and women from power has thus in fact stripped them of the social armor by which they could most effectively defend themselves.

Robert Nisbet captures the irony this way: "The genius of totalitarian leadership lies in its profound awareness that human personality cannot tolerate moral isolation. It lies, further, in its knowledge that absolute and relentless power will be acceptable only when it comes to seem the only available form of community and membership."[18] Fictitious legal persons, though secure in their rights, reside in no particular neighborhood, belong to no particular clubs, identify with no particular clan or tribe or nation, and are part of no particular community. Therein lies their personhood. Yet therein, also, lies their vulnerability. Universality is an abstraction of little value to particular men. Barred from legitimate community by abstract liberty, the universal person may be all too ready to abdicate his actual liberty for the benefits of an illegitimate community. There is, in Nisbet's poignant phrase, "a fatal affinity of power and individual loneliness." And so today's anarchist becomes tomorrow's authoritar-

16. De Tocqueville, *Democracy*, vol. 2, p. 380.

17. Once again, it is Reinhold Niebuhr who pinpoints the schizophrenia of the liberal orientation: "Preoccupation with the perils of collective forms of ambition produce social theories which emphasize freedom at the expense of order, ending finally in the philosophy of anarchism. Preoccupation with the perils of inordinateness on the other hand, allows the fear of anarchy to bear the fruit of connivance with tyranny" (*The Children of Light and the Children of Darkness* [New York: Charles Scribner's Sons, 1944], p. 47).

18. Nisbet, *Quest*, p. 204.

ian, and the fear of his own freedom drives him into the arms of hospitable tyrants.[19] In this fashion, the pathologies of anarchism are transmuted into the pathologies of realism.

THE REALIST DISPOSITION AND THE PATHOLOGIES OF POWER

The convincingly lunatic logic enunciated by Shigalov in Dostoevski's *The Possessed* offers a caricature of thin democracy's polarized obsession with absolute liberty and absolute power: "Starting from unlimited freedom," Shigalov reports, "I arrived at unlimited despotism." Nonetheless, he adds, "there is no other solution."

Indivisible sovereign power can be the only way of guaranteeing inalienable individual liberty: that has been the lesson of liberal thought from Hobbes to Lenin (who in *State and Revolution* makes "centralized power" the only reliable servant of liberty).[20] Bertrand Russell, like many liberals, was torn between the absolute demands of pure freedom and the need for central power as freedom's guarantor; he was drawn this way and that by the conflicting claims of each. In *The Practice and Theory of Bolshevism*, he inclines toward anarchism: "Government and the law, in their very essence, consist of restrictions on freedom, and freedom is the greatest of political goals."[21] Yet in *Power* he yields to realism—not in order to refute anarchism but to offer a paradoxical corollary to it. "There must be power," he writes, "either that of government or that of anarchical adventurers. There must even be naked power, so long as there are rebels against government, or even ordinary criminals."[22] For the liberal democrat, there is always freedom: that is the end, the aim,

19. The authoritarian streak in the moral teachings of the anarchists is evident in Emma Goldman's insistence that the anarchist must be "a great TEACHER of the new values." Nechayev's *Revolutionary Catechism* reeks not only with violence and rage but with purifying righteousness.

20. Lenin, *State and Revolution* (New York: International Publishers, 1932), pp. 62 et passim. "Where the state exists," writes Lenin, sounding remarkably like an anarchist, "there is no freedom. Where there is freedom, there will be no state" (*ibid.*, p. 79). But Lenin is of course caught precisely in that liberal dilemma whereby it seems that total freedom can be achieved only through total power—in this case, through the Dictatorship of the Proletariat.

21. Bertrand Russell, *The Practice and Theory of Bolshevism* (London: Allen and Unwin, 1962), p. 82. For a full discussion of Russell as a liberal and a minimalist, see my "Solipsistic Politics: Russell's Empiricist Liberalism," in George Roberts, ed., *Bertrand Russell: The Memorial Volume* (London: Allen and Unwin, 1978).

22. Bertrand Russell, *Power: A New Social Analysis* (London: Allen and Unwin, 1938), p. 106.

and the object of politics, and politics is its only instrument. Yet there must also be power, for that is the essence of the political instrument and thus the necessary condition for the preservation of liberty. This conjunction poses the chief dilemma of polarized liberalism. How can we preserve liberty without falling into anarchism? How can we use power without falling into tyranny?

Russell acknowledges that the "two dangers" facing "every community" are "anarchy and despotism," which are "alike disastrous."[23] Liberty, in denying tyranny, engenders anarchy; power, in thwarting anarchy, engenders tyranny. This polarization is built into liberalism's social-contract premises and gives to thin democracy its characteristic ambivalence toward both liberty (a virtue fraught with danger) and power (a danger that can serve virtue).

A further danger for political life lurks in the realist disposition. Liberals have regarded power as in the first instance an instrument—a device of prudence by which natural liberty is secured politically. Hobbes thus begins analyzing power in Chapter 10 of *Leviathan* by portraying it as strictly relational, the "present means to some future good." Yet he moves quickly from this guarded instrumentalism to the striking claim that life for human beings is but a "ceaseless search for power after power unto death." Power as an instrument gives way to power as a deep human need. Power and with it glory become ends in themselves, part of a more basic definition of human nature that associates individuality with aggression and acquisition and that transforms the abstract solitary person into a voracious predator.

Bertrand Russell's own view of human nature, which during his early years was imbued with the rationalist's faith in enlightenment and progress, was transformed in the course of his career into a pessimism heavy with the weight of Freud's and Conrad's irrationalism. Man degenerates into beast, and is given bestial desires that are "essentially boundless and incapable of complete satisfaction."[24] Man's grandeur becomes one with his perversity: in Russell's words, a "titanic combination of nobility and impiety" drives man to "be God." Man is a paradox, an awesome animal who evokes our approbation even as he excites our fears: his "primitive lusts and egoisms" are to be curbed, but his saving individuality must be cher-

23. Ibid., p. 211.
24. Bertrand Russell, *Roads to Freedom* (London: Allen and Unwin, 1966), p. 73.

ished and protected. The object of modern liberal democratic theory has thus become to rescue the individual from the beast, to save freedom from itself, to find and nurture the fictitious legal person in the rabid misanthrope, to subdue the id without destroying its life-sustaining potency.

What liberalism lacks is precisely what could facilitate the miracle—namely, a theory of citizenship. What is missing is politics, the only legitimate form that our natural dependency can take. In practice politics is of course unavoidable even for the liberal, but in theory it seems too messy, too cumbersome, and too susceptible to passion and opinion to be a safe repository for the rights and liberties of individuals. Better to rely on benevolent legislators, on good laws, and on sound principles. Participatory politics is seen as particularly villainous because depredations supposedly multiply beyond the number of individuals when the animals run in herds. "The motion of the people," warned Montesquieu, a paragon of early liberalism, "is always either too remiss or too violent. Sometimes with a hundred thousand arms they overturn all before them; and sometimes with a hundred thousand feet they creep like insects."[25] How often has the language of the herdsman and the shepherd been used to depict the benevolent masters of a nation's liberties. How much more often have plebs and commoners been called sheep—or stampeding cattle, when they have proven themselves less docile.

Liberal theory is hard pressed to resolve these dilemmas because it visualizes so little middle ground between liberty (anarchy) and power (despotism), so little space for citizenship—which is the only legitimate form of common life that insulates the individual from the animal within by linking him in civic relations to every other individual.

A society that centralizes power in the name of liberty but at the cost of self-government, and that at the same time pursues the rhetoric of pure individualism and absolute freedom without providing for a politically free citizenry, is a society ripe for both anarchy *and* tyranny—or for that rapid succession from the former to the latter that has typified some of the past century's ill-fated experiments in thin democracy.

25. Montesquieu, *The Spirit of the Laws*, ed. T. Nugent (New York: Hafner Editions, 1949), p. 101.

The Minimalist Disposition
and the Pathologies of Passivity

On its face, minimalism appears to be a good deal more secure from the pathologies of absolute liberty and absolute power than are the anarchist and realist dispositions of liberal democracy. Eschewing the dogmas of idealism and empiricism, it makes possible (in Russell's words) "a diffused liberal sentiment, tinged with skepticism" in which "social cooperation [is] much less difficult, and liberty correspondingly more possible."[26] Yet agnosticism is not a particularly useful defense against fanaticism, and tolerant skeptics who think that nothing can be known are ineffectual allies of civilization when zealots who think they know everything are on the march. The minimalist disposition can immunize us against anarchy and tyranny and as such is an important preventative, but it does little to fortify democrats or liberals in their struggle against the extremisms they face. Tolerance is a beneficent and admirable posture, but in itself it can stop nothing. It refrains from doing harm but may permit harm to be done.

Sir Karl Popper and others have seen in fallibilism an important bulwark of democratic liberty: if falsification rather than positive proof is the real test of scientific knowledge, then political knowers will hardly dare claim a stronger base for their opinions than prejudice or interest. Yet this doctrine in its prudent negativism attempts to draw practical lessons from epistemological failure, and in doing so it makes two errors. The first is to think that politics must conform to epistemology, rather than replace it (see Chapter 8). The second is to found a praxis, which should be vigorous and resilient, on a metaphysical mood whose foundation in skepticism renders it self-doubting and pusillanimous. Hume knew well enough that his skepticism was to be thought rather than lived, but minimalists apparently want to live skepticism in (of all places) the political arena.

The minimalists' strategy is to provide individual liberty with a sanctuary: if Truth and Principle are forever uncertain, they cannot be legitimately deployed against the beliefs of individuals. But real freedom may suffer as much in this refuge as it is benefited. The struggle for liberty requires an energized faith that, it has often been said, only young and vigorous peoples can possess. Certainly a

26. Bertrand Russell, *Power*, p. 308.

spirit of weary equivocation born of metaphysical doubt aids the practical struggle but little.

Perhaps the dilemma can be construed in terms of citizenship: the free individual may wish that his fellow citizens would refrain from imposing their opinions upon him in the name of some "objective" truth, but citizens so tame as to shrink from the consequences of what they take to be public justice and common interest are scarcely citizens at all and are unlikely to be capable of defending freedom in any form. Freedom may need to be protected from the tyrannies of putatively immutable "Truth," but it also requires a spirited defense of provisional social truths. Skepticist minimalism affords protection, but only at the price of undermining activity. Citizenship cannot thrive where citizens are without conviction; and without citizens, freedom must in practice remain in jeopardy—however secure it seems to be from the intrusions of careening majorities or self-proclaimed technocrats.

If the minimalist pays too little heed to the requirements of citizenship, he also thinks too little of the political paralysis facing the skeptic who refuses to acknowledge the possibility of public interests and concerted action. In such caution lies the peculiar thinness of liberal democracy. Afraid of overstepping the prudent boundaries set by skeptical reason, the liberal is politically paralyzed. Because he is uncertain of his beliefs, he hesitates to act. But in a world of necessary actions and ineluctable consequences (see Chapter 6), the liberal's diffidence cannot mean that nothing happens, only that *he* causes nothing to happen. He may modestly abstain from acting on behalf of public goods that he does not think can be legitimated, but his reticence only means that private and clearly illegitimate forces will control his destiny unopposed. Refusing to impose himself or a public will on others, he willy-nilly permits market forces, which are neither public nor just, to ride roughshod over his fellow citizens. Thus can skepticism, candidly embraced and consistently pursued, open the door to philosophies of power—to cant and dogma, since the skeptic has given up on public reason; to opinion and prejudice, which the skeptic cannot distinguish from right; and to private power and illegitimate coercion, because the Thrasymachean self that shadows every skeptic admits of no genuine "public" power and views legitimacy itself as a hypocritical ruse. Uproot principle, deny the possibility of mutual knowledge or public goods, and what is left except bigotry and brute force?

How often have their philosophical good will and their reluctance to claim the right to act where they lack the ability to know led thoughtful liberals from a useful political temperance into a damaging political nihilism—an attitude better known as philosophical anarchism? Thus, in an earlier anarchist incarnation, Robert Paul Wolff was compelled by the logic of his own line of questions to a skeptical extreme for which he had little use: "There is not, and there could not be," he seemed forced to allow, "a state that has a right to command and whose subjects have a binding obligation to obey."[27] Once political rationality—that is, the very possibility of public judgment—is denied, even the most obvious distinctions become insupportable. Thus a thinker as sensitive as Herbert Read could be seduced by his skepticism into the nonsensical claim that there was "nothing to choose" between Churchill and Hitler.[28]

Abstention from political action may secure the skeptic against any untoward disposition to treat his own opinions as truths, but it will do little to secure the public at large against the tyranny of opinion. Quite the contrary. In the absence of public judgments, private judgments will prevail. Where the community will not act for itself, the market will act for it. And it is the market rather than some limbo of inaction to which minimalists acquiesce when they refuse to participate in political judgment. Certain minimalists openly acknowledge that they defer to a market—which, they claim, will be fairer and more egalitarian than any community judgment could possibly be.[29] This sort of skeptic, when he cedes the resolution of conflict to the private realm, means to cede it to a realm of natural equality and bilateral exchange in which individuals will, each representing himself, resolve their differences amicably and voluntarily.[30]

Yet in reality, this procedure only cedes all conflict resolution to a

27. Robert Paul Wolff, "On Violence," *Journal of Philosophy* 66, 19 (1969): 607. Wolff was concerned here about the illegitimate violence used by the state in the 1960s. Elsewhere, he has expressed his interest in community: see *The Poverty of Liberalism* (Boston: Beacon Press, 1968).

28. In his *To Hell with Culture* (New York: Schocken Books, 1964), Read writes "I am concerned to show that from a certain point of view there is nothing to choose between fascism and democracy" (p. 49).

29. Milton Friedman, for example, writes that "a major objection to a free economy is precisely that . . . it gives people what they want instead of what a particular group thinks they ought to want. Underlying most arguments against the free market is a lack of belief in freedom itself" (in *Capitalism and Freedom* [Chicago: University of Chicago Press, 1962], p. 15).

30. This is the position Robert Nozick takes in his previously cited *Anarchy, State, and Utopia*; it either presupposes the equal power of the participants in the market or is indifferent to whether the outcome is equitable.

realm of arbitrary power and unequal wills. In exchange for the sometimes questionable judgment of the people, the liberal gets the always nefarious judgment of the joint-stock corporation; for the accountable will of the sometimes extravagant majority, he gets the unaccountable willfulness of the always self-interested pressure group; for the educable reason of the sometimes misinformed citizenry, he gets the uneducable prejudice of the information-manipulating media. He does not escape judgment or intrusion or prejudice masquerading as truth, but he does surrender the accountability and publicity by which such evils can be mitigated.

Other minimalists, more naïve still, seem to believe that if they do not act and if the public can be made to recognize its epistemological limits, there will be no action. They lean toward complete anarchism, viewing the public not only as the source of arrogance and coercion but as the cause of conflict itself. To them, tolerance is a problem only because of the intolerant state: individuals if left alone would leave each other alone, whereas the state with its dubious claims to public right and popular responsibility is always trying to do things "for"—which means "to"—individuals. This sort of minimalist calls for toleration only because abolition of the state seems historically impossible. If the political community cannot be extirpated altogether, it must at least be made to do as little as possible—to "tolerate" individual beliefs and actions unless it can "prove" that they pose an obvious danger (something it is difficult to do in light of the skeptics' doubt about the possibility of proof).

Now strong democratic theory also denies that an absolute principle (or independent ground) can serve as the basis of political judgment, and insofar as minimalists advance only that claim one may prefer them to idealist anarchists and empiricist realists. However, the strong democrat would argue that the proper response to uncertainty and metaphysical failure is not passivity or toleration of all private judgments but rather a quest for forms of political judgment that do not depend on metaphysics, epistemologies, or independent grounds. The antidote to the loss of metaphysical faith is, precisely, politics, the cultivation of community judgment, rather than skepticism, anarchism, or that acquiescence of the modest that is called "tolerance." In the absence of an independent ground, random coercion and arbitrary force will seize hold of our common destinies. Only an active politics and a democratic citizenry can prevent the transformation of relativism into nihilism or of philosophical skepticism into political impotence (the Weimar Republic comes to mind).

Minimalism in its skeptical and tolerationist variations thus evades the extremes of realism and anarchism. But it does not, finally, provide the basis for a positive politics capable of resisting the tyrannies that have arisen as faith, tradition, kinship, and the benevolent authoritarianism of metaphysical politics have given way to modernity. To elucidate such a politics, which goes by the name of *strong democracy* here, is the task of the second half of this study.

LIBERALISM AND THE TOTALITARIAN TEMPTATION

Liberalism's three dispositions do not exist independently of one another, and it is not really fair to indict them in isolation. In practice, the three complement and check one another, each affording the others a certain immunity to the pathologies to which they might otherwise be disposed. Minimalism's distrust of collective power resists realism's inclination to abuse individual rights in the name of popular power (Hobbes's "authorized sovereign"). Realism's perception of anarchism's impotence to contest private coercion and market inequality supports the idea of legitimate state power. The anarchist disposition underscores the primacy of the individual in every social relationship and is a caution against investing representative institutions, the symbolic collectivity, or the idea of the community with an intrinsic value that can only be the property of individuals.

Indeed, it is the hybrid character of American democratic liberalism that gives it its greatest versatility and its ability to resist degeneration. One would be hard pressed to think of another system that honors freedom so generously even as it concentrates power so efficiently. Certainly, by the standards of world history the liberal democracies of America, England, and parts of continental Europe have remained extraordinary exceptions to the tyrannical proclivities of the human species.

Yet even in the hybrid form, liberalism has suffered certain corruptions that appear to derive from its defining character. Liberal regimes have proven themselves unequal to the challenge of a tyranny imposed from within in Germany, Spain, Italy, France (between Republics), and elsewhere, and they have been maintained in America and England only at an escalating cost and with increasing difficulty.

Because liberal democracy makes an ideology of radical individualism, it depends heavily on the idea of private property, held both by individual and corporate persons. Private life is secured for some, but a public life in which all would participate becomes impossible. In wedding itself to social structures defined by inequality, liberalism is compelled to eschew a consistent theory of distributive justice. Once one defines democracy as "guaranteeing individual freedom" (Milton Friedman), then "a society which is socialist cannot also be democratic."[31] Which is to say, democracy remains solely a means for the preservation of individual rights (including property) and so cannot tolerate planning, public ownership, or for that matter equality itself.[32]

It would be ludicrous to attribute all of the pathologies of modern liberal regimes to the intrinsic philosophical deficiencies of liberalism. High crime rates, public lying, private and public fraud, systemic inegalitarianism, economic chaos, exploitation, mean-spiritedness, commercialism, privatism, persistent racism, and the atrophying of public life in the neighborhoods as well as in the central government owe their existence to myriad causes—so many that one may perhaps blame modernity itself.[33] But the liberal spirit is part of the modern spirit, and with the credit for material progress and economic emancipation it must bear some blame. When individuals act like "free-riders" by refusing to pay (or even to take responsibility) for services provided by an abstract public to which they feel no obligation;[34] when the middle class grows weary of the problems of minorities and of other oppressed groups and begins to sermonize about self-reliance to victims of structural inequality;[35]

31. Friedman, *Capitalism*, p. 8.
32. Frederick Hayek makes the polemical case for this argument in *The Road to Serfdom* (Chicago: University of Chicago Press, 1944) and the philosophical case in *Law, Legislation and Liberty*, vol. 2 of *The Mirage of Social Justice* (Chicago: University of Chicago Press, 1976).
33. For discussions of modernity and of its role in the corruption of man see Alasdair MacIntyre, *After Virtue* (Notre Dame, Ind.: University of Notre Dame Press, 1981); Richard Sennett, *The Fall of Public Man* (New York: Knopf, 1974); and Marshall Berman, *All That Is Solid Melts into Air: The Experience of Modernity* (New York: Simon and Schuster, 1982). The locus classicus of all such works is Rousseau's second discourse, *On the Arts and Sciences*, which he wrote in 1751.
34. The free-rider problem is discussed in Chapter 8.
35. The practice of attributing the problems of the poor or of women to their own native character rather than to systemic impediments or social discrimination has become widespread; see, for example, George Gilder, *Wealth and Poverty* (New York: Basic Books, 1980), and Colette Dowling, *The Cinderella Complex* (New York: Summit Books, 1981).

when responsible government officials insist either that there is nothing to be done (the Carter administration) or that all public rights and goods can be better served and better used by private interests (the Reagan administration);[36] when social scientists argue that the health of democracy depends on the passivity of its citizens and liken the call of oppressed groups for justice to a democratic distemper[37]—then, it would seem, at least some responsibility for our worsening crises belongs to liberal democratic thinking.

If, in the Western world, hope is accompanied by despair, if along with freedom there is meaninglessness, purposelessness, and ano-mie, if a too-active bureaucracy has left citizens in a torpor and too-active courts have usurped the law-making functions of frightened legislators who in turn distrust their own constituents, then it may be that liberalism has come face to face with itself. It may be that it now confronts the weakness built into its strength, the selfishness built into its privacy, the passivity built into its tolerance, the anar-chism built into its liberty, the bureaucratism built into its realism, and the indifference to citizenship built into its enervating and antipolitical instrumentalism.

Politics, more even than nature, abhors a vacuum. Where citizens will not act, judges, bureaucrats, and finally thugs rush in. Bernard Henri-Lévy, that scourge of leftist extremism, has written, "totali-tarianism is not the police but the savants in power."[38] But when citizens are dispossessed of their power, or offer it up willingly, who will be left to rule but savants or thugs? And who can be surprised if the savants quickly come to act like thugs, or if the thugs claim they are wise men? Henri-Lévy has written, "totalitarianism is not force unleashed but truth put in chains."[39] One might better say that skepticism unleashed will imprison political judgment and paralyze political action. Henri-Lévy has written, "he who says total power says, in effect, total knowledge."[40] Yet without denying this Bacon-

---

36. The plan of Reagan's former Secretary of the Interior, James Watt, to "return" roughly five percent of nationally held lands to the private sector is a tribute to the power of this kind of thinking. A theoretical defense is given in Charles L. Schultz, *The Public Use of Private Interest* (Washington, D.C.: Brookings Institution, 1977), al-though—as one might expect from President Carter's Secretary of the Treasury—Schultz makes important allowances for the public use of private power through the incentive system.

37. For examples of this argument, see Chapter 1, n. 5 above.

38. Bernard Henri-Lévy, *La Barbarie à visage humain* (Paris: Bernard Grasset, 1977), p. 170 (my translation).

39. Ibid.

40. Ibid.

ian equation of truth and mastery, one might better say that total
agnosticism is as dangerous as total truth in a world where power is
at work and decisions must be taken. In fact, the abstract polarization of Truth and Skepticism to which liberals are so often reduced
is itself part of the problem. It imposes philosophical categories
upon political life, and in doing so excludes the practical middle
ground of discourse, common work, and community-building, activities that in the real world of politics serve the function of such
constructs as Truth and Objective Knowledge.

The totalitarian temptation thrives not only in the political vacuum left by skepticism but also in the spiritual vacuum left by radical
individualism. Individualism, with its myths of solitary beatitude
(godliness), has persistently underrated the human need for association, community, and species identification. By failing to provide
healthy forms of social interaction, it has inadvertently promoted
unhealthy ones. It is not just artists, romantics, and poets (in this
instance, D. H. Lawrence) who have acknowledged:

> I am part of the sun as my eye is part of me. That
> I am part of the earth my feet know perfectly,
> And my blood is part of the sea. My soul knows that
> I am part of the human race, my soul is an organism,
> Part of the great human soul. . . .
> There is nothing of me that is alone and absolute
>   except my mind . . . it is only the surface of the waters.[41]

The liberal reads "blood," and crimson tyrannies of the spirit
spring into his mind—he sees Robespierre putting on Rousseau's
romantic mantle or Goebbels writing out the destiny of the German
Volk in blood. And with good reason: the unconscious is a dangerous place and blood brotherhood is a dangerous myth. Yet it is dangerous as well to ignore the claims of commonality. Totalistic man
may be the product not of the unconscious mind served but of the
unconscious mind thwarted, not of community totemized but of
community spurned.

The human yearning for union and for communion cannot be
"demythologized" away. It is real and must be answered responsibly by nourishing, nontoxic forms of democratic community if it is
not to be answered by deformation of the human spirit. Our
interdependence as members of the human species requires us to
belong—if not to free associations, then to totalistic collectivities.

41. D. H. Lawrence in *Kangaroo*. One is reminded here of the American Indian
aphorism: "The White Man says, the land belongs to us; we say, we belong to the
land."

If liberalism undervalues the need for kinship, it also is oblivious to what Richard M. Titmuss, in his study of blood donors in America and England, has called "the need for gift relationships."[42] Titmuss argues that "modern societies now require more rather than less freedom of choice for the expression of altruism in the daily life of all social groups."[43] The reality, however, is that contractual and exchange relations have driven out almost every vestige of altruism. Recent social philosophers have in fact been at pains to exclude altruism and other "supererogatory" theories of the good from their consideration of morals and justice for reasons that, while philosophically sensible, misconstrue the political role of the excluded terms.[44] Whether philosophy is here following practice or practice is following philosophy, relationships founded on motives other than self-interest narrowly defined have clearly fallen outside the pale of liberal political theory—with the consequence again that such motives are left to those least likely to treat with them in a judicious and legitimate fashion.

The need to give, when stymied by conventional institutions, can transmute into the need to sacrifice or be martyred (Jonestown is a troubling example). Gift relationships, when excluded by normal social rules, can take on an obsequious or fanatical character, turning love into possessiveness and membership into the loss of personal identity. Giving, like belonging, can have either healthy or pathological forms. A society blind to the need in either form is likely to reap the worst of both worlds: to harbor the meanness of market relations, where private interest is the only measure of human worth, as well as the fanaticism of sacrificial relations, where altruism—because it is not permitted healthy expression in the dominant culture—reappears in the insidious form of subcultural zealotry. The problem of the totalitarian temptation is then the problem of emptiness. And if emptiness is the peculiarly modern condition, liberalism is the peculiarly political form of emptiness.

For all of this, the question remains: is there a viable and safe alternative? The liberal may nod in response to the criticisms developed here and still be skeptical. And because liberalism has done more to secure the freedom and to win the material liberation of

42. Richard M. Titmuss, *The Gift Relationship* (New York: Pantheon Books, 1971), p. 170.
43. Ibid.
44. This is, for example, John Rawls's strategy in *A Theory of Justice* (Cambridge, Mass.: Harvard University Press, 1971).

women and men in the West than any other regime form, liberals have earned the right to pose the following series of questions and demands—which comprise the setting within which the second part of this book must be treated:

If not through liberalism, how will you secure liberty? What form of democratic politics can you describe that will nourish community without destroying autonomy? Show me a form strong enough to overcome what you call the passivity and emptiness of liberalism that is nonetheless safe enough to defend individuals against opinion run amok, or majorities crying for blood, or the people's will trying to substitute itself for the rule of law. Invent for me a form of political discourse that detaches public decision and action from the claims of truth and the quest for certainty without then falling prey to relativism, arbitrariness, or subjective prejudice. Since you decry contractualism, show me a community that brings citizens together without extirpating their differences, that permits the realization of common ends without deforming autonomous wills, that displays what you call human interdependency without sacrificing individual identity and the freedom it secures. In short, show me an activism that is not dogmatic, a relativism that is not arbitrary, a citizenry that is not whimsical and prone to error and arrogance. Show me a community that does not oppress individuals, a consensus that respects dissent, a politics that recognizes conflict without enthroning permanent factions, and a democracy that is strong without being unitary, rich without being fragmented, and consensual without being monolithic. Until you can show me this, I will accept each of your criticisms and still believe that liberal democracy is the best arrangement that free men and women can make.

In the balance of this book, I hope to make an argument for politics in the participatory mode—for a form of "strong" democracy that not only answers these wise challenges but that offers genuine hope for democratic practice in the new age.

II

Strong Democracy:
The Argument for Citizenship

Chapter Six

Strong Democracy:
Politics as a Way of Living

> *Democracy is not an alternative to other
> principles of associated life. It is the idea
> of community life itself. . . . [It is] a
> name for a life of free and enriching
> communion.*
>
> (John Dewey)

> *We have in mind men whose state of vir-
> tue does not rise above that of ordinary
> people . . . who seek not an ideally per-
> fect constitution, but first a way of
> living.*
>
> (Aristotle)

Strong democracy is a distinctively modern form of participatory democracy. It rests on the idea of a self-governing community of citizens who are united less by homogeneous interests than by civic
education and who are made capable of common purpose and mutual action by virtue of their civic attitudes and participatory institutions rather than their altruism or their good nature. Strong democracy is consonant with—indeed it depends upon—the politics
of conflict, the sociology of pluralism, and the separation of private
and public realms of action. It is not intrinsically inimical to either
the size or the technology of modern society and is therefore wedded neither to antiquarian republicanism nor to face-to-face parochialism. Yet it challenges the politics of elites and masses that
masquerades as democracy in the West and in doing so offers a relevant alternative to what we have called thin democracy—that is,
to instrumental, representative, liberal democracy in its three
dispositions.

Strong democracy has a good deal in common with the classical democratic theory of the ancient Greek polis, but it is in no sense identical with that theory. It also shares much with its cousin liberal democracy, and in practical terms it is sometimes complementary to rather than a radical alternative to the liberal argument. Yet it is distinctive in a number of crucial ways and is a powerful foil for American democratic practice.

It is a much less total, less unitary theory of public life than the advocates of ancient republicanism might wish, but it is more complete and positive than contemporary liberalism. It incorporates a Madisonian wariness about actual human nature into a more hopeful, Jeffersonian outlook on human potentialities. As portrayed here, it is a new theory drawn from a variety of established practices and nourished by classical theories of community, civic education, and participation.

The theory of strong democracy does not quite envision politics in the ancient sense of a "way of life," and it is explicitly hostile to the still more extravagant claim that politics is *the* way of life. It has no share in the republican nostalgia of such commentators as Hannah Arendt or Leo Strauss. Modern men and women know too well the dangers of a unitary politics that lays claim to all the human soul and affects to express man's "higher nature." "How small of all that human hearts endure / That part which laws or kings can cause or cure," wrote Samuel Johnson, in what should be the epigraph of every tract urging greater democracy.

Yet while recognizing the dangers of totalism, we need not accept the wan residualism of liberal democratic pluralism, which depicts politics as nothing more than the chambermaid of private interests. The history of the twentieth century should have taught us that when democracy cannot respond to the need for community with anything more than a pusillanimous privatism, other, more oppressive political ideologies will step in. That, indeed, was the theme of the previous chapter of this book.

The theory of strong democracy offers a different and more vigorous response: it envisions politics not as a way of life but as a way of living—as, namely, the way that human beings with variable but malleable natures and with competing but overlapping interests can contrive to live together communally not only to their mutual advantage but also to the advantage of their mutuality.

Because democratic politics makes possible cooperation and an approximation of concord where they do not exist by nature, it is potentially a realm of unique openness, flexibility, and promise. It is in fact the quintessential realm of change that, while it is occasioned by conflict and by the inadequacy of man's higher nature, becomes the occasion for mutualism and the superseding of his lower nature. This is perhaps why John Dewey was moved to call democracy not a form of associated life but "the idea of community life itself."[1]

There is an element of hubris in Dewey's almost Periclean vision of political life, but there is moderation as well. Neither the solitary, nearly divine philosopher nor the solitary Hobbesian predator fully embodies that odd creature *Homo politicus* who inhabits both the ancient and modern worlds of democracy: dependent, yet under democracy self-determining; insufficient and ignorant, yet under democracy teachable; selfish, yet under democracy cooperative; stubborn and solipsistic, yet under democracy creative and capable of genuine self-transformation.

The stress on transformation is at the heart of the strong democratic conception of politics. Every politics confronts the competition of private interests and the conflict that competition engenders. But where liberal democracy understands politics as a means of eliminating conflict (the anarchist disposition), repressing it (the realist disposition), or tolerating it (the minimalist disposition), strong democracy also aspires to transform conflict through a politics of distinctive inventiveness and discovery. It seeks to create a public language that will help reformulate private interests in terms susceptible to public accommodation (see Chapter 8); and it aims at understanding individuals not as abstract persons but as citizens, so that commonality and equality rather than separateness are the defining traits of human society (see Chapter 9).

Open to change and hospitable to the idea of individual and social transformation, strong democracy can overcome the pessimism and cynicism, the negativity and passivity that, while they immunize liberalism against naïve utopianism and the tyranny of idealism, also undermine its cautious hopes and leave its theory thin and threadbare and its practice vulnerable to skepticism and dogmatism. Under strong democracy, politics is given the power of human promise. For the first time the possibilities of transforming private into public, dependency into interdependency, conflict into coop-

1. John Dewey, *The Public and Its Problems* (New York: Holt, 1927), p. 148.

eration, license into self-legislation, need into love, and bondage into citizenship are placed in a context of participation. There they are secure from the manipulation of those bogus communitarians who appeal to the human need for communion and for a purpose higher than private, material interests only in order to enslave humankind.

Strong democratic politics is finally not so different from the political condition depicted by Michael Oakeshott when he wrote of sailors on "a boundless sea [where] there is neither harbor nor shelter nor floor for anchorage, neither starting-point nor appointed destination, [and where] the enterprise is to keep afloat on an even keel."[2] This imagery speaks not only to conservatives, for it depicts a politics free of crass instrumentalism, a politics that is to a degree an end in itself rather than one that only has ends. Where democracy is end as well as means, its politics take on the sense of a journey in which the going is as important as the getting there and in which the relations among travelers are as vital as the destinations they may think they are seeking.

Yet though strong democracy can be made to sound attractive, rhetoric alone is an insufficient argument for it. Having introduced the idea in a very general way, I must now try to give it a more formal expression. I have suggested that strong democracy is the only form of democracy that can provide an adequate response to the dilemmas of modern politics. I want now to go further and argue that among democratic regime forms, it alone accounts for and responds to what we may call the basic conditions of politics—i.e., the circumstances that give rise to politics in the first place. This argument must begin by stipulating the conditions of politics. Then it will be possible to give a formal definition of strong democracy (and of several other competing forms) in terms of these conditions.

DEFINING THE CONDITIONS OF POLITICS

One can understand the realm of politics as being circumscribed by conditions that impose *a necessity for public action, and thus for reasonable public choice, in the presence of conflict and in the absence of private or independent grounds for judgment.*

A political question thus takes the form: "What shall we do when something has to be done that affects us all, we wish to be reason-

2. Michael Oakeshott, *Rationalism in Politics* (New York: Basic Books, 1962), p. 127.

able, yet we disagree on means and ends and are without independent grounds for making the choice?" This formulation suggests that the ultimate political problem is one of action, not Truth or even Justice in the abstract. The vital advantage of this viewpoint, which Machiavelli recognized and Burke celebrated, is that it eschews metaphysics and circumvents philosophical issues of Final Truth and Absolute Morals. It requires a proximate solution for real problems that will persist whether or not an ultimate measure of judgment is available. The disadvantage, which such pure philosophers as Kant and Rawls have found it difficult to overcome, is that *some* reasonable answer must be found, even where none can be philosophically warranted. For when one is confronted by the logic of consequences (see "Necessity" below), making no decision at all becomes a decision. This means that the political actor, unlike the speculative philosopher, can afford neither the luxury of agnosticism nor the Olympian nonchalance of skepticism. To be political is to *have* to choose—and, what is worse, to have to choose under the worst possible circumstances, when the grounds of choice are not given a priori or by fiat or by pure knowledge (*epistemē*). To be political is thus to be free with a vengeance—to be free in the unwelcome sense of being without guiding standards or determining norms yet under an ineluctable pressure to act, and to act with deliberation and responsibility as well.

This is the true dilemma of Plato's Cave, the problem that philosophers have called Right Opinion, where we are without final truth and absolute knowledge yet wish to act in a manner that conforms to right. We hope our choice to be something more than arbitrary or impulsive or merely self-interested yet we must choose without the guidance of impartial truth. Under these conditions, the cave can hardly be a tidy place.[3] No wonder it is so disdained by the philosopher. It is grimy with the muddled activity of reluctant doers who must nonetheless do as best they can. It is dark and confused and tumultuous because it is peopled by creatures who are defined by

---

3. Montaigne captures perfectly the untidy, practical spirit of politics when he writes:

> The virtue assigned to the affairs of the world is a virtue with many bends, angles, and elbows, so as to join and adapt itself to human weakness; mixed and artificial, not straight, clean, constant, or purely innocent. . . . [H]e who walks in a crowd must step aside, keep his elbows in, step back or advance, even leave the straight way, according to what he encounters. (*On Vanity*, in *The Complete Essays of Montaigne*, trans. Donald M. Frame [Stanford: Stanford University Press, 1958], p. 758)

what they do rather than by how they think, by the search for proximate good rather than for immutable certainty, and by the need to
discover a reasonable basis for their commonality rather than an unimpeachable foundation for their individuality. Enshrouded in ambivalence, it is a world constrained to reject Thrasymachean ideologies of pure interest without being able to achieve Socratic
philosophies of pure right.

These points may be more readily acknowledged if we isolate the
several key constituents of this definition of the political condition
and examine them individually. The definition can be rephrased in
a fashion that highlights its crucial constituent elements (in italics),
as follows: the need for politics arises when some *action* of *public*
consequence becomes *necessary* and when men must thus make a
public choice that is *reasonable* in the face of *conflict* despite the *absence
of an independent ground* of judgment. The key concepts in need of
elaboration are then *action, publicness, necessity, choice, reasonableness,
conflict*, and the *absence of an independent ground*.

Action. The realm of politics is first and foremost a realm of human
action. While there is a sense in which every human thought, every
event, every utterance (called "speech acts" by certain philosophers) can be regarded as an action, our definition intends a somewhat narrower and more common usage. *Action* here suggests
building or closing a hospital, starting or concluding a war, taxing
or exempting a corporation, initiating or deferring a welfare plan—
in other words, doing (or not doing), making (or not making) something in the physical world that limits human behavior, changes the
environment, or affects the world in some material way. Where
there is no action (or no nonaction of consequence), there is no
politics.

This assimilation of politics to action may seem obvious enough,
but at least within the liberal democratic tradition there has been a
tendency to see politics as a thing or a place or a set of institutions—
as, at best, something done by others (politicians, bureaucrats,
party workers, voters)—and to undervalue the degree to which action entails activity, energy, work, and participation. Thus, when
Hannah Arendt defined politics as the active life (*vita activa*) in her
book *The Human Condition*, what was curious was not the definition
itself but the degree to which her colleagues received it as a radical
antiquarian critique of modern liberal democracy, as if action had

nothing to do with modern politics. Liberal democrats have too often permitted their concern with accountability, representation, passively maintained individual rights, and abstract autonomy to suffuse their conception of the political with torpor. Nonetheless, politics remains something we do, not something (such as power, for example) that we possess or use or watch or think about. Politics is action and is about action. In states defined by watching rather than doing—in "watchdog" or "watchman" states—citizens, like spectators everywhere, may find themselves falling asleep.

Publicness. Politics describes a realm of action, but not all action is political. We may more properly restrict politics to *public* action: i.e., to action that is both undertaken by a public and intended to have public consequences. Politics describes the realm of *we*. Determining whether gold makes a useful filling for cavities is a private choice (action) undertaken by a special group of authorities, in this case dentists, and is of concern only to individual dental patients. Determining whether gold is a useful monetary standard is a public choice (action) with clearly public consequences and must be decided by duly constituted public authorities. Matters of taste, to take another example, may be both contentious and of consequence, but unless they have public results (such as a public mural or a national anthem) they are not, strictly speaking, political matters.[4]

Some apparently private actions and choices, such as tobacco smoking, turn out to have public consequences, such as polluting the common air. Other actions are private when examined one at a time but have public consequences when taken in the aggregate: for example, siting private homes where they can have the greatest solitude and the widest vistas, at the expense of destroying solitude and vistas for everyone else.[5]

The failure of such philosophers as Robert Nozick to distinguish between private and public acts is a major reason why they have been unable to develop a convincing concept of the political. Of course the thin line between public and private is often obscured or controversial. Indeed, it is one primary function of political activity

4. The recent half-hearted but earnest proposals that songs by John Lennon and Bruce Springsteen be adopted as, respectively, the American national anthem and the official state song of New Jersey illustrate how questions of private esthetics can become questions of public policy.

5. Fred Hirsch, in *Social Limits to Growth* (Cambridge, Mass.: Harvard University Press, 1978), calls this the problem of "positional goods." The theme is at the heart of his powerfully argued case for a *public* interpretation of the dilemmas of growth.

to provide a continuing forum for the discussion and definition of these terms. Conditions change, and along with them the notion of the public. A flexible politics demands that we be sensitive to such change and constantly willing to reformulate what is and what is not public. "What is political?" is always a fundamental question of politics.

If what affects the public is political, then much more obviously what the public does as a whole community is political. If all actions with public consequences are political, then all public (common or community) actions are necessarily so. When *I* act, the publicness of the act can only be measured by the publicness (or privacy) of its consequences; when *we*—the community, the people, the nation— act, the act is public regardless of its consequences.

Necessity. Politics encompasses the realm not simply of action but of necessary action. It is enmeshed in events that are part of a train of cause and effect already at work in the world. This engagement guarantees that even the choice not to make some political decision will have public consequences. Recent political science has given the odd name "nondecision" to this behavior. A nondecision is still a species of decision because as a passive component of ongoing events it has specifiable public consequences: it reinforces a status quo or permits a train of action already in process to gain momentum.

Nondecisions are thus part of the logic produced by what we may call the first law of inertial politics: that events set in motion in the public realm will continue to their logical conclusion (their inertial terminus) if there are no contrary inputs from conscious political actors. "Nonactors" thereby bear responsibility for whatever results their nondecisions have allowed the momentum of events to produce.

There is little that is startling in the first law of inertial politics. It is the political analogue of consequentialism, which is the moral posture that evaluates conduct on the basis of the actual effects it has in the world rather than on the basis of its intentions or the good (or bad) will motivating it—and as such it has had a long history in the Western political tradition. Its most illustrious, or notorious, modern proponent was perhaps Machiavelli, who in *The Prince* warned princely nonactors that their failure to take timely action might permit the unfolding of an untoward chain of events with grave consequences for themselves and their principalities. In his most vivid example, Machiavelli chides the overly scrupulous prince who in his shortsighted mercy abstains from executing the children of enemies who have betrayed him and his principality; for once, owing to this small act (or nonact) of Christian mercy, the children mature into men, they will transform the wrongs of their childhood into a sword of vengeance and provoke civil war and renewed fratricide. And will not these consequences, Machiavelli concludes, be far more devastating than any that a timely infanticide might have occasioned?[6] Cruel as their conduct seems when measured by the deontological standards of private moral conduct, public actors are always necessarily weighing the benefits of short-term noninterference against its long-term costs. "It is a fearsome thing to kill," confesses a shuddering character in Brecht's *Man Is Man*, "but it is not granted to us not to kill."[7]

In recent times, market liberals have insisted that to do nothing (laisser faire) is to eschew both action and its costs. But in fact market forces produce all kinds of outcomes, including many that are unfair, many that are unintended, and many that reflect the working of specifiable historical forces that are skewed, or Darwinian, or otherwise inequitable.[8] Liberals thus often remain oblivious to realities

6. In chap. 17 of *The Prince*, Machiavelli states the general principle as follows:

A Prince, therefore, must not mind incurring the charge of cruelty for the purpose of keeping his subjects united and faithful; for, with a very few examples, he will be more merciful than those who, from excess of tenderness, allow disorders to arise, from whence spring bloodshed and rapine; for these as a rule injure the whole community, while the executions carried out by the Prince injure only the individual.

At issue is the contest between deontological and consequentialist morals: Machiavelli's point (and ours) would seem to be that in politics, where the fate of living communities rather than the souls of individual women and men is at stake, consequentialist reasoning is unavoidable.

7. Like Machiavelli, Brecht here pursues a consequentialist logic that sees men as confronted with a choice between actual evils that are distinguished only by degree, rather than between an ideal good and an ideal evil.

8. Markets are many things, but they are never free. The sociological critique of market liberalism is too well known to require rehearsing here, but this passage from John Ruskin suggests the tone of all subsequent critiques:

In the community regulated only by laws of demand and supply, but protected from open violence, the persons who become rich are, generally speaking, industrious, resolute, proud, covetous, prompt, methodical, sensible, unimaginative, insensitive, and ignorant. The persons who remain poor are the entirely foolish, the entirely wise, the idle, the reckless, the humble, the thoughtful, the dull, the imaginative, the sensitive, the well-informed, the improvident, the irregularly and impulsively wicked, the clumsy knave, the open thief, and the entirely merciful, just, and Godly person. (*Unto This Last*, ed. L. J. Hubenka [Lincoln: University of Nebraska Press, 1967], pp. 74–75)

that statesmen cannot fail to grasp. A country suffering invasion can decide to resist or not to resist, but it cannot abstain from deciding, for that would be tantamount to deciding not to resist. A government facing runaway inflation can impose wage-price controls or not impose them, but it cannot defer to the market and pretend that it has not acted at all, for deference to a market that has itself produced inflation clearly amounts to a decision to permit or even to encourage inflation. Policy-makers understand this well enough. They often choose not to act precisely as part of a conscious political strategy aimed at getting inertial forces already at work to play themselves out. They may for example permit prices to "float" upward, in the hope of controlling demand, or permit profits to soar, in the hope of expanding the base for economic productivity and thus increasing national and individual wealth (the Kemp-Roth Supply-Side strategy suggesting that all boats rise on a rising tide).

The logic of consequences is thus always a public logic and is always an element in the conditions that underlie politics. The inertial momentum of history makes political decision inevitable.

Choice. In the political arena, to speak about doing is to speak about choosing—about deliberating, determining, and deciding. Action that is impulsive, arbitrary, or unconsidered is not yet political action. Just as we would not understand a sleepwalker to be a human agent or a hysteric to be a human actor, so a rabble is not an electorate and a mob is not a citizenry. If action is to be political, it must ensue from forethought and deliberation, from free and conscious choice. Anyone can be an actor. Only a citizen can be a *political* actor.

The political condition thus requires that we have some working notion of citizenship, one that incorporates both autonomy and volition. To speak of those who choose with deliberation and act with responsibility is in the political realm to speak of citizens. In a monarchy, as Hegel notes, only a despot or a king may be a citizen (i.e., a responsible political actor), whereas in a democracy the entire adult population may qualify; but in both cases, only free choosers count as political actors. "Masses" would by these measures seem not to count—not even when they "vote." Freedom is integral to politics, and for there to be politics there must be a living notion of the free, choosing will. It is thus hardly an accident that positivist social science, having liberated itself from the messy idea of freedom, finds itself incapable of comprehending politics.

This is not to argue that all actors in a political community are free (are citizens) or that there cannot be a real politics when choices of public consequence are made by a minority of citizens or by a single ruler. The question is not *who* chooses (for that issue is a feature of political regimes, not of the political condition to which regimes respond) but whether those who choose do so freely. Political actors are always citizens, although this fact forces every actual polity to confront the vital problem of defining the class of citizens (the class of free choosers—see Chapter 9).

Reasonableness. This criterion is to a degree already implicit in the idea of deliberate choice. Citizens construed as free choosers are by definition reasonable—nonimpulsive, thoughtful, and fair. But reasonableness is not simply a characteristic of deliberate choosers and actors but a distinguishing mark of political choices and actions, and as such it requires independent elaboration.

To say that politics is the search for reasonable choices, which must be made in the face of conflict and in the absence of independent grounds for judgment, is to say that politics seeks choices that are something less than arbitrary even though they cannot be perfectly Right or True or Scientific. Abstract rationality is not at stake, for that concept suggests some prepolitical standard of truth, some agreement on at least formal norms, of the sort that Rawls proposes or that Habermas would seem to have in mind. Yet in reality it is precisely the absence of such norms that gives rise to politics. Reasonableness as used here is a rather more commonsensical notion, whose color is practical rather than metaphysical. A reasonable choice or a reasonable settlement is not necessarily rational at all, but it will be seen as deliberate, nonrandom, uncoercive, and in a practical sense fair.

The word *reasonable* bespeaks practicality. It suggests that persons in conflict have consented to resolve their differences in the absence of mediating common standards, to reformulate their problems in a way that encompasses their interests (newly and more broadly conceived) even while it represents the community at large in a new way. "Well, I guess that's reasonable," admits an adversary who has not gotten his way but has been neither coerced nor cajoled into the agreement he has consented to. He is neither victor nor loser; rather, he has reformulated his view of what constitutes his interests and can now "see" things in a new manner.

Reasonable choices are generally public choices. That is to say, they are choices informed by an extension of perspective and by the reformulation of private interests in the setting of potential public goals. To be reasonable is therefore not to deny Self, but to place Self in the context of Other and to inform it with a sense of its dependence on the civic polity.

Conflict. It is not news to liberal democrats that politics arises out of conflict and takes place in a realm defined by (inter alia) power and interest. The entire tradition of liberal thought from Hobbes to Laswell supports the idea that politics is conflict resolution. Yet the paradox of consensus remains: if one claims that the condition of unanimity and consensus that politics wishes to achieve by art already exists by nature, then politics loses its purpose and becomes superfluous.

Rousseau makes the point with his customary incisiveness in the *Social Contract.* He anticipates and remonstrates with enthusiasts who would imagine that the General Will not only achieves an artificial community but is engendered by and acts as a mirror to a natural consensus. "If there were no different interests," he writes, "the common interest would be barely felt, as it would encounter no obstacle; all would go on of its own accord, and politics would cease to be an art."[9] Where there is natural consensus there cannot be conflict or power or need for reasonableness. Angels need not be reasonable (they are angelic); mutualists need not learn to think communally (they are defined by their communality). The garden where there is no discord makes politics unnecessary; just as the jungle where there is no reasonableness makes politics impossible.

Conflict, of course, must have limits in any political setting; otherwise, the war of all against all would preclude society in toto. Theorists have traditionally distinguished substantive, quotidian conflict (the raison d'être of politics) from procedural, long-term consensus (the sine qua non of politics). The latter, in the form of basic law, a constitution, the social contract itself, makes the former tolerable.

Formal consensus is sometimes described as "agreeing to disagree," but a more accurate description would be "agreeing on *how*

9. Jean-Jacques Rousseau, footnote to chap. 3, book 2 of *The Social Contract.* The paradox noted here (and clarified in the next chapter) is evident, for example, in Jane J. Mansbridge's otherwise excellent study of participation in a Vermont town and in an urban crisis center (*Beyond Adversary Democracy* [New York: Basic Books, 1980]).

CALL FOR PROPOSALS

4th Annual Conference on
Intellectual Skills Development

"Liberal Learning and Intellectual Skills Development"

October 24-25, 1985
Western Michigan University

Proposals are welcome for presentations and workshops on the theory and classroom practice of intellectual skills development, especially as related to current discussions on liberal learning. Suggested topics include higher order thinking in content area, writing and reading courses; improving reading and writing skills across the curriculum; quantitative reasoning; evaluation techniques; software review; developing tests and assignments.

Please forward proposals (maximum two pages) by July 1, 1985 to: Dr. Lynne McCauley, Director, Intellectual Skills Development Program, Western Michigan University, Kalamazoo, Michigan, 49008 (616) 383-8062.

**Conference will incorporate annual meeting of the Intellectual Skills Development Association.

**Abstracts of Proceedings from the 3rd Annual Conference are available for $3.00 each. Please make check payable to: W.M.U.- Intellectual Skills Development Association.

Coming Events

Continued from Preceding Page

6-8—Piaget: "Constructivism in the Computer Age," annual symposium, Jean Piaget Society, Philadelphia. Contact: Peter B. Pufall, Department of Psychology, Smith College, Northampton, Mass. 01063; (413) 584-2700, ext. 3921.

6-10—Urban studies: "Making Cities Livable," conference, Center for Urban Well Being, Venice, Italy. Contact: Suzanne H. Crowhurst Lennard, CUWB, Box QQQ, Southampton, N.Y. 11968; (516) 283-0207.

6-13—Literature and phenomenology: "The Origins of the Work of Art: Phenomenological Approaches," symposium, International Society for Phenomenology and Literature, Cerisy-la-Salle, France. Contact: Marlies Kronegger, Department of Romance and Classical Languages, Michigan State University, East Lansing, Mich. 48824.

7—Non-credit programs: "Marketing Non-Credit Courses," seminar, Learning Resources Network, Denver. Contact: LERN, 1221 Thurston, Manhattan, Kan. 66502; (913) 539-LERN.

7-8—Science education: "Science Teacher Education at Museums," workshop, Association of Science-Technology Centers, Cranbrook Institute of Science, Bloomfield Hills, Mich. Contact: Ellen Horowitz, ASTC, 1413 K Street, N.W., Washington 20005-3405; (202) 371-1171.

7-9—History: New York State history conference, Hofstra University, Hempstead, N.Y. Contact: Cultural Center, Hofstra University, Hempstead, N.Y. 11550; (516) 560-5669.

7-9—Women: "Paths to Performance," annual meeting, Women in Organizations, Keuka Park, N.Y. Contact: Susan Cameron, Administrative and Adult Studies, 550 Huntington Hall, School of Education, Syracuse University, Syracuse, N.Y. 13210; (315) 423-4763.

8—July 19—Job market: "Career Opportunities Institute for Ph.D.'s," University of Virginia, Charlottesville, Va. Contact: Career Opportunities Institute, 444C Cabell Hall, University of Virginia, Charlottesville, Va. 22903; (804) 924-3838.

9-11—Facilities: Regional conference, Association of College and University Housing Officers, North Dartmouth, Mass. Contact: Chuck Lamb, University of Southern Maine, Gochman, Me. 04038.

9-11—Faculty: "Dignity and Meaning in the Teaching Profession," faculty institute, Council of Independent Colleges, Pittsburgh. Contact: Jan Gilmer, CIC, Suite 320, One Du... Washington 20036; (202)...

10-14—Computers: ...ers' Group, Chica... Group, Suite 510, ... Park, Md. 20740;

10-18—Medicine: A... betes Association ... Two Park Avenue ... 7444.

10-21—Administrati... for Higher Educa... shop, Pennsylvania ... Park, Pa. Contac... Higher Education ... University, 328 P... 16802; (814) 863-2...

10-21—Communica... faculty members i... ton Program of An... cations, Washingt... Program Manager... nenberg Schools, ... nue, S.W., Washi...

10-21—Teaching: ... Teaching," short ... Ithaca, N.Y. Con... of Education, Cor... Hall, Ithaca, N.Y...

10-28—Computers: ... tute: Retraining i... England Regional ... Mass. Contact... Street, Braintr...

11-13—Higher e... tury: Changing ... tion," worksh... tion, Fort ... Contact: A... 20036; (2(...

11-14—C... house ... pus A... Ker... fa... 5...

19...

to disagree": on whether, that is, to deal with conflict by suppressing it, ameliorating it, tolerating it, resolving it, or transforming it. It is around these political modes and the institutions connected with them that the several versions of democracy laid out in the next chapter revolve.

Absence of an Independent Ground. Among the several components proposed here for the political condition, the absence of an independent ground for judgment is probably the most novel and the most central. It certainly is a crucial criterion in distinguishing strong democracy from its competing regime types. Yet it has been litttle considered in previous discussions of democratic theory.

As we have seen, to choose and act politically is to choose and act responsibly, reasonably, and publicly yet without the guidance of independent consensual norms. Where there is certain knowledge, true science, or absolute right, there is no conflict that cannot be resolved by reference to the unity of truth, and thus there is no necessity for politics.[10]

Politics concerns itself only with those realms where truth is not—or is not *yet*—known. We do not vote for the best polio vaccine or conduct surveys on the ideal space shuttle, nor has Boolean algebra been subjected to electoral testing. But Laetrile and genetic engineering, while they belong formally to the domain of science, have aroused sufficient conflict among scientists to throw them into the political domain—and rightly so. Where consensus stops, politics starts.[11]

Liberal political theorists have always been afflicted by paradox

10. A lunatic may insist that lightning is a manifestation of Zeus's spitefulness and fire a cannon into the clouds to wreak vengeance; but the *political* question here is not the physical nature of lightning but only the erratic behavior of the lunatic, inasmuch as such behavior has public consequences.

11. There is of course a lively debate about whether scientific communities are themselves ultimately political. Thomas Kuhn has advanced the well-known argument that scientific debates within such communities are settled by power (by means of the position and prestige enjoyed by scientific elites and the inertia of their theories) rather than by scientific judgment. See Thomas S. Kuhn, *The Structure of Scientific Revolutions* (Chicago: University of Chicago Press, 1962).

But whether scientific communities are political has no effect on the claim made here, which is that political communities are never scientific (i.e., rooted in objective consensus). Indeed, a good illustration of this point is that the failure of scientists to reach consensus can take a controversy out of the domain of science and place it in the domain of politics. Thus genetic engineering, the possible effects of which are currently a matter of fundamental and seemingly irresolvable scientific debate, has become a legitimate concern of public policy makers—with respect not just to the possible public consequences but to the very course of inquiry and experiment.

when they consider the role of independent "natural" norms in politics. Although they understand that uncertainty and conflict are the occasion for politics, they share the human aspiration to certainty and find themselves drawn to putative absolutes of one kind or another that might facilitate "scientific" or "rational" or "natural" solutions to political questions. They look hopefully to theoretical reason (Kant's categorical imperative or Rawls's principles of justice, for example); or to natural law (John Locke and the American tradition of judicial review, for example); or to a naturalistically grounded theory of absolute right (Hobbes or Robert Nozick); or to some notion of communicative rationality (Habermas); or to true knowledge (Plato's *epistemē*). In each case, philosophy is required to provide norms external to the political process with which political problems can then be resolved. The consequences for the political process are, however, paralytic. In conflating epistemology and action, the liberal can no longer distinguish the needs of the reasonable actor from those of the speculative metaphysician. The tendency in recent American jurisprudence to substitute formal reasoning and the abstract principles it yields for political processes is a perfect illustration.[12]

The seductiveness of abstract principle in the face of uncertainty is perfectly understandable given the muddy ambiguities typical of the actual political realm. Even when he has lost the metaphysical ladder on which he hoped to ascend out of the cave, the philosopher is loath to say with Yeats,

> Now that my ladder's gone
> I must lie down where all the ladders start
> In the foul rag and bone shop of the heart.[13]

But politics is a rag and bone shop of the practical and the concrete, the everyday and the ambiguous, the malleable and the evanescent. There is no firm stairway to nature or to some higher realm from which one can borrow shaping norms and fixed standards to lend abstract order to inchoate experience. If there is political truth, it can only be the kind of truth that, in William James's phrase, "is made in the course of experience."

It is, similarly, not so much Burke's conservatism as his sense of

12. For an excellent critical discussion see John Hart Ely, *Democracy and Distrust* (Cambridge, Mass.: Harvard University Press, 1980).
13. William Butler Yeats, "The Circus Animals' Parade."

the concreteness of politics that leads him to the conviction that "the science of constructing a commonwealth, or renovating it, or reforming it, is, like every other experimental science, not to be taught a priori."[14] In speaking thus, Burke merely echoes the traditional republican wariness of universal principles and abstract reasoning. He speaks for Machiavelli, for Montesquieu, and even for his nemesis Rousseau when he warns of the "multitude of misfortunes" that can be traced to "considering certain general maxims without attending to circumstances, to time, to places, to conjectures and to actors"; for, he concludes, "if we do not attend scrupulously to these, the medicine of today becomes the poison of tomorrow."[15]

The political condition is engendered by history, circumstance, and context. Real political actors, confronted with controversies and dilemmas issuing out of fundamental conflicts of interest and value in a changing society, are required to make responsible and reasonable choices. The philosopher, like Minerva's owl, comes too late to help. Or, if he has somehow arrived promptly, the dilemmas are superseded by virtue of his arrival and the need for politics disappears. The citizen wishes in any case only to act rightly, not to know for certain; only to choose reasonably, not to reason scientifically; only to overcome conflict and secure transient peace, not to discover eternity; only to cooperate with others, not to achieve moral oneness; only to formulate common causes, not to obliterate all differences. Politics is what men do when metaphysics fails; it is not metaphysics reified as a constitution.

STRONG DEMOCRACY AS A RESPONSE TO THE POLITICAL CONDITION

Every political regime, even those that are ultimately politics-denying, can be characterized as arising out of a response to the seven components of the political condition elucidated above. I will offer a typology of democratic regime types in the next chapter, but here I want to introduce strong democracy—a regime form that has the particular virtue of responding directly to the dilemmas posed by

14. Edmund Burke, *Reflections on the Revolution in France* (London: Dent, 1910), p. 58.

15. Ibid., p. 277. It is ironic that Burke contemns Rousseau along with the other Philosophes for an attachment to metaphysics that Rousseau himself despises. Indeed, in books 3 and 4 of *The Social Contract*, as well as in the essays on Poland and Corsica, Rousseau exhibits an almost Burkean concern with time, place, and circumstance.

the political condition. This condition obtains, it will be recalled, when there is *a necessity for public action, and thus for reasonable public choice, in the presence of conflict and in the absence of private or independent grounds for judgment.*

The response to these conditions is strong democracy, which can be formally defined as *politics in the participatory mode where conflict is resolved in the absence of an independent ground through a participatory process of ongoing, proximate self-legislation and the creation of a political community capable of transforming dependent, private individuals into free citizens and partial and private interests into public goods.*

We shall see in the next chapter how this definition distinguishes strong democracy from its rival forms, and in subsequent chapters we shall examine what strong democracy entails for common talk and action, citizenship, and community and for the institutions these things require. This chapter can thus be ended with only some brief remarks on strong democracy's aptness as a response to the seven conditions of politics.

Action. Aristotle was persuaded in the *Eudaimonian Ethics* that man was defined above all by action. Voltaire and Rousseau, who agreed on little else, might have written with a single pen this thought (actually Voltaire's): "Man is born for action as the sparks fly upward. Not to do anything is the same for man as not to exist."[16] Or this (Rousseau's): "Man is born to act and to think, not to reflect."[17] Yet in recent centuries, as C. B. Macpherson has noted, "the notion that activity itself is pleasurable, is a utility, has sunk almost without a trace under [the] utilitarian vision of life."[18] Hannah Arendt spent much of her productive career deploring the disappearance of the *vita activa* as a central element in political life. Indeed, the thin conception of democracy depends so much on a passive and inarticulate citizenry that Bernard Berelson and his colleagues have asked, "How could a mass democracy work if all the people were deeply involved in politics?"[19]

The centrality of process, transformation, and creation to the idea

16. Voltaire, *Philosophical Letters*, no. 23 (Indianapolis: Bobbs-Merrill, 1961).

17. Jean-Jacques Rousseau, "Preface to Narcisse," trans. Benjamin R. Barber and Janis Forman, *Political Theory* 6, 4 (November 1978): 13.

18. C. B. Macpherson, *The Real World of Democracy* (Oxford: Oxford University Press, 1966), p. 38.

19. B. R. Berelson et al., *Voting* (Chicago: University of Chicago Press, 1954), p. 318.

of action in the strong democratic definition of democracy is not, then, a standard feature of democratic thinking. In strong democracy, politics is something done by, not to, citizens. Activity is its chief virtue, and involvement, commitment, obligation, and service—common deliberation, common decision, and common work—are its hallmarks.

Publicness. Strong democracy creates a public capable of reasonable public deliberation and decision and therefore rejects traditional reductionism and the fiction of atomic individuals creating social bonds ex nihilo.[20] But it also rejects the myth of corporatism and collectivism that posits an abstract community prior to individuals and from which individuals derive their significance and purpose. Strong democracy is thus hostile to that reductive historical sociology that makes an individual's class or race or social movement the sole determinant of his actions and that tries to reconstruct conscious human beings as pure species beings. Far from positing community a priori, strong democratic theory understands the creation of community as one of the chief tasks of political activity in the participatory mode. Far from positing historical identity as the condition of politics, it posits politics as the conditioner of given historical identities—as the means by which men are emancipated from determinative historical forces.

With John Dewey, strong democracy recognizes that "the public has no hands except those of individual human beings"; yet it also recognizes "that the essential problem is that of transforming the action of such hands so that it will be animated by regard for social ends." It thus focuses attention on the question, "How can a public be organized?"[21] Or in our language, how can a civic community be created? The creation of community here becomes a concomitant of the creation of public goods and public ends. Conversely, the creation of public ends depends on the creation of a community of citizens who regard themselves as comrades and who are endowed with an enlarging empathy. Community, public goods, and citizen-

20. Bruce Ackerman alludes to (and to some extent represents) this tradition of atomism when he refers to the liberal definition of women and men as "asocial monads" (*Social Justice and the Liberal State* [New Haven: Yale University Press, 1980], p. 100).

21. John Dewey, *The Public*, pp. 82 and 14.

ship thus ultimately become three interdependent parts of a single democratic circle whose compass grows to describe a true public.[22]

Necessity. Because it is rooted in participatory action and in a keen sense of the public character of politics, strong democracy is particularly sensitive to the element of necessity in public choice. Its concrete sense of the interconnectedness of events and of the embeddedness of citizens in a changing polity safeguard it from that dangerous innocence with which liberals disclaim responsibility for historical laws and events not of their own making. Like the realist, the participationist sees power as inevitable—as a presence with which every politics must reckon. But he also recognizes that power legitimized and power used are what make social freedom and political equality possible.

In sum, strong democracy not only places agency and responsibility at the center of political activity, it understands them as an indispensable response to man's need to act in the face of conflict—which is the precipitating condition of politics itself.

Choice. Participation as a political mode obviously presupposes citizens capable of meaningful and autonomous choice, as do all coherent theories of democracy. Consent without autonomy is not consent. But participation enhances volition in that it lends to choice the direct engagement of the deliberating mind and the choosing will. While clients or voters or constituents or masses may be characterized in ways that omit their free agency, participants cannot: individual volition is the heart of the idea of self-legislation through participation. In this emphasis, strong democracy may be said to go beyond the simple idea of free agency shared by all democratic theories.[23]

22. Gandhi employs the metaphor of the democratic circle with poetic if extravagant effect:

> Life will not be a pyramid with the apex sustained by the bottom. But it will be an oceanic circle whose centre will be the individual always ready to perish for the village, the latter ready to perish for the circle of villages, till at last the whole becomes one life composed of individuals, never aggressive in their arrogance but ever humble, sharing the majesty of the oceanic circle of which they are integral units. (M. K. Gandhi, *Democracy: Real and Deceptive*, compiled by R. K. Prabhu [Ahmedabad: Navajivan, 1942], pp. 73–74)

23. Since every democratic theory requires a commitment to the reality of human agency—of meaningful volition in a world of choice that is not (*pace* B. F. Skinner) beyond freedom and dignity—the only legitimate debate concerns the degree and

Reasonableness. I have suggested that public choices and actions, which must be more than arbitrary or merely self-interested yet cannot be expected to be scientific or certifiable by the standards of abstract philosophy, must at least be "reasonable." The way in which participatory processes of ongoing, proximate self-legislation meet this criterion goes to the heart of the strong democratic project. Much of Chapter 8 is devoted to specifying what *reasonable* means from the perspective of strong democratic talk and action. Here it should be noted only that reasonableness is not an abstract precondition of politics but an attitude that strong democratic politics itself engenders.

Conflict. Every form of pluralist democracy perceives conflict as central to politics, but pluralists have often charged that participatory and communitarian theories slight conflict in favor of consensualism. Consensual democracy resolves conflict by defining it out of the political picture from the outset. Strong democracy is different. It is unique among nonrepresentative forms in that it acknowledges (and indeed uses) the centrality of conflict in the political process. This recognition differentiates it radically from "unitary" modes of democracy and insulates it from collectivist and unitary abuses of communitarianism.

At the same time, strong democracy resists the liberal idea that conflict is intractable and at best vulnerable only to adjudication or toleration. Instead, it develops a politics that can transform conflict into cooperation through citizen participation, public deliberation, and civic education. Strong democratic theory begins but does not end with conflict: it acknowledges conflict but ultimately transforms rather than accommodates or minimizes it.

Absence of an Independent Ground. It is perhaps the greatest virtue of strong democracy, and certainly the one that makes it unique, that it yields a truly autonomous politics. The procedures of self-legislation and community-building on which it relies are self-contained and self-correcting and thus are genuinely independent of external norms, prepolitical truths, or natural rights. Strong democratic politics, it would be foolish to deny, does operate in a world of

---

character of volition under various social circumstances. See for example Christian Bay's *The Structure of Freedom* (Stanford: Stanford University Press, 1958). In the end, however, as John Stuart Mill noted long ago, the philosophical debate about free will simply does not bear on the political debate about free choice.

values and truth claims, and participants in the political process naturally have their own ideas about right and interest and truth. This form of politics is anything but "value-free" in the sense attributed to politics by the positivists. But the autonomy of the democratic process under strong democracy equalizes value inputs. It gives to each individual's convictions and beliefs an equal starting place and associates legitimacy with what happens to convictions and beliefs in the course of public talk and action rather than with their prior epistemological status. The legitimacy of a value is thus a feature of its publicness, of how it is refined, changed, or transformed when confronted with a public and the public norms which that public has already legitimized through its politics. Politics in the participatory mode does not choose between or merely ratify values whose legitimacy is a matter of prior record. It makes preferences and opinions earn legitimacy by forcing them to run the gauntlet of public deliberation and public judgment. They emerge not simply legitimized but transformed by the processes to which they have been subjected.

The basic difference between the politics of bargaining and exchange and the politics of transformation is that in the former, choice is a matter of selecting among options and giving the winner the legitimacy of consent, whereas in the latter, choice is superseded by judgment and leads men and women to modify and enlarge options as a consequence of seeing them in new, public ways. For this reason, decision without common talk always falls short of judgment and cannot be the basis of strong democratic politics. The test of legitimacy is whether an individual value has been changed in some significant way to accommodate larger—that is, more common or public—concerns. If a value emerges from the political process entirely unchanged by that process, then either it remains a private value masquerading as a public norm or it denotes a prior consensus that has been revealed by the political process. In neither case has participatory politics accomplished its task of legitimation.

For this reason, there can be no strong democratic legitimacy without ongoing talk. Where voting is a static act of expressing one's preference, participation is a dynamic act of imagination that requires participants to change how they see the world. Voting suggests a group of men in a cafeteria bargaining about what they can buy as a group that will suit their individual tastes. Strong democratic politics suggests a group of men in a cafeteria contriving new menus, inventing new recipes, and experimenting with new diets in the effort to create a public taste that they can all share and that will supersede the conflicting private tastes about which they once tried to strike bargains. Voting, in the bargaining model, often fixes choices and thereby stultifies the imagination; judging, in the model of strong democracy, activates imagination by demanding that participants reexamine their values and interests in light of all the inescapable others—the public.

The rightness of public acts depends then neither on a prepolitical notion of abstract right nor on a simple conception of popular will or popular consent.[24] For what is crucial is not consent pure and simple but the active consent of participating citizens who have imaginatively reconstructed their own values as public norms through the process of identifying and empathizing with the values of others. This perspective enables strong democratic theory to substitute for the usual discussion of Abstract Right versus Popular Will a more concrete and institutionally pertinent discussion of the character of citizenship and of its implementation as political judgment. How this discussion evolves is examined in Chapters 8 and 9.

This brief review was meant to show that at least on first analysis strong democracy would seem to meet the conditions of politics with particular aptness (although this is not to claim that it is the sole appropriate response).[25] To extend and deepen our understanding of the theory of strong democracy, we now need to place it in the context of the rival forms of democracy—that is, to place it within a formal typology of democratic regime forms that includes

24. Michael Walzer, a sensitive and incisive radical democrat, portrays the problem as a "tension between philosophy and democracy," between Rational Right as purveyed by philosophy and legitimate will as exhibited in popular choice ("Philosophy and Democracy," *Political Theory* 9, 3 [August 1981]: 379–99). But the problem is not Right versus Opinion but achieving right opinion. What is required is a self-regulating will, not a will subordinated to abstract reason.

25. Were strong democracy the *only* possible response to the seven conditions of politics enumerated here, critics could say that those conditions were analytically indistinguishable from it—that I had loaded the definition of politics so as to preclude any outcome other than the desired (strong democratic) one. A problem of this sort afflicts the relationship between Rawls's two principles of justice and the conditions of the "original position" to which they are supposedly a response. I have charged Rawls with this error in my "Justifying Justice: Problems of Psychology, Measurement, and Politics in Rawls," *American Political Science Review* 69, 2 (June 1975), and am thus naturally anxious to avoid committing it here myself.

representative democracy and its constituent variations as well as "unitary" democracy as a competing form of participatory politics. The next chapter thus concludes the effort to give strong democracy an ideal formal definition. The subsequent chapters will attempt to give substance to the ideal.

Chapter Seven

A Conceptual Frame:
Politics in the Participatory Mode

Life requires a more organic and mutual form than bourgeois democracy provides for it; but the social substance of life is richer and more various, and has greater depths and tensions than are envisaged in the Marxist dream of social harmony.

(Reinhold Niebuhr)

The keynote of democracy as a way of life may be expressed . . . . as the necessity for the participation of every mature human being in the formation of values that regulate the living of men together; which is necessary from the standpoint of both the general social welfare and the full development of human beings as individuals.

(John Dewey)

Strong democracy is one of several democratic responses to the political condition.[1] The typology offered here (see Figure 1) distinguishes strong democracy both from the several kinds of thin or representative democracy and from unitary democracy, with which it is often confounded. The three variations on representative democracy are the authoritative, the juridical, and the pluralist, which are related to the dispositions explored in Part I but are by no means

1. A complete typology would have to include both democratic and nondemocratic regimes. However, the nondemocratic response to conflict in the absence of independent grounds is incoherent in relation to the conditions of politics discussed in the previous chapter: nondemocratic regimes would "solve" the political problem by eliminating politics. This places such regimes outside of the categories with which we are concerned here.

identical with them. The two more direct forms are the unitary and the strong; the former of which turns out to have certain characteristics in common with thin forms of democracy, despite its appearance as a variation on communitarianism.

All five forms are ideal types in two important senses. First, they are distinguished by features that are abstract and ideal: no actual regimes correspond perfectly with the types. Second, these forms are presented separately, yet most actual regimes are composite and combine features from each type. The three thin forms are in fact part of a single democratic praxis typical of American (and to a lesser degree, European) political experience. Using Figure 1 as our guide, we can describe each of the five alternative democratic forms as follows.

Authoritative Democracy. The authoritative model of democracy is defined by the deployment of power by a centralized executive on behalf of security and order, which are among its chief justifying norms. Authoritative democracy relies on a deferential citizenry and the excellence of a governing elite, although it is still representative in that it remains accountable to the people or to the "masses" who select it. Considered as a response to the dilemmas of the political condition, as laid out in the previous chapter, authoritative democracy can be given this formal definition: *democracy in the authoritative mode resolves conflict in the absence of an independent ground through deferring to a representative executive elite that employs authority (power plus wisdom) in pursuit of the aggregate interests of its electoral constituency.*

Burke's ideal English constitution and America under the imperial presidency are possible examples of democracy operating in a predominantly authoritative mode. The government posture is centralized and active, and the citizen posture is deferential but unified (by the elite's interpretation of the citizens' interests). The institutional bias favors executive power, although the executive in authoritative systems tends to play a prominent legislative role as well (in the New Deal or the Great Society, for example).

We can summarize some of the criticisms that were leveled at representative democracy generally (in Part I) of this book in terms of our typology here. Authoritative democracy, then, is deficient because it tends toward hegemony, is incompletely egalitarian, and has a weak view of citizenship (which is limited to the selection of

FIGURE 1. *Democratic Regimes (Ideal Types)*

Regime Form	Political Mode	Value	Institutional Bias	Citizen Posture	Government Posture	"Independent Ground" Disguised as
Representative Democracy						
Authoritative	authority (power/wisdom)	order	executive	deferential unified	centralized active	noblesse oblige wisdom
Juridical	arbitration and adjudication	right	judicial	deferential fragmented	centralized limited	natural right higher law
Pluralist	bargaining and exchange	liberty	legislative	active fragmented	decentralized active	invisible hand natural equality market rules
Direct Democracy						
Unitary	consensus	unity	symbolic	active unified	centralized active	the collective the general will
Strong	participation	activity	populist	active centralizing	decentralizing active	(no independent ground)

elites).[2] It is also deficient because of two greater difficulties that it shares with each of the other weak forms of democracy: its dependence on representation and its reintroduction into the domain of politics, under the camouflage of "wisdom," an independent ground that becomes a surrogate for autonomous politics. The virtue of politicians thus comes to replace the activity of politics, and the excellence (*aretē*) of policy is made to do the work of an engaged citizenry.

Juridical Democracy. The juridical model of democracy is defined by the arbitration, adjudication, and protection of right (its chief justifying norm) by a representative but independent judiciary that governs indirectly by placing limits and constraints on the explicit organs of government.[3] Like the authoritative model, the juridical relies on a deferential citizenry that considers the courts an institution capable of mediating and enforcing basic (i.e., nonpolitical) norms that justify civil society and limit the scope and purposes of all governmental activity.

Considered as a response to the dilemmas of the political condition, juridical democracy can be given the following formal definition: *democracy in the juridical mode resolves conflict in the absence of an independent ground through deferring to a representative judicial elite that, with the guidance of constitutional and preconstitutional norms, arbitrates differences and enforces constitutional rights and duties.* Philosophical jurisprudence of the kind practiced so persuasively by John Rawls, Ronald Dworkin, and most recently Bruce Ackerman typifies the theory of juridical democracy.[4] The American Supreme Court in its

2. Joseph Schumpeter's definition of democracy illustrates these weaknesses: "The democratic method is that institutional arrangement for arriving at political decisions in which individuals acquire the power to decide by means of a competitive struggle for the people's vote" (*Capitalism, Socialism, and Democracy* [London: Allen and Unwin, 1943], p. 269).

3. Franz Neumann first used the phrase "juridical liberty" to describe a political order in which law is used to protect the abstract freedom of individuals from governmental infringement. See "The Concept of Political Freedom," in *The Democratic and Authoritarian State* (Glencoe, Ill.: Free Press, 1957), pp. 162–63 et passim.

More recently, Theodore J. Lowi has offered "juridical democracy" as an alternative to "interest group liberalism." He argues that the former, which he labels "the rule of law operating in institutions," "is the only dependable defense the powerless have against the powerful" (*The End of Liberalism*, 2d ed. [New York: Norton, 1979], p. 298).

My definition draws on the legalism of these prior uses but is not otherwise intended to reflect them.

4. See John Rawls, *A Theory of Justice* (Cambridge, Mass.: Harvard University Press, 1971); Ronald Dworkin, *Taking Rights Seriously* (Cambridge, Mass.: Harvard

activist phases and, in a quite exotic fashion, the legalists of the Han dynasty exemplify a potential juridical praxis.

The governmental posture here is centralized but more limited than in the authoritative mode. The citizenry is deferential but, in keeping with the atomistic character of rights, more often fragmented than unified. The institutional bias is juridical, even though the judiciary often comes to usurp and to exercise what might otherwise be perceived as legislative functions.

Juridical democracy is deficient because it subverts the legislative process and has a corrosive impact on citizen activity and also because it is dependent on representative principles and reintroduces independent grounds into the political realm—in this case disguised as natural right, higher law, and the constitution.

Pluralist Democracy. The pluralist model of democracy is defined by the resolution of conflict through bargaining and exchange in "free markets" under the governance of a "social contract" that makes promises binding. Liberty is both the operating principle of markets and their chief objective, making it the chief justifying norm of politics in the market mode. Unlike authoritative and juridical democracy, the pluralist model relies on an engaged and active citizenry that, fragmented into individuals, groups, and parties (political and otherwise), formulates and aggressively pursues private interests within a framework of competitive legislative bargaining.

Considered as a response to the dilemmas of the political condition, pluralist democracy can be given the following formal definition: *pluralist democracy resolves public conflict in the absence of an independent ground through bargaining and exchange among free and equal individuals and groups, which pursue their private interests in a market setting governed by the social contract.*

Examples of pluralist democratic theory include the economic and interest-group theories of democracy advanced by Anthony Downs or Mancur Olson, Robert Dahl's "polyarchy" model, and the plu-

---

University Press, 1978); and Bruce Ackerman, *Social Justice in the Liberal State* (New Haven: Yale University Press, 1980). Useful antidotes to this jurisprudential perspective can be found in John Hart Ely, *Democracy and Distrust* (Cambridge, Mass.: Harvard University Press, 1980) and Michael Walzer, *Radical Principles* (New York: Basic Books, 1980), as well as in Walzer's review of Ackerman in *The New Republic*, 25 October 1980.

ralism of mainstream American political science.[5] Laissez-faire England in the nineteenth century (if there was such a thing) and pluralist America before the New Deal (if there was such a thing) are usually taken as examples of the praxis. To the extent that the market is a real thing (which is a controversial claim, as we have seen), the market model is the freest of the three variations on representative democracy: the government is decentralized (often federal) and though active, also deferential to a citizenry that, if fragmented, is much more active than in the other two cases. The institutional bias is toward legislation, although legislation is more an output of the dominant system of bargaining and exchange than an input into it.

Pluralist democracy is deficient because it relies on the fictions of the free market and of the putative freedom and equality of bargaining agents; because it cannot generate public thinking or public ends of any kind; because it is innocent about the real world of power; and (as with the first two models) because it uses the representative principle and reintroduces into politics a covert independent ground—namely, the illusions of the free market and of the invisible hand and the simplistic utilitarianism (Mandeville, Smith, and Bentham) by which the pursuit of private interests is miraculously made to yield the public good.

These first three democratic modes are evidently related to what I depicted in Part I as the realist, the anarchist, and the minimalist dispositions of liberal democracy, and for this reason their defects need not be recapitulated in detail here. Focusing on power and order, the authoritative mode conforms in many ways to realism; the juridical mode, in its emphasis on rights and its concern with the limits of government, recalls the bases of minimalism and anarchism; and pluralism, as a theory of bargaining and exchange that

5. The modern locus classicus for the pluralist model is David B. Truman, *The Governmental Process* (New York: Knopf, 1957). In its more recent incarnation, the theory has been assimilated by economic modeling and rational-decision theory. See for example Anthony Downs, *An Economic Theory of Democracy* (New York: Harper Bros., 1957); Mancur Olson, Jr., *The Logic of Collective Action* (Cambridge, Mass.: Harvard University Press, 1965); and Kenneth J. Arrow, *Social Choice and Individual Values*, 2d ed. (New Haven: Yale University Press, 1963).

Two recent defenses of traditional pluralism are in William H. Riker, *Liberalism against Populism* (San Francisco: Freeman, 1982), which also contains a vigorous attack on participatory democracy; and Robert A. Dahl, *Dilemmas of Pluralist Democracy: Autonomy versus Control* (New Haven: Yale University Press, 1982). Dahl, however, has begun to question the capacity of pluralism (which he calls *polyarchy*) to deal with questions of economic and social justice—hence the "dilemma," which did not appear in his earlier *A Preface to Democratic Theory* (Chicago: University of Chicago Press, 1956).

presupposes freedom and tolerance, shares in some of the biases of minimalism. Yet these interesting convergences are not decisive, and the typology does not pretend to construct a perfect correspondence among the three dispositions of liberal democracy and its more generic democratic modes.

What remains clear, however, is that the authoritative, juridical, and pluralist modes of democracy—with their complementary emphases on, respectively, order, right, and freedom—have all played a part in liberal democracy as practiced in the West over the last two centuries. Their peculiar weaknesses have thus contributed to the weakness of liberal democracy *tout simple.*

Before we move on to examine the direct democratic alternatives to liberalism, it may be useful for us to pause and review in summary form the two weaknesses that, I have asserted, are shared by all three modes of liberal democracy: namely, representation and the reintroduction into supposedly autonomous politics of surreptitious independent grounds.

A well-known adage has it that under a representative government the voter is free only on the day he casts his ballot. Yet even this act may be of dubious consequence in a system where citizens use the franchise only to select an executive or judicial or legislative elite that in turn exercises every other duty of civic importance. To exercise the franchise is unhappily also to renounce it. The representative principle steals from individuals the ultimate responsibility for their values, beliefs, and actions. And it is far less hospitable to such primary Western values as freedom, equality, and social justice than weak democrats might wish.

Representation is incompatible with freedom because it delegates and thus alienates political will at the cost of genuine self-government and autonomy. As Rousseau warned, "The instant a people allows itself to be represented it loses its freedom."[6] Freedom and citizenship are correlates; each sustains and gives life to the other. Men and women who are not directly responsible through common deliberation, common decision, and common action for the policies

6. Jean-Jacques Rousseau, *The Social Contract*, book 3, chap. 15. A later philosopher writing in the same vein insists upon "the logical impossibility of the 'representative' system." Since "the will of the people is not transferable, nor even the will of the single individual, the first appearance of professional leadership marks the beginning of the end" (Robert Michels, *Political Parties: A Sociological Study of the Oligarchical Tendencies of Modern Democracy* [Glencoe, Ill.: Free Press, 1915; reprinted, 1949], pp. 33–34).

that determine their common lives are not really free at all, however much they enjoy security, private rights, and freedom from interference.

Representation is incompatible with equality because, in the astute words of the nineteenth-century French Catholic writer Louis Veuillot, "when I vote my equality falls into the box with my ballot—they disappear together."[7] Equality, construed exclusively in terms of abstract personhood or of legal and electoral equity, omits the crucial economic and social determinants that shape its real-life incarnation. In the absence of community, equality is a fiction that not merely divides as easily as it unites but that raises the specter of a mass society made up of indistinguishable consumer clones.

Representation, finally, is incompatible with social justice because it encroaches on the personal autonomy and self-sufficiency that every political order demands, because it impairs the community's ability to function as a regulating instrument of justice, and because it precludes the evolution of a participating public in which the idea of justice might take root.[8]

Freedom, equality, and justice are in fact all *political* values that depend for their theoretical coherence and their practical efficacy on self-government and citizenship. They cannot be apprehended or practiced except in the setting of citizenship. They are not coterminous with the condition of politics, they are aspects of a satisfactory response to the condition of politics. They cannot be externally defined and then appropriated for political use; rather, they must be generated and conditioned by politics.

This point relates directly to the problem of the independent ground. In each of the three versions of weak democracy, the banished independent ground (in whose place a mode of politics is supposed to operate) is covertly reintroduced in the guise of such no-

---

7. Cited by Michels, *Political Parties*, p. 39; my translation. Victor Considerant, a forerunner of Michels, commented on the central principle of representative government, delegation, that "in delegating its sovereignty, a people abdicate it. Such a people no longer governs itself but is governed. . . . Turning Saturn on his head, the principle of sovereignty ends up being devoured by its daughter, the principle of delegation" (*La Solution, ou le gouvernement direct du peuple* [Paris: Librairie Phalansterie, 1850], pp. 13–15; my translation).

8. Court-ordered busing programs, which are "right" by every legal standard, nonetheless manage to remedy the effects of public prejudice only by destroying public responsibility and activity in a realm (schooling) that is traditionally associated with vigorous neighborhood civic activity. Here the principle of right collides with the principle of participation, and the damage done to the latter imperils, in the long run, the possibility of sustaining the former by democratic means.

tions as noblesse oblige (the wisdom of an authoritative elite), or the free market (the absolute autonomy of the individual as an irrefutable premise of pluralist market and contract relations). Yet the definition of the political condition developed above would suggest that it is precisely such notions as "wisdom," "rights," and "freedom" that need to be given meaning and significance within the setting of democratic politics. These terms and others like them are essentially contestable: their meaning is subject to controversy at a fundamental level and cannot be discovered by abstract reasoning or by an appeal to external authority.[9] This is why they become the focus of discourse in democratic politics: they do not define but are defined by politics.

Representative democracy suffers, then, both from its reliance on the representative principle and from its vulnerability to seduction by an illicit rationalism—from the illusion that metaphysics can establish the meaning of debatable political terms. By permitting, even encouraging, the reintroduction of independent grounds, representative modes of democracy subvert the very political process that was supposed to meet and overcome the absence of such grounds. By subordinating the will and judgment of citizens to abstract norms about which there can be no real consensus, these modes demean citizenship itself and diminish correspondingly the capacities of a people to govern itself. And by allowing heteronomous notions of right to creep into the politics of self-legislation, they fatally undermine the autonomy on which all real political freedom depends. Citizens become subject to laws they did not truly participate in making; they become the passive constituents of representatives who, far from reconstituting the citizens' aims and interests, usurp their civic functions and deflect their civic energies.

To the extent that these criticisms apply, thin democracy is not very democratic, nor even convincingly political. For all the talk about politics in Western democratic regimes, it is hard to find in all the daily activities of bureaucratic administration, judicial legislation, executive leadership, and party policy-making anything that resembles citizen engagement in the creation of civic communities and in the forging of public ends. Politics has become what politi-

---

9. The idea of "essential contestability," first developed in a philosophical setting by W. B. Gallie, has been given an illuminating political context by William Connolly in *The Terms of Political Discourse* (Lexington, Mass.: Heath, 1974).

cians do; what citizens do (when they do anything) is vote for the politicians.

Two alternative forms of democracy seem to hold out some hope that these difficulties can be alleviated through the activation of citizenship and community. The first, which I call *unitary democracy*, is motivated by the need for consensus but ultimately betrays the democratic impulse—particularly when it is separated from the small-scale institutions out of which it arose. The second, *strong democracy*, seems able to remedy a number of the shortcomings of weak democracy without falling prey to the excesses of unitary democracy. It is the argument of this book that the strong form of democracy is the only form that is genuinely and completely democratic. It may also be the only one capable of preserving and advancing the political form of human freedom in a modern world that grows ever more hostile to traditional liberal democracy.

Unitary Democracy. The unitary form of democracy is defined by politics in the consensual mode and seems at first glance to eschew representation (if not politics itself) in pursuit of its central norm, unity. It calls for all divisive issues to be settled unanimously through the organic will of a homogeneous or even monolithic community—often identified symbolically as a race or nation or people or communal will. The government posture here is centralized and active, while the posture of the citizenry is ambiguous, since the individual citizen achieves his civic identity through merging his self with the collectivity, that is to say, through self-abandonment. Although this surrender assures a certain equality (another characteristic norm of unitary and strong democracy), it is obviously corrupting to autonomy and thus ultimately to citizenship itself.

The institutional bias of unitary democracy is symbolic, i.e., government is associated with the symbolic entity in which the community will is embodied. In subordinating participation in a greater whole to identification with that whole and autonomy and self-legislation to unity and group self-realization, unitary democracy becomes conformist, collectivist, and often even coercive. In small face-to-face communities it is relatively benign, and it has historically served both equality and citizenship reasonably well in places where they might otherwise not have been served at all.[10] In such

10. Peter Laslett provides the "face-to-face" society with a sociology and a history in his seminal work *The World We Have Lost* (London: Methuen, 1965).

settings, unitary democracy relies on voluntary self-identification with the group, peer pressure, social conformism, and a willing acceptance of group norms—mechanisms that, to be sure, have their own perils but that are for the most part well immunized against the virulent modern strains of infectious totalism.[11]

In larger settings, however, where the community becomes an impersonal abstraction and individuals relate anonymously and anomically with masses of strangers, unitary democracy can turn malevolent, can be perilous to freedom and citizenship and ruinous to democracy. In its final phase, the French Revolution seemed to aspire to the unitary ideal in its most obnoxious form. Thus Hippolyte Castille glorified the reign of terror in these startling words: "The most perfect community would be where tyranny was an affair of the whole community. That proves fundamentally that the most perfect society would be one where there is the least freedom in the satanic [i.e., individualist] meaning of this word."[12] It is this unitary perversion of "direct" democracy that has aroused so many liberals to condemn participation and community as well as the arguments for "political freedom" with which their proponents justify these ideals.

To bring it into our typology, we may give unitary democracy, considered as a response to the dilemmas of the political condition, the following formal definition: *democracy in the unitary mode resolves conflict in the absence of an independent ground through community consensus as defined by the identification of individuals and their interests with a symbolic collectivity and its interests.*

As I have suggested, whether the consensual community is large and abstract (as in the case of fascism in its pure, national form) or small and face-to-face (as in the case of the homogeneous eighteenth-century New England town or the rural Swiss commune) will determine whether unitary democracy becomes vicious or merely irrelevant.[13] But in neither case is it consistently participa-

11. I have tried to give an account of the strengths and the dangers of face-to-face democracy in the Swiss German Alps in my *The Death of Communal Liberty* (Princeton: Princeton University Press, 1974). Readers may refer to this work for a fuller discussion.

12. Hippolyte Castille, *History of the Second Republic*, cited by Edouard Bernstein, *Evolutionary Socialism*, ed. Sidney Hook (New York: Schocken Books, 1961).

13. Even in such benign settings as the Vermont town meeting or an urban crisis cooperative, direct democracy can be problematic. See for example Jane J. Mansbridge's sociologically astute study *Beyond Adversary Democracy* (New York: Basic Books, 1980).

tory (since it undermines self-legislation) or genuinely political (since it "wills" away conflict). For the identification of individual with collectivity—which permits a government in the unitary mode to speak not only for but *as* "The People"—conceals and obscures the representative relationship that actually obtains between citizens and governing organs. Moreover, the symbolic collectivity denoted by such abstract terms as *the nation* or *the Aryan Race* or *the communal will*—since it is no longer circumscribed by the actual wills (or choices) of individual citizens acting in concert—usually turns out to be a cipher for some surreptitious set of substantive norms. It turns out, in other words, to be camouflage for the reintroduction of independent grounds, a stalking horse for Truth in the midst of politics, a Trojan Horse carrying Philosophers, Legislators, and other seekers of Absolute Certainty into the very inner sanctum of democracy's citadel. And so, in the place where we expect finally to hear the voices of active citizens determining their own common destiny through discourse and deliberation, we hear instead the banished voice of hubris, of would-be-truth and of could-be-right, which were unable to get a hearing on their own merits. Had they done so, the occasion for politics, democratic or otherwise, would never have arisen.

Thus does the promise of unitary democracy fade: unable to escape weak democracy's dependency on representation and the covert independent ground, it adds to them all the grave risks of monism, conformism, and coercive consensualism. No wonder that liberal democrats cringe at the prospect of "benevolent" direct democratic alternatives. With the perils of unitary democracy in mind, they justifiably fear the remedy for representation more than its ills.

The central question for the future of democracy thus becomes: Is there an alternative to liberal democracy that does not resort to the subterfuges of unitary democracy? In the absence of a safe alternative, it is the better part of prudence to stick by the representative forms of democracy, deficiencies and all.

STRONG DEMOCRACY: POLITICS IN THE PARTICIPATORY MODE

The future of democracy lies with strong democracy—with the revitalization of a form of community that is not collectivistic, a form of public reasoning that is not conformist, and a set of civic institutions that is compatible with modern society. Strong democracy is defined by politics in the participatory mode: literally, it is self-government by citizens rather than representative government in the name of citizens. Active citizens govern themselves directly here, not necessarily at every level and in every instance, but frequently enough and in particular when basic policies are being decided and when significant power is being deployed. Self-government is carried on through institutions designed to facilitate ongoing civic participation in agenda-setting, deliberation, legislation, and policy implementation (in the form of "common work"). Strong democracy does not place endless faith in the capacity of individuals to govern themselves, but it affirms with Machiavelli that the multitude will on the whole be as wise as or even wiser than princes and with Theodore Roosevelt that "the majority of the plain people will day in and day out make fewer mistakes in governing themselves than any smaller body of men will make in trying to govern them."[14]

Considered as a response to the dilemmas of the political condition, strong democracy can be given the following formal definition: *strong democracy in the participatory mode resolves conflict in the absence of an independent ground through a participatory process of ongoing, proximate self-legislation and the creation of a political community capable of transforming dependent private individuals into free citizens and partial and private interests into public goods.*

The crucial terms in this strong formulation of democracy are *activity, process, self-legislation, creation,* and *transformation.* Where weak democracy eliminates conflict (the anarchist disposition), represses it (the realist disposition), or tolerates it (the minimalist disposition), strong democracy *transforms conflict.* It turns dissensus into an occasion for mutualism and private interest into an epistemological tool of public thinking.

Participatory politics deals with public disputes and conflicts of interest by subjecting them to a never-ending process of deliberation, decision, and action. Each step in the process is a flexible part of ongoing procedures that are embedded in concrete historical conditions and in social and economic actualities. In place of the search for a prepolitical independent ground or for an immutable rational

14. "The People are wiser and more constant than Princes," writes Machiavelli in his *Discourses on Livy,* book 1, chap. 58. Roosevelt is cited in R. A. Allen, "The National Initiative Proposal: A Preliminary Analysis," *Nebraska Law Review* 58, 4 (1979): 1011.

plan, strong democracy relies on participation in an evolving prob-
lem-solving community that creates public ends where there were
none before by means of its own activity and of its own existence as
a focal point of the quest for mutual solutions. In such communities,
public ends are neither extrapolated from absolutes nor "discovered" in a preexisting "hidden consensus." They are literally forged
through the act of public participation, created through common deliberation and common action and the effect that deliberation and
action have on interests, which change shape and direction when
subjected to these participatory processes.

Strong democracy, then, seems potentially capable of transcend-
ing the limitations of representation and the reliance on surreptitious independent grounds without giving up such defining democratic values as liberty, equality, and social justice. Indeed, these
values take on richer and fuller meanings than they can ever have in
the instrumentalist setting of liberal democracy. For the strong democratic solution to the political condition issues out of a self-sustaining dialectic of participatory civic activity and continuous community-building in which freedom and equality are nourished and
given political being. Community grows out of participation and at
the same time makes participation possible; civic activity educates
individuals how to think publicly as citizens even as citizenship informs civic activity with the required sense of publicness and justice. Politics becomes its own university, citizenship its own training
ground, and participation its own tutor. Freedom is what comes out
of this process, not what goes into it. Liberal and representative
modes of democracy make politics an activity of specialists and experts whose only distinctive qualification, however, turns out to be
simply that they engage in politics—that they encounter others in a
setting that requires action and where they have to find a way to act
in concert. Strong democracy is the politics of amateurs, where
every man is compelled to encounter every other man without the
intermediary of expertise.

This universality of participation—every citizen his own politi-
cian—is essential, because the "Other" is a construct that becomes
real to an individual only when he encounters it directly in the political arena. He may confront it as an obstacle or approach it as an
ally, but it is an inescapable reality in the way of and on the way to
common decision and common action. *We* also remains an abstrac-

tion when individuals are represented either by politicians or as symbolic wholes. The term acquires a sense of concreteness and simple reality only when individuals redefine themselves as citizens and come together directly to resolve a conflict or achieve a purpose or implement a decision. Strong democracy creates the very citizens it depends upon *because* it depends upon them, because it permits the representation neither of *me* nor of *we*, because it mandates a permanent confrontation between the *me* as citizen and the "Other" as citizen, forcing *us* to think in common and act in common. The citizen is by definition a *we*-thinker, and to think of the *we* is always to transform how interests are perceived and goods defined.

This progression suggests how intimate the ties are that bind participation to community. Citizenship is not a mask to be assumed or shed at will. It lacks the self-conscious mutability of a modern social "role" as Goffman might construe it. In strong democratic politics, participation is a way of defining the self, just as citizenship is a way of living. The old liberal notion, shared even by radical democrats such as Tom Paine, was that a society is "composed of distinct, unconnected individuals [who are] continually meeting, crossing, uniting, opposing, and separating from each other, as accident, interest, and circumstances shall direct."[15] Such a conception repeats the Hobbesian error of setting participation and civic activity apart from community. Yet participation without community, participation in the face of deracination, participation by victims or bondsmen or clients or subjects, participation that is uninformed by an evolving idea of a "public" and unconcerned with the nurturing of self-responsibility, participation that is fragmentary, part-time, half-hearted, or impetuous—these are all finally sham, and their failure proves nothing.

It has in fact become a habit of the shrewder defenders of representative democracy to chide participationists and communitarians with the argument that enlarged public participation in politics produces no great results. Once empowered, the masses do little more than push private interests, pursue selfish ambitions, and bargain for personal gain, the liberal critics assert. Such participation is the work of prudent beasts and is often less efficient than the ministra-

---

15. Tom Paine, "Dissertation on First Principles of Government," in *Writings*, ed. N. D. Conway (New York: G. P. Putnam's Sons, 1894–1896, 8 vols.), vol. 3, p. 268.

tions of representatives who have a better sense of the public's appetites than does the public itself. But such a course in truth merely
gives the people all the insignia and none of the tools of citizenship
and then convicts them of incompetence.[16] Social scientists and political elites have all too often indulged themselves in this form of
hypocrisy. They throw referenda at the people without providing
adequate information, full debate, or prudent insulation from
money and media pressures and then pillory them for their lack of
judgment. They overwhelm the people with the least tractable
problems of mass society—busing, inflation, tax structures, nuclear
safety, right-to-work legislation, industrial waste disposal, environmental protection (all of which the representative elites themselves
have utterly failed to deal with)—and then carp at their uncertainty
or indecisiveness or the simple-mindedness with which they mud-
dle through to a decision. But what general would shove rifles into
the hands of civilians, hurry them off to battle, and then call them
cowards when they are overrun by the enemy?

Strong democracy is not government by "the people" or government by "the masses," because a people are not yet a citizenry and
masses are only nominal freemen who do not in fact govern themselves. Nor is participation to be understood as random activity by
maverick cattle caught up in the same stampede or as minnow-
school movement by clones who wiggle in unison. As with so many
central political terms, the idea of participation has an intrinsically
normative dimension—a dimension that is circumscribed by citizenship. Masses make noise, citizens deliberate; masses behave, cit-

16. Ironically, as many leftists as conservatives have criticized populist democracy. See for example Peter Bachrach, "Testimony before the Subcommittee on the
Constitution," *Committee on the Judiciary*, on S. J. Res. 67, 95th Congress, 1st session,
13–14 December 1977. Robert Michel anticipated this antipopulism of the left when
he wrote:

> Where party life is concerned, the socialists for the most part reject . . . practical
> applications of democracy, using against them conservative arguments such as we
> are otherwise accustomed to hear only from the opponents of socialism. In articles
> written by socialist leaders it is ironically asked whether it would be a good thing
> to hand over the leadership of the party to the ignorant masses simply for love of
> an abstract democratic principle. (Michels, *Political Parties*, p. 336)

Marxists have nurtured the concept of "false consciousness," by which they generally mean the unwillingness of the people to do as the scientific laws of history
dictate they ought to. People are thus trusted in the abstract but disenfranchised concretely in favor of elites and vanguards who have a better grasp of what history
requires.

izens act; masses collide and intersect, citizens engage, share, and contribute. At the moment when "masses" start deliberating, acting, sharing, and contributing, they cease to be masses and become citizens. Only then do they "participate."

Or, to come at it from the other direction, to be a citizen *is* to participate in a certain conscious fashion that presumes awareness of and engagement in activity with others. This consciousness alters attitudes and lends to participation that sense of the *we* I have associated with community. To participate *is* to create a community that governs itself, and to create a self-governing community *is* to participate. Indeed, from the perspective of strong democracy, the two terms *participation* and *community* are aspects of one single mode of social being: citizenship. Community without participation first breeds unreflected consensus and uniformity, then nourishes coercive conformity, and finally engenders unitary collectivism of a kind that stifles citizenship and the autonomy on which political activity depends. Participation without community breeds mindless enterprise and undirected, competitive interest-mongering. Community without participation merely rationalizes collectivism, giving it an aura of legitimacy. Participation without community merely rationalizes individualism, giving it the aura of democracy.

This is not to say that the dialectic between participation and community is easily institutionalized. Individual civic activity (participation) and the public association formed through civic activity (the community) call up two strikingly different worlds. The former is the world of autonomy, individualism, and agency; the latter is the world of sociability, community, and interaction. The world views of individualism and communalism remain at odds; and institutions that can facilitate the search for common ends without sabotaging the individuality of the searchers, and that can acknowledge pluralism and conflict as starting points of the political process without abdicating the quest for a world of common ends, may be much more difficult to come by than a pretty paragraph about the dialectical interplay between individual participation and community. Yet it is just this dialectical balance that strong democracy claims to strike. To justify this claim in detail is the task of the remaining part of this study. But first we need to clarify the status of the argument thus far and to compare its logic with the preconceptual logic portrayed in Part I.

Politics as Process: Overcoming the Generic Logic
of Preconceptual Frames

Our analysis to this point has compared and clarified different conceptions of democracy, but it has not posited a set of preconceptual
premises for strong democracy that could be compared with the
Newtonian preconceptual frame developed for liberal democracy in
Chapter 2. This omission was not accidental; for the argument of
Chapter 2 was that thin democracy suffered as much from the belief
in preconceptual reasoning as from the substantive biases yielded
by that reasoning. The idea that reasoning about politics is generic
or deductive and is best conceived as analogous to concatenation, it
turned out, is linked to many of liberalism's most glaring weaknesses.

Because it acknowledges that the condition of politics is the absence of an independent ground by which conflicts might otherwise
be settled or common goods fashioned, strong democracy avoids
reintroducing external criteria into the political process. Its central
value is the autonomy of politics, and it therefore requires that participants put whatever moral codes, principles, interests, private
ideas, visions, and conceptions of the good they may bring into the
process as individuals or groups to the test of politics itself. This
does not mean that values and ideas will not be drawn from religious and metaphysical systems of the kind offered by Christians or
liberals. Rather, it means that such values will acquire their legitimacy from their political fecundity—from their acceptance into and
transformation through the democratic political process. Instead of
focusing on the prepolitical roots or the epistemological status of
conceptions of freedom or law or right or justice in the abstract,
strong democracy regards these terms as rudimentary symbols for
competing ideas and perspectives, as encapsulations of normative
paradoxes that are constantly being adjudicated, challenged, modi-
fied, transposed, reinterpreted, emended, unpacked and repacked,
depreciated and revalued, and edited and transformed in accordance with the historical circumstances and evolving needs of concrete political communities.[17]

17. Liberal political philosophers have in the last decade come to see political language as a malleable and evolving product of social and political forces. (See for example Quentin Skinner, *Foundations of Political Thought*, 2 vols. (Cambridge: Cambridge University Press, 1979), and J. G. A. Pocock, *The Machiavellian Moment*

Democratic politics cannot assume a paradigmatic language that is rooted in prepolitical syntax because it is itself *about* paradigmatic language. Through participatory deliberation and ongoing public talk it contrives to define and redefine the crucial terms that we use in turn to define and redefine our common lives. The language of politics is thus necessarily compound, protean, and controversial. Is self-interestedness tantamount to avarice and to be regarded as a deadly sin—as medieval political thinkers claimed? Or is it the engine by which the great market forces of the free economy can be set in motion, as the economists of the Scottish Enlightenment preferred to think? Are we today to call abortion infanticide or an exercise of women's right to control their own bodies? Is *busing* a term for equal educational opportunity or for community-busting? Does *freedom* denote the absence of governmental intervention in our lives, or does it mean the presence of rational self-legislation? Can the act of voting be understood to describe the whole of equality, or must social and economic factors be brought within the definition?

Not one of these questions can be answered a priori or by reference to some abstract philosophical lexicon. For what we *want* the terms *freedom* and *equality* and *justice* and *right* to stand for is what politics is about. It is no different for us than it was for Adam: what we call things is what they become, and so politics is first of all about what we call things. As we shall see in the next chapter, when values have been named, issues identified, agendas set, and options delineated, most of what is meaningful in politics has already taken place. And by the same token, if we agreed on how to use words like freedom and justice, there would be no political debate in the first place and thus no need for politics—only for a political dictionary that any astute political scientist (if such exists) could compose during a sabbatical.

If essential contestability is the premise of politics, and citizenship rather than epistemology is the key to the resolution of conflicts over values and ends, then political *judgment* is evidently much more crucial to democracy than liberal democrats have believed.[18] Indeed,

---

(Princeton: Princeton University Press, 1975). Yet they often seem to treat actual political discourse (as against its history) as an ideal type with a fixed vocabulary and a permanent syntax—as if the current usage were somehow outside of history.

18. One of the few recent works that tries to take up the problem of political judgment is Ernst Vollrath, *Die Rekonstruction der politischen Urteilskraft* (Stuttgart: Ernst Klett, 1977). This work depends heavily on the classic source, Immanuel Kant's *Critique of Judgment* (*Kritik der Urteilskraft*, 1786).

participation has as its primary function the education of judgment. The citizen is the individual who has learned how to make civic judgments and who can evaluate goods in public terms. We often rank politicians and statesmen by their capacity for judgment. It is no different with citizens, whose responsibility it is not merely to choose but to judge options and possibilities. As we discuss citizenship and participation in subsequent chapters, the centrality of political judgment to the strong democratic political process will become increasingly evident.

OBJECTIONS AND CAVEATS

There are two particularly credible lines of argument that can be developed against strong democracy's substitution of the politics of process for prepolitical and preconceptual reasoning. The first is that in securing participatory politics against the abstract and the absolute, strong democracy sets it adrift, so that the lines to all principled moorings are severed. When this happens, self-reliance becomes a euphemism for subjectivism and relativism, and the right to community self-legislation becomes a mask for majoritarian tyranny and irrationalism.[19] The second objection is the other side of the same coin: in barring the certitude of independent grounds and preconceptual frames from political life, the strong democrat merely mimics the cautious demeanor of such skeptical weak democrats as Bertrand Russell and Karl Popper, who have turned philosophical skepticism into an excuse for political passivity and whose restraint was associated with the thinness of liberal democracy in the first part of this book.

Strong democracy is vulnerable to both lines of criticism, but it incorporates checks that prevent it either from falling back into minimalism (as per the second objection) or from slipping forward into majoritarian tyranny (as per the first objection).

The first line of argument worries that a politics unhinged from abstract reason can deteriorate into a politics of unreason and that a people loosed from all grounds other than its own will can easily degenerate into a permanently assembled mob. However doctrinaire and metaphysical the Bill of Rights may be in origin, it has

19. The fear of unconstrained majoritarianism, first expressed by James Madison in *Federalist* no. 51, has remained a leitmotif of American political writing through de Tocqueville down to Walter Lippmann and, most recently, Samuel Huntington.

served as a vital check on whimsical majorities, public willfulness, and popular prejudice. Judicial activism may curtail civic activity by preempting civic legislation, but it also protects civil rights with a wariness that the people often lack. And if there is no appeal to prior standards, who can legitimately prevent a people from democratically abdicating its own right to self-rule? With will as its only guide, anything is possible. Under these circumstances the "totalitarian temptation" may prove irresistible.[20]

But these perversions are, as we have seen, more aptly associated with unitary than with strong democracy. When safeguards are ignored, when impatience for utopia overwhelms the need for a proximate resolution of transient conflicts, when the ideals of duty, fraternity, and community and the sovereignty of politics over society and of public over private are deployed without their indispensable strong democratic concomitants—equality, autonomy, pluralism, tolerance, and the separation of private and public—then to be sure democracy can become unitary and collectivistic. This is the problem with conservative attempts to extrapolate from feudalism and tribalism guiding principles for modern community—which then becomes inseparable from hierarchy (as in Robert Nisbet's account, for example).[21] It is also the problem with the radical utopian's critique of tolerance and civility as impediments to the formation of a harmonious community, which they consider the condition rather than the product of political discourse (this is Herbert Marcuse's view, for example).[22] And it is the problem with the moralists' desire to transform the General Will into an efficient ally of public morals (see Lord Devlin, for example)[23] or to subsume individual citizens to a corporate totality or a unitary will (see Rocco or Gentile, for example).

Communal politics can verge on the profane and can tempt even

20. This line of argument is summed up in the title of Jean-François Revel's polemic against postwar communism in France: *La Tentation totalitaire* (Paris: Editions Robert Laffont, 1976). It can be traced to J. L. Talmon's *The Origins of Totalitarian Democracy* (New York: Praeger, 1961) and to Sir Karl Popper's *The Open Society and Its Enemies*, 2 vols. (London: Routledge and Kegan Paul, 1951). As suggested above in Chapter 5, I prefer the term *totalism*.

21. Robert A. Nisbet, *The Quest for Community* (New York: Oxford University Press, 1953 and 1969).

22. Herbert Marcuse, *One-Dimensional Man* (Boston: Beacon Press, 1964); also see Herbert Marcuse, Barrington Moore, Jr., and Robert Paul Wolff, *A Critique of Pure Tolerance* (Boston: Beacon Press, 1965).

23. Patrick Devlin, *The Enforcement of Morals* (Oxford: Oxford University Press, 1959).

good-willed democrats into perilous experiments with collectivism unless the central role of reasonableness and public talk is recognized. The Bill of Rights may actually do less to constrain a mob than would an appeal to the citizenship of its members, reminding them that they are embarked on a public course of action that cannot meet the objections of reasonable public discourse. Lynchings are carried out but they are not often defended. They may be more successfully interdicted by an appeal to the civic and human ties that connect the participants under normal circumstances than by an invocation of the "rights" of the victim. In reasonableness, commonality, participation, and citizenship lie the most powerful constraints on irrationalism and mob behavior that a political system can possess. Their cultivation is one of strong democracy's defining traits.

Liberal democracy also defends against mob rule (although it simultaneously invites the totalitarian to exploit its psychological and sociological weaknesses, as we saw in Chapter 5). The difference is, strong democracy forestalls mob rule by developing internal checks rather than by developing a system of external limits on government. Strong democracy enjoins a politics of *self-regulation* in which flywheel mechanisms dampen the extremes of popular passion and in which ongoing public talk and participation in public action induce in the people a spirit of reasonableness that becomes a governor on the public engine. To design institutions that are truly popular yet also deliberate and reasonable is obviously the first order of business in a strong democratic state, and that effort will occupy our attention in subsequent chapters.

In any case, there is no certain way to prevent a people intent on abdicating its liberty from doing so. Such institutional checks as the separation of powers may permit a more leisurely and painless demise, but external restraints cannot ultimately deter a society from civic self-destruction. The need is rather to create a citizen community that regards the preservation of autonomy as even more sacred than its exercise and that will therefore never sacrifice the former to the latter.

The second line of argument noted above contends that in its attempt to exclude truth and certitude from the domain of politics, strong democracy merely echoes the ineffective fallibilism of minimalism. The claim has some force, inasmuch as minimalism, in its skepticism about the place of dogmatic metaphysics in politics, does evoke the climate of strong democracy much more palpably than either anarchism or realism. Mill's version of fallibilism is thus no less hospitable to strong democracy than to the politics of liberalism: "That mankind are not infallible; that their truths, for the most part, are only half-truths; that unity of opinion, unless resulting from the fullest and freest comparison of opposite opinions, is not desirable, and diversity not an evil but a good . . . are principles applicable to men's mode of action, not less than to their opinions."[24]

Despite this congruence, however, strong democracy dissents from the liberal reading of fallibilism at both its philosophical and its political ends. To the liberal, philosophical fallibilism entails political minimalism: if we cannot *know* anything for certain we surely cannot *do* anything for certain. The assumption is that reflection and action answer to the same defining norms.[25] Strong democracy begins with the contrary assumption that it is precisely the difference between reflection and action that distinguishes politics from philosophy. Whereas philosophy can be either skeptical or dogmatic, public action will always be both contested (rooted in conflict) and consequential (of certain and inexorable consequences). Politics takes up where philosophy leaves off, but it has nothing to learn from philosphy's failure. It aims at reasonable public action based on community consent, and the default of philosophy that leads to contest and conflict to begin with is not its concern.

At the political end of the argument, the strong democrat understands that while politics begins with conflict and uncertainty, it always ends with what we may call the consensus of action—with a decision that is singular and historically determinative, however conflicted and plural was the process of arriving at it. Out of the diversity of the process comes the unity of the deed. Philosophy (or reflection) of course involves no deeds and hence no drama of the unitary outcome.

Now this understanding permits the strong democrat to see far more clearly than his liberal fallibilist colleague (who is a fallibilist because he perceives continuity, not disjunction, between reflection and action) that skepticism about the possibility of objective truth

24. John Stuart Mill, *On Liberty* (London: Dent, 1910), p. 14.
25. Bertrand Russell has thus argued that to believe, as a liberal empiricist must believe, that "almost all knowledge . . . is in some degree doubtful" will have "in the sphere of practical politics . . . important consequences." These include tolerance, an unwillingness to inflict present pain in the name of future good, and similar liberal values ("Philosophy and Politics," in Russell, *Unpopular Essays* [London: Unwin Books, 1968], p. 23).

cannot justify agnosticism about political outcomes. The strong democrat wants to transform uncertainty into reasonable group action, not to protect the individual (in the name of uncertainty) against all group action; he wants to find ways of using conflict as a means to achieve cooperation, rather than as a barrier to all common endeavor.

These are not nitpicking differences, for they lead to fundamental distinctions in political style and emphasis that go to the heart of the distinction between strong and weak democracy. In a word, liberals insist that knowing nothing for certain means doing nothing for certain, whereas strong democrats insist that knowing nothing for certain, when something must nevertheless be done (this is the political condition), means substituting for the missing certain knowledge an autonomous logic of public action—substituting reasonableness for reason, judgment for knowledge, and common will for truth. Active, creative, mutualistic, transforming, imaginative, and profoundly public in nature, strong democratic politics is obviously a far cry from the placid minimalism of the wary liberal fallibilist.

The claims of strong democracy to be the soundest of the democratic regime forms are extensive; yet if the theory yielded by our typology seems attractive, theory alone is not sufficient. The next three chapters will attempt to develop a convincing praxis to go with the theory. The heart of the argument for strong democracy is to define what it means by public talk, public action, citizenship, and community and to outline the concrete institutions in which these ideals can be made relevant to the modern American experience. The theory cannot be fully judged until this elaboration is offered in detail.

Thus, in the next chapter we will focus on the participatory process itself as it nurtures public talk, civic judgment, and the citizenship on which they depend. In the following chapter, we will take up the theme of community. Our final chapter will then explore how to devise actual institutions that can realize strong democracy in the modern world.

Chapter Eight

Citizenship and Participation: Politics as Epistemology

As regards the conduct of our life, we are frequently obliged to follow opinions which are merely probable, because the opportunities for action would in most cases pass away before we could deliver ourselves from our doubt. And when as frequently happens with two courses of action, we do not perceive the probability of the one more than the other, we must yet select one of them.

(Descartes)

Reasoning should not form a chain which is no stronger than its weakest link, but a cable whose fibers may be ever so slender, provided they are sufficiently numerous and intimately connected.

(Charles Sanders Peirce)

It is one of the ironies of the history of philosophy that skepticism as a metaphysical tool has been closely associated with a certain form of dogmatism and that those like Descartes and Hume who employed the skeptical method never once deluded themselves into believing that it had the slightest bearing on human conduct. Unfortunately, others have been more credulous. Both liberals and minimalists have come to believe that uncertainty in the realm of metaphysics must mean inaction in the realm of human conduct. Descartes was more careful. When in his *Discourse on Method* he embarked on his spectacular voyage of doubt, he did not fail to equip himself with a "code of morals for the time being" drawn from the laws, customs, and religion of France, in which he "had been instructed" since his childhood.[1] It is not possible, he told his readers, to pull down and rebuild the house we inhabit "unless we have also provided ourselves with some other house where we can be comfortably lodged during the time of building."[2] After all, one cannot become "irresolute in [one's] actions"; one has to "carry on" with life.

David Hume makes the same prudent allowance in his *Dialogues Concerning Natural Religion*. Cleasthenes taunts the skeptic Philo: "Whether your skepticism be absolute and sincere as you pretend, we shall learn by and by, when the company breaks up; we shall then see whether you go out at the door or the window; and whether you really doubt, if your body has gravity or can be injured by its fall, according to popular opinion derived from our fallacious senses and more fallacious experience."[3] Hume constructed his own political maxims, his skeptical metaphysics notwithstanding, on a foundation of history, custom, and necessity reinforced with a thin mortar of utility.

Conservatives in politics have always acknowledged the chasm between philosophy and the realm of action. Michael Oakeshott, for example, insists that maxims of conduct are "abridgements of tradition" rather than metaphysical abstractions; and Burke remarks that "the science of constructing a commonwealth, or renovating it, or reforming it, is, like every other experimental science, not to be taught a priori."[4]

In fact, skepticism and certainty are two sides of a single error: that of thinking that knowledge about the conduct of life or the creation of community can be derived from abstract reasoning or justified by appeal to the epistemological status of truth. Charles Peirce concluded that skeptical doubt was always a sham. "We cannot begin with complete doubt," he countered; "we must begin with all the prejudices which we actually have. . . . skepticism will be a mere self-deception and not real doubt; and no one who follows the

1. René Descartes, *Discourse on Method*, in *Philosophical Works*, ed. E. S. Haldane and G. R. T. Ross (Cambridge: Cambridge University Press, 1970), vol. 1, p. 95.
2. Ibid.
3. David Hume, *Dialogues concerning Natural Religion* (1779), in *Hume on Religion*, ed. Richard Wollheim (London: Fontana Library, 1963), p. 104.
4. Michael Oakeshott, *On Human Conduct* (New York: Oxford University Press, 1975), p. 66; and Edmund Burke, *Reflections on the Revolution in France* (London: Dent, 1910), p. 58.

Cartesian method will ever be satisfied until he has formally re-covered all those beliefs which in form he has given up."[5]

In the effort to achieve useful political and moral knowledge that will permit proximately just (public) human conduct, the real challenge is practical. One must conceive maxims that can motivate action and create consensus while having the malleability, flexibility, and provisionality of historically conditioned and thus ever-changing working rules. These rules may be abridgments of tradition, but they will also be abridgments of community—of that which is yielded by public deliberation.

Peirce sees in the thinker wedded to skepticism a foolish traveler who journeys to Constantinople via the North Pole, in order to "come down regularly upon a meridian."[6] Such metaphysicians cannot move without absolute Newtonian coordinates to guide them. For them, to conceive a maxim is to constitute an incorrigible ontology and a corresponding epistemology and then to deduce from them principles of conduct. The complete skeptic never finds the North Pole at all and therefore denies that the trip to Constantinople can be made. It is little wonder that Burke deems the philosophers "metaphysically mad" for thinking that they can rule human conduct with "no better apparatus than the metaphysics of an undergraduate and the mathematics and arithmetic of the exciseman."[7]

The political journey, which may lack even a Constantinople, begins in a given present and is conditioned by a contingent history and by the contours of a changing geography. There are no fixed coordinates and even destinations may have to be invented. Under the circumstances, the citizen cannot afford to suspend his opinions. Rather, he must seek to justify and to transform them while living amid competing others who are at once both potential supporters and potential adversaries. Like the conservative, the democratic citizen acknowledges the shaping force of history and the uncertainty of politics. Unlike the conservative, however, he under-

5. Charles Sanders Peirce, *Philosophical Writings of Peirce*, ed. Justus Buchler (New York: Dover Books, 1975), p. 229. Peirce concludes: "To make single individuals absolute judges of truth is most pernicious. The result is that metaphysics has reached a pitch of certainty far beyond that of the physical sciences;—only they can agree on nothing else."

6. Ibid.

7. Edmund Burke, *Speech on the Petition of the Unitarians*, in *Works of the Right Honourable Edmund Burke* (London: Bohn, 1877–1884), vol. 6, p. 21.

stands that an autonomous politics is the way out of historical determinism—that it provides a way for him to treat with historical
contingency without becoming a historicist and a way for him to
accept that human dilemmas cannot be resolved by metaphysical
logic without becoming a relativist. Writers such as Hannah Arendt
who have celebrated the world of the ancient polis have offered a
vision of a politics that while embedded in culture nevertheless enhances the possibilities of human freedom. This vision, although it
is not conservative, is as clear as conservatism has been about the
difference between political knowledge and truth. "Culture and politics, then," writes Arendt, "belong together because it is not knowledge or truth which is at stake, but rather judgment and decision,
the judicious exchange of opinion about the sphere of public life and
the common world, and the decision what manner of action is to be
taken in it, as well as how it is to look henceforth, what kinds of
things are to appear in it."[8]

If metaphysics, either through the assertion or the denial of ultimate principle, should not be the basis of political judgment, and if
at the same time we are unwilling to cede politics to mere history
and necessity, then political judgment must itself become the basis
for principle. This conclusion suggests that the task of democracy
must be to invent procedures, institutions, and forms for citizenship
that nurture political judgment and succor common choice and action in the absence of metaphysics. The two previous chapters have
incorporated these requirements into the basic definition of strong
democracy. In this chapter we will spell these requirements out.
This effort will require us to depict an epistemology in political
terms. In fact, it will mean conceiving politics *as* epistemology and
thereby inverting the classical liberal priority of epistemology over
politics.

Strong democracy places politics as epistemology at the very heart
of its practice. Peirce's striking metaphor of truth as a cable woven
together from many slender strands is a perfect representation of
strong democratic politics. Many citizens are bound together intimately through their common citizenship, and they interact guided
by opinions that in themselves are slender and provisional but that
when woven together into a communal will and a public purpose
inspire powerful conviction. A citizenry cannot speak truth to

8. Hannah Arendt's vision is elaborated and criticized by Hanna F. Pitkin, "Justice: On Relating Private and Public," *Political Theory* 9, 3 (August, 1981): 330–39.

power because it does not pretend to know what truth is. What it does instead is simply to speak to power in a voice rich with affect and commonality, a voice colored by its origin in autonomous wills seeking imaginative self-expression and by the public medium through which it is conveyed.

In what follows, we will explore the several aspects of politics as its own epistemology. First I will sketch a rough portrait of a political epistemology, using the ideas of public seeing and political judgment to arrive at a recognizable profile. Then we will look more closely at the details: nine features of talking and listening in public, the strong democratic process of political judgment as public willing, and common action as a necessary extension of common seeing and public judgment.

PUBLIC SEEING AND POLITICAL JUDGMENT

When politics in the participatory mode becomes the source of political knowledge—when such knowledge is severed from formal philosophy and becomes its own epistemology—then knowledge itself is redefined in terms of the chief virtues of democratic politics. Where politics describes a sovereign realm, political knowledge is autonomous and independent of abstract grounds. Where politics describes a realm of action, political knowledge is applied or practical and can be portrayed as praxis. Where politics concerns itself with evolving consciousness and historically changing circumstances, political knowledge is provisional and flexible over time. Where politics is understood as the product of human artifice and contrivance, political knowledge is creative and willed—something made rather than something derived or represented. And, finally, where politics is the preeminent domain of things public (*res publica*), political knowledge is communal and consensual rather than either subjective (the product of private senses or of private reason) or objective (existing independently of individual wills).

The distinction between political epistemology understood as practical judgment and the formal epistemology of pure reason is summarized in Figure 2, which is offered as a convenient shorthand introduction to the discussion that follows.

It is the pragmatic and self-regulating character of democratic politics that makes democratic political knowledge autonomous. Whereas knowledge in philosophy is deemed to depend on and de-

children both Paine and Hamilton, both Jefferson and Madison. And Burke himself proved that honoring the integrity of indigenous traditions can have radical consequences (e.g., his defense of American independence and East Indian autonomy) no less than conservative ones (e.g., his better-known defense of the French monarchy against the Revolution). A democratic community is inevitably obliged to create its past no less than its future, and the justice with which it does so will be one measure of its political judgment. Moreover, by constantly recapturing its own past in words and maxims, a community demonstrates its autonomy and its political vigor: in allowing itself to be shaped by the past, it also reshapes the past and so builds a foundation for its future.

If talk can give the dead back their voices, it can also challenge the paradigms of the living and bring fundamental changes in the meaning or valuation of words. Major shifts in ideology and political power are always accompanied by such paradigmatic shifts in language usage—so much so that historians have begun to map the former by charting the latter.[42] The largely pejorative meaning that the classical and early Christian periods gave to such terms as *individual* and *privacy* was transformed during the Renaissance in a fashion that eventually produced the Protestant Reformation and the ethics of commercial society. Eighteenth-century capitalism effected a transvaluation of the traditional vocabulary of virtue in a manner that put selfishness and avarice to work in the name of public goods. (George Gilder's *Wealth and Poverty* is merely the last and least in a long line of efforts to invert moral categories.) The history of democracy itself is contained in the history of the word *democracy*. The battle for self-government has been fought over and over again as pejorative valuations of the term have competed with affirmative ones (pitting Plato or Ortega or Lippmann or modern political science against Machiavelli or Rousseau or Jefferson). The terms *ochlocracy*, *mob rule*, *tyranny of the majority*, and *rule of the masses* all reflect hostile constructions of democracy; *communitarianism*, *participationism*, *egalitarianism*, and—it must be admitted—*strong democracy* suggest more favorable constructions.

Poverty was once a sign of moral weakness; now it is a badge of environmental victimization. *Crime* once proceeded from original sin; now it is an escape from poverty. *States' rights* once bore the

---

42. I have in mind the contextualist work of J. G. A. Pocock, Quentin Skinner, and John Dunn, inter alia (cited in earlier chapters).

stigma of dishonor, then signified vigorous sectionalism, then was a code word for racism, and has now become a byword for the new decentralized federalism. *Busing* was once an instrument of equal educational opportunity; now it is a means of destroying communities. The shifts in the meaning of these and dozens of other key words mirror fundamental national shifts in power and ideology. The clash of competing visions—of social Darwinism versus collective responsibility and political mutualism, of original sin and innate ideas versus environmentalism, of anarchism versus collectivism—ultimately plays itself out on the field of everyday language, and the winner in the daily struggle for meaning may emerge as the winner in the clash of visions, with the future itself as the spoils of victory.

An ostensibly free citizenry that leaves this battle to elites, thinking that it makes a sufficient display of its freedom by deliberating and voting on issues already formulated in concepts and terms over which it has exercised no control, has in fact already given away the greater part of its sovereignty. How can such a citizenry help but oppose busing if busing means the wrecking of communities and only the wrecking of communities? How can it support the right to abortion if abortion means murder, period? To participate in a meaningful process of decision on these questions, self-governing citizens must participate in the talk through which the questions are formulated and given a decisive political conception. The anti–Vietnam War movement of the 1960s did just this, of course; it won no elections, it participated in no votes, and it contributed to no legislative debates. But it radically altered how most Americans saw the war and so helped bring it to an end.

If language as a living, changing expression of an evolving community can both encapsulate and challenge the past, it also provides a vehicle for exploring the future. Language's flexibility and its susceptibility to innovation permit men to construct their visions of the future first in the realm of words, within whose confines a community can safely conduct its deliberations. Language can offer new solutions to old problems by altering how we perceive these problems and can make new visions accessible to traditional communities by the imaginative use (and transvaluation) of familiar language. This is the essence of "public thinking." The process moves us perforce from particularistic and immediate considerations of our own and our groups' interests, examined in a narrow temporal framework ("Will there be enough gasoline for my summer vacation trip?" for example), to general and long-term considerations of the nature of the communities we live in and of how well our life plans fit in with that nature ("Is dependence on oil a symbol of an overly materialistic, insufficiently self-sufficient society?" for example).

In sum, what we call things affects how we do things; and despite the lesson of Genesis, for mortals at least the future must be named before it can be created. Language is thus always the crucial battlefield; it conserves or liquidates tradition, it challenges or champions established power paradigms, and it is the looking glass of all future vision. If language is alive, society can grow; if it is dialectical, society can reconcile its parts—past and future no less than interest and interest or class and class. As Jürgen Habermas has understood, democracy means above all equal access to language, and strong democracy means widespread and ongoing participation in talk by the entire citizenry.[43] Left to the media, the bureaucrats, the professors, and the managers, language quickly degenerates into one more weapon in the armory of elite rule. The professoriate and the literary establishment are all too willing to capture the public with catch phrases and portentous titles. How often in the past several decades have Americans been made to see themselves, and thus their futures, through the lens of a writer's book title? Recall *The True Believer, The Managerial Society, The End of Ideology, The Other America, The Culture of Narcissism, The Greening of America, The Totalitarian Temptation, The Technological Society, The Two Cultures, The Zero-Sum Society, Future Shock.* We are branded by words and our future is held hostage to bestseller lists.

9. Community-Building as the Creation of Public Interests, Common Goods, and Active Citizens. All of the functions of talk discussed above converge toward a single, crucial end—the development of a citizenry capable of genuinely public thinking and political judgment and thus able to envision a common future in terms of genuinely common goods. This function of talk raises a host of new questions, of which the most important are perhaps, What is a "public"? And what is the political relationship between goods and interests? These issues are the subject of the next chapter. We need only note

43. In *Towards a Rational Society* (Boston: Beacon Press, 1970), Habermas attacks speech specialization and the expertise of "technical-rational" elites, which permits them to become forces of domination over and repression of society. His recent work focuses on "ideal speech situations" where expression is uncoerced and access to expression equally available. See *Communication and the Evolution of Society* (Boston: Beacon Press, 1979) and *Sprachpragmatik und Philosophie* (Frankfurt: Suhrkamp, 1976).

here that talk is ultimately a force with which we can create a community capable of creating its own future and that talk is nourished by community even as it helps establish the conditions for community.

DECISION-MAKING: PUBLIC WILLING AND POLITICAL JUDGMENT

Liberal representative democrats commonly assume that democracy means democratic *choice*. In an otherwise admirable little essay on the dilemmas of modern democracy, Stanley Hoffmann thus assures us that "politics is about choice."[44] And of all the institutions that we associate with democratic government in the West, none seems so central as voting, which many social scientists construe as choice epitomized. Talk to these thinkers is little more than a deliberative preliminary to the act of choosing. Representation, on the one hand, plays a dominant role for them because with representation votes can be counted, positions can be quantified, and power can be delegated. The deliberative process, on the other hand, lends itself neither to quantification nor delegation.

Those who identify democracy with decision-making through choice or voting capture the urgency of action without which politics becomes an abstract process that touches neither power nor reality. Yet to limit democracy to a selection among preferences and to think of efficient decision-making as its sole measure is to ignore all but the thinnest features of democracy. The reduction of democracy to voting implies that a ready-made agenda exists when none does and prompts the replication of private interests at higher levels where they are called *majorities* and *minorities* and where, as a consequence, they do even more damage. Majoritarianism is a tribute to the failure of democracy: to our inability to create a politics of mutualism that can overcome private interests. It is thus finally the democracy of desperation, an attempt to salvage decision-making from the anarchy of adversary politics. It is hardly surprising then that majoritarianism is often regarded as one of the great banes of democracy. In every age critics have had to do little more than link democracy to this threat in order to persuade the thinking and the wary that popular rule could only be a way station on the road to tyranny.

Conceiving of decision as majoritarian preference not only re-

44. Stanley Hoffmann, "Some Notes on Democratic Theory and Practice," *The Tocqueville Review* 2, 1 (Winter 1980): 69.

duces public goods to weak aggregations of private interests and mutualism to the rambling willfulness of transient majorities, it also is unresponsive to intensity and commitment. Unable to recognize qualitative differences in voters' motivations, it precipitates one of representative democracy's classical dilemmas: that the weak and complacent majority can unthinkingly overrule an impassioned and obdurate minority and thereby destabilize the regime. Talk may seem inconsequential, but it measures intensity. Voting does not.

The briefest survey of the theoretical and the empirical literature suggests that thin democracy—which reduces decision-making to voting for elected representatives and relies on the institutions of majoritarianism and adversary politics (the single-member district, the two-party system, the convention system)—is anything but the generic of democratic decision-making. Brian Barry lists seven models of decision in his *Political Argument*: decision by combat, by bargaining, by discussion on merits, by voting, by chance, by contest, and by authoritative determination.[45] In recent years, students of comparative politics have introduced a provocative distinction between competitive (adversary) systems and "consociational" systems. The latter are defined by a "non-competitive 'cartelized' pluralist pattern" in which "amicable agreement" plays the leading role.[46] The consociational model avoids the fractiousness of majority decision through a process of what we might call holistic bargaining, where agreements are limited to issues on which a genuine mutualism is possible. Another model is that of authoritative interpretation. Here a chairperson's "sense of the meeting" displaces actual votes and obviates the need for factions to form around adversary interests, or an executive rendering of the results of a complex balloting process imposes consensus upon diversity (as happened in the eighteenth-century Republic of Raetia).[47]

Strong democracy offers an alternative model that incorporates

45. Brian Barry, *Political Argument* (London: Routledge and Kegan Paul, 1965), chap. 5.

46. For the most recent interpretation of the theory of consociationalism, see Jurg Steiner and Robert H. Dorff, *A Theory of Political Decision Modes: Intraparty Decision-Making in Switzerland* (Chapel Hill, N.C.: University of North Carolina Press, 1980). Steiner's classification here includes his three earlier forms (majority decision, amicable agreement, and nondecision) as well as a new mode he calls "decision by interpretation"—what I call in the text "authoritative interpretation."

47. In the communes of eighteenth-century Raetia, votes took the form of position papers that were like judicial briefs. An executive council was empowered to extrapolate a common outcome from these several position papers, a procedure that obviously left a great deal of room for interpretative manipulation.

certain of the virtues of liberal democracy's view of decision as choice in the face of necessity but promotes a richer, more mutualistic understanding of what it means to develop political judgment and to exercise political will. Indeed, strong democratic decision-making is predicated on will rather than choice and on judgment rather than preference. Strong democracy understands decision-making to be a facet of man as maker and as creator and consequently focuses on public willing. Liberal democrats, like the economists and analytic philosophers they have taken into their service, conceive the decision exclusively in terms of rational choice. Thus they render the critical democratic question as "What will we choose?" Strong democracy poses the alternative question, "How do we will?" The challenge here is not how to make correct choices but how to make choices correctly, and this in turn is a question of judgment. Following Jean-Jacques Rousseau, strong democrats prefer the language of legitimate willing to the language of right choosing. To render a political judgment is not to exclaim "I prefer" or "I want" or "I choose such and such" but rather to say, "I will a world in which such and such is possible." To decide is thus to will into being a world that the community must experience in common: it is to create a common future, if only for selfish ends. In place of "I want Y," the strong democrat must say "Y will be good for us," a locution that is tested not by the incorrigibility of Y's philosophical origins but by the assent it finds in the community that must live with it.

It may now be evident that decision as willing belongs to the domain of power and action in a way that decision as choosing cannot. To will is to create a world or to bring about events in a world, and this act entails (and thus defines) power—the ability to create or modify reality. Our preferences are merely contemplative or speculative until we make them subjects of our wills and transform them into actions. In treating decision-making as an activity of the will, strong democrats honor the tradition of Rousseau and Kant, for whom the aim was not to choose common ends or to discover common interests but to will a common world by generating a common will. Legitimacy here is awarded not to the virtuous interest but to the general will, the will that incarnates a democratic community that is comprised in turn of the wills of autonomous citizens. The issue is not "I want" versus "you want" but "I want" versus "we will." More than a play of words is involved here, for conflicts of interest, while subject to bargaining, are finally intractable: my interest and your interest are separated forever by the particularity of me and you. The conflict of wills, on the other hand, is a contest over competing visions of a single possible future. However incompatible our wants, the world we will into existence can only be one world—a common arena in which our wants and interests will be satisfied or thwarted.

The fact that there can only be one world (whereas there can be innumerable interests) makes the contest of wills far more difficult and far more consequential than the contest of interests; but by the same token, it is much more tractable. From the perspective of radical individualism, every interest may seem equally legitimate. Interests can all coexist in the world of reflective reason; one is as good as the next. But wills cannot all be equally legitimate in the same sense, because by willing one affects the world, and the world is finally one—our world—and can only be as legitimate as the process that willed it into being. With interests, we may ask: "Do you prefer A or B or C?" With wills, we must ask: "What sort of world do you will our common world to be?"

The second question may seem on the surface little more than a reformulation of the first. But it is a crucial reformulation because it subjects otherwise incommensurable interests to the test of something very much like the categorical imperative; that is to say, it builds the Kantian test of universalizability into the political process. As private persons we may prefer all sorts of things, but as citizens we must be ready to will into existence a world in which our preferences can be gratified, and that turns out to be a quite different matter. I may want a big, fast, lead fuel–powered automobile, but I may not be prepared to will into existence a world with polluted air, concrete landscapes, depleted energy resources, and gruesome highway death tolls; and so as a citizen I may act contrary to my private preferences. By definition, no felt private interest can ever fail the test of preference, but many fail the test of will, which universalizes by virtue of its effect on reality. This fact should remind us again that politics in the participatory mode is the art of public seeing and of political judgment—of envisioning a common world in which every member of the community can live. It is the realm of "we will" rather than of "I want," and every attempt to reduce its role to the adjudication of interests will not only demean it but will rob it of any possibility of genuine public seeing.

If public seeing requires public willing, and if public willing cannot be reduced to mere choosing, then it seems evident that voting is the weakest rather than the strongest expression of the spirit of democracy and that the majority principle corrupts rather than nourishes political judgment. Rousseau suggested that the will of the majority (even the will of all) was not necessarily an expression of the general will. Particular interests can be counted and aggregated, but a will that is general entails a seeing that is common—which is something that numbers can neither measure nor certify.

Public seeing and political judgment are served, on the other hand, by political talk. Talk engenders empathy, nourishes affection, and engages imagination. From it are drawn the myriad visions that compete for the common will; in it are found the past abridged and the future dreamed. As in a marriage ceremony, where the couple's "I do" bespeaks a relationship already established and commitments already made, so in the process of decision under a strong democracy the "we will" certifies a vision already commonly imagined. Like the marriage vows, it is also a test of whether promises will be translated into actions and a vision of the future into present reality. Talk creates, but it creates conditionally: its visions are provisional and the shared consequences they promise are hypothetical. As in a simulation, the stakes are not yet real. The decision converts promise into reality and compels us to give irrevocable shape and life to what were initially only imaginings. It tests us by asking whether we can *will* that which until now we have only imagined, whether we are willing to mold the contours of a future still rich in possibility to the austere shape of our one dream.

In politics lies man's true hubris, although it is an inescapable hubris; for in politics we will not just for ourselves but for all. Yet we have no other choice, for not to will is also to will—to will the arbitrary or the determined or the natural.

A number of the dilemmas and paradoxes of liberal democratic theory lose some of their force when transcribed in the language of strong democratic politics. An examination of four of them may help clarify the nature of strong democratic citizenship. The four paradoxes are (1) that human preferences are incommensurable yet must be articulated, selected, ranked, and thus compared and evaluated; (2) that efforts to make politics more representative only produce a fragmented, inefficient system that is increasingly elitist (this is the so-called iron law of oligarchy); (3) that voters are equal in the number of votes they can cast (one each) but may be widely unequal in the intensity of their feelings about the issue being voted on; and (4) that the plurality of any individual's roles and interests weakens and privatizes citizenship and robs it of its ordering (sovereign) role. For purposes of shorthand, we may deal with these four sets of dilemmas under the headings "Incommensurability and Ranking," "The Iron Law of Oligarchy," "Intensity and Voting," and "Pluralism and Civic Fragmentation."

1. *Incommensurability and Ranking.* As long as decision-making is associated with choosing, the question of how to formulate topics, interests, and issues for the public agenda will raise a host of rational-choice dilemmas. There is the problem of overload: an infinite number of alternatives placed on what is a finite agenda. There is the problem of ordering choices: the sequence and position of alternatives on the ballot can affect the decisions of the voter. There is the problem of transitivity: if A is preferred to B, which is preferred to C, will A also be preferred to C (as the rule of transitivity dictates)? Or are preferences A, B, and C incommensurable, so that (paradoxically) A may be preferred to B, B to C, and C to A?[48] And finally there is the problem of how to create a single, interpersonal index, how to set exchange values for the multitudinous interests, goods, plans, and values envisaged in individual life plans.[49] Can personal dignity be measured by personal wealth? Is power commensurable with happiness? What is the exchange rate between glory and property? Is liberty lexically prior to all other goods, as Rawls and many traditional liberals assert?

These questions lead to paradoxes in part because liberal democrats pose them in the vacuum of abstract rationality, where they are stripped of historical and political context and removed from the arena of will and political judgment. The perspective of rationality, wedded to the rigorous distinctions of logic and statistical principle, quite naturally yield logical and statistical paradoxes. These dilem-

48. For a standard account of ranking and ordering problems, see Kenneth J. Arrow, *Social Choice and Individual Values*, 2d ed. (New Haven: Yale University Press, 1963). The transitivity problem is sometimes referred to as "Arrow's dilemma," although it is in fact as old as the logic of choice and probability theory.

49. Typical of the problems that modern social theorists face is John Rawls's attempt to construct an interpersonal index of goods by which to measure "least advantaged persons"; see his *A Theory of Justice* (Cambridge, Mass.: Harvard University Press, 1971). My objections to his argument and to the general issue of interpersonal indices are expressed in my "Justifying Justice: Problems of Psychology, Measurement, and Politics in Rawls," *American Political Science Review* 69, 2 (June 1975).

mas have been taken up by logicians and statisticians from the time of Borda and Condorcet in the eighteenth century and treated as models of political choice. The more recent work of Duncan Black, Kenneth Arrow, Mancur Olson, Anthony Downs, James Buchanan, William Riker, and many others who are laboring in the public-choice field retains the early commitment to "the possibility of forming a pure science of Politics."[50] There is evidence of course that rational models can correspond to certain forms of social behavior and that they help explicate problems of choice in committees and elsewhere. This is particularly true for liberal democratic systems, which have themselves evolved under the influence of theories of rationality.

Nevertheless, in a strong democratic system some of the dilemmas of rational choice are muted or circumvented. Agendas there are integral to the process of talk and deliberation, and options are as much created as chosen and are in any case subjected to the test of a single vision of the common future (in which implicit hierarchies of values can be found). Intransitivity is a problem in liberal democracy because it suggests incommensurable preferences. But if values and interests are incommensurable it is because they have neither been harmonized by an integrated will nor put to the test of being willed into a single common world (which, perforce, orders interests and goods in a natural, existential hierarchy whether we want it so or not). In other words, intransitivity paradoxes often merely conceal incoherently conceived options or a subliminal substitution of one scale for another with respect to choices that would otherwise be perfectly coherent and transitive. The gourmand who says, "I

50. This is the claim made by Duncan Black (p. xi). His book, an early work but one which won the 1983 Lippincott award of the American Political Science Association, is useful because it surveys the history of rational-choice dilemmas starting with Borda and Condorcet in the eighteenth century and because it discusses the abstract dilemmas in the context of the concrete data about choice in committees; see Duncan Black, *The Theory of Committees and Elections* (Cambridge: Cambridge University Press, 1958). Kenneth Arrow's seminal work is cited in note 48 above. Other works, including studies by authors cited in the text, are: James Buchanan and Gordon Tullock, *The Calculus of Consent* (Ann Arbor: University of Michigan Press, 1962); Anthony Downs, *An Economic Theory of Democracy* (New York: Harper and Row, 1956); Peter C. Fishburn, *The Theory of Social Choice* (Princeton: Princeton University Press, 1973); Douglas Rae, *The Political Consequences of Electoral Laws* (New Haven: Yale University Press, 1971): and William H. Riker, *The Theory of Political Coalitions* (New Haven: Yale University Press, 1963), and his recent *Liberalism against Populism: A Confrontation between the Theory of Democracy and the Theory of Social Choice* (San Francisco: Freeman, 1982). In this last book Riker suggests that although some critics claim to distinguish the rational models associated with choice theory from the political realities addressed by democratic theory, there are crucial issues between these realms.

like steak better than ice cream; I like ice cream better than vodka; but I like vodka better than steak" may have a classification rather than a preference problem. He may mean that he likes steak best as measured by nutrition, ice cream best as measured by taste, and vodka best as measured by effect. When asked for a choice, we get the paradox of transitivity; when asked for a clarification, we may get information that leads out of the paradox (including, perhaps, a ranking of nutrition, taste, and effect, which would permit us to discover which he would choose—and when, since time and circumstances might play a role).

The problem with reducing decision-making to mere voting is that information is minimized and the paradoxes of fixed options are maximized. Talk enables us to examine rank orders, commensurable scales, and the effect of time and place; it allows us to get at what we really want as individuals and as a community. Voting freezes us into rational dilemmas. Those who believe that democracy is a Pythagorean puzzle that becomes invalid if it cannot be "solved" by the theorems of logic and statistics confound problems of numbers and words with problems of willing and judgment. It is not just that judges and citizens finally have to choose; it is that their choices are generally more coherent and less paradoxical than the logical dilemmas extrapolated from them, especially if the choices are informed by a process of strong democratic talk.

2. *The Iron Law of Oligarchy.* There has been considerable debate in recent years about how to make the American system "more representative." The trouble is that "more representative" can mean "more oligarchic." Exponents of "democratization" argued for and won reforms in the Democratic Party's process of selecting presidential candidates that moved the weight of choice from the party convention ("elite") to the primary system.[51] Now the pendulum is swinging the other way, but there is little evidence that the reforms of 1968 through 1976 have had any lasting effect on elite/mass politics. The iron law of oligarchy, which claims that when citizens delegate power they create the conditions for oligarchy and therefore

51. For a complete discussion of the democratic reform movement and of party politics in the spirit of the argument offered here, see my "The Undemocratic Party System: The Problem of Citizenship in an Elite/Mass Society," in Robert Goldwyn, ed., *Political Parties in the Eighties* (Washington, D.C.: American Enterprise Institute, 1980). For another recent discussion that reflects the liberal representative position, see Cyrus R. Vance, "Reforming the Electoral System," *New York Times Magazine*, 22 February 1981.

that representative government is always doomed to become oligarchical, has not been overcome by such reforms. If anything, it has been vindicated.

At least since John Stuart Mill publicly advocated the Hare system of proportional representation (PR), critics of the single-member (winner-take-all) district system (SMD) have maintained that multi-member districts offer a "more democratic" form of representation. And again, although the effect on party politics has been decisive—PR has everywhere produced multiparty systems and some resulting governmental instability (Italy, for example), while SMD organization has produced stable but centrist two-party systems—it is not at all clear that PR has really had a democratizing effect on the nations that have used it.

On the whole, attempts at democratization conducted within the confines of thin democracy work only to further polarize elites and masses while cloaking oligarchic manipulation in a mantle of popular sovereignty. PR may multiply the number of special-interest and one-issue political groups represented in the adversary system, but it can only fragment the citizenry and further impede efforts at public seeing. The Democratic Party's convention rule changes brought Americans into the selection process who had previously been excluded, but it encouraged them to see themselves as special-interest constituencies and fostered the selection of nominees incapable of winning elections (McGovern) or of leading the nation when they did win (Carter). By challenging only the mechanics but not the premises of representative democracy, attempts at democratization tend to undermine the strengths of liberal democracy (the brokered, compromise conventions; the wisdom of back-room politics; the efficiencies of machines) without nurturing political judgment and public seeing by a responsible citizenry. With this in mind, strong democrats can sympathize with the old-guard liberals who believe that the old-style politics of machine elites was preferable to the new-style politics of "democratic" special-interest groups. Neither style is hospitable to strong democracy, but old-style politics avoided the hypocrisy of the new and permitted political wisdom and political judgment to be exercised by (at least) an elite. The new politics destroys judgment without achieving democracy—surely the worst of both worlds.

3. Intensity and Voting. The intensity problem afflicts every mode of democracy, but it is a greater problem for representative majoritarianism, where decision-making means vote-counting, than for strong democracy, whose focus on participation and talk gives more opportunity for a qualitative measurement of conviction and commitment. A listening citizenry is more likely than a voting special-interest group to hear the voices of inspiration and imagination that vote tallies cannot measure. Martin Luther King could cast only one vote, but by moving the imagination of millions of whites he gave a voice to millions of blacks who had been silent; and in doing so he helped forge a new common will in the struggle against America's deeply ingrained racism. Though strong democracy may respond practically no better than liberal democracy to the immediate crises of the desperate and the powerless, its politics of public seeing and common willing is better suited than the politics of private interests to envisioning their status in a common future.

The division of a citizenry into majority and minority is a necessary feature of representative democracy, an evidence of its effective functioning. But it is a rebuke to strong democracy, for it is evidence of democracy's failure to create a common future in which every citizen can envision himself or herself living—and living *well*. Where the liberal is proud of his divisions and of the weary good will with which minorities acquiesce in the preferences of those who outnumber them, the strong democrat regrets every division (though there may be many) and regards the existence of majorities as a sign that mutualism has failed. Wherever possible, the strong democrat will try to defer decisions on which there is not yet agreement rather than to win a majority victory that leaves behind a legacy of dissatisfaction. Individuals will not always be content with a public vision; we are splintered into fragments, and few of us are ever satisfied with ourselves. But for us to accede to a political judgment that we have helped formulate is less alienating than having to accede to a majority that has outvoted us.

4. Pluralism and Civic Fragmentation. The social-science literature on comparative democratic theory is rife with the dilemmas of faction, role, and cleavage; of multiple individual identities that cut across different groups; and of majorities and minorities that are constantly in flux in liberal democracy.[52] At the heart of these dilem-

52. Robert Dahl states these dilemmas in paradigmatic form in his *Preface to Democratic Theory* (Chicago: University of Chicago Press, 1956) and places them in comparative perspective in his anthology, *Political Oppositions in Western Democracies* (New Haven: Yale University Press, 1966). His most recent book returns to the central dilemmas: *Dilemmas of Pluralist Democracy* (New Haven: Yale University Press, 1982). A classic case study is Harry Eckstein, *Division and Cohesion in Democracy: A Study of Norway* (Princeton: Princeton University Press, 1966).

mas—and of the intensity problem as well—is the fragmentation of
man by a host of private and public roles. In each role, man is compelled to don a different mask, to belong to and identify with a different group, and to speak with a different, often forked, tongue.
The long-time family man living on Mulberry Street in New York
whose grandfather came from Bologna and who is a shop steward
in the sheet-metal workers' union is a portrait in pieces: his life is
splintered into quarters and fifths, his politics is a compound mass
of incompatible interests. As a union man he votes Democratic, but
as an insecure blue-collar worker he leans toward moral-majority
Republicanism. As a city-dweller he understands the problems of
teenage pregnancy but as a Catholic he abhors abortion. As a wage-
earner he shares the goals of the hard-working Hispanics and blacks
at his workplace, but as an ethnic white he fears their inroads into
his community and their disruptive impact on his neighborhood. As
a father and husband he wants *his* women to act like traditional
women, but as a shop steward he is sensitive to his female cowork-
ers' complaints about sex discrimination and sexual harassment on
the job. As a taxpayer he resents the mammoth social-security de-
ductions taken off his paycheck, but as a twenty-five-year man and
potential retiree he feels deeply anxious about the possible bankruptcy of the Social Security Administration. When asked to participate politically by "voting his interests," how can such a fractured
soul exhibit anything but cognitive dissonance and political schizophrenia? Certainly his overlapping membership in so many groups
and constituencies makes him aware that the majority is fragile and
that his affiliations and interests are crosscutting. The result, however, is not just the "stability" prized by liberals but a pervasive
sense of confusion and political apathy that is corrosive to citizenship and to democracy.

Strong democratic political processes aim to strengthen the role
of "citizen"—to reestablish its sovereignty over other roles—and
thereby to provide a political means by which the multiple identities
of the individual in the private marketplace can be ordered and
made consistent with political judgment. By emphasizing the politics of common will and deemphasizing the politics of brokered interests, strong democracy makes interaction, listening, and common judgment the allies of civic and psychic integration. The citizen
emerges from the struggle of partisan interests as a whole person.
The Italian-American begins to think about what is required of him

as a citizen. He finds himself measuring his private interests by the yardstick of public interests in which, as citizen, he has a growing investment. Citizenship here serves to transform interests and to reorient identity; the dilemmas of pluralist sociey are not thereby addressed, they are challenged head on.

COMMON ACTION AS COMMON WORK AND COMMON DOING

If common decision is the test of common talk, then common action is the test of common decision. Common work is a community doing together what it has envisioned and willed together. Thus might the citizens of an eighteenth-century Swiss village have decided to declare war on a harassing neighbor and then armed themselves and conducted that war, thereby implementing their vote with their muskets. Thus might the members of a union talk their way to a strike decision and then embark jointly upon common strike action. Thus might pioneers in a frontier community decide they need a new schoolhouse and then raise it together, sealing their decision with their own labor. Thus might an urban neighborhood take over an abandoned lot and convert it with the equity of their sweat into an urban farm.

In each of these cases common action exerts a powerful integrating influence on the doers even as they are achieving common goals. So great is the power of common military service to build a community spirit that some have traced the birth of modern nationalism to such experiences and the philosopher William James was moved to call for a "moral equivalent of war" that might inspire in a people at peace the fraternal passions associated with common defense. Georges Sorel was no great friend of democracy, but he did perceive in the General Strike not so much an efficient engine of economic improvement as a sanctified incubator from which might emerge a "new Socialist man."[53] The "language of movement" that Sorel discovered in the strike in fact characterizes every common action aimed at realizing a common good.

A community that will not affix to its decisions the seal of common implementation, whether it pleads the rights of privacy or mere incompetence, may quickly lose its grip on the decision process. Deference to "experts" and "professionals" in government begins with

53. Georges Sorel, *Reflections on Violence*, trans. T. E. Hulme and J. Roth (New York: Collier Books, 1961), pp. 127–28.

the executive branch, but it can spread to the legislative branch and leave citizens feeling like "amateurs" who can play no other role than client in the civic process. The failure of democracy at the level of common action ultimately jeopardizes democracy at the level of decision and talk.

In practical terms, wherever conditions facilitate common legislation, there is the possibility of common execution and implementation. In urban neighborhoods the possibilities are endless: common action could transform trash lots into pocket parks or urban farms; rehabilitate unused storefronts as community education and recreation centers; develop neighborhood teams skilled in carpentry, masonry, plumbing, and electricity to cooperate with tenants and owners in urban homesteading ("sweat equity") programs; organize block associations, "crime-watch" units, school crossing guards; and so forth. The potential of course depends on the vitality of the neighborhood (a topic taken up in the next chapter), but such projects are not only feasible but already in place in a number of cities.

Smaller towns and rural areas could engage in still more ambitious public projects, on the model of the traditional barn-buildings and roof-raisings. In 1974, for example, the town of Thebes, Illinois, used a grant from the Department of Agriculture to rebuild a historic courthouse, using local labor from the ranks of the unemployed to complete the project. "Workfare" is a controversial idea that in practice has been widely abused, but it rests on a promising idea: that government clients can become contributing citizens by participating in common civic work for public ends.[54] In any case, common work ought to engage all citizens, the fully employed as well as the unemployed. It is not a substitute for private labor on behalf of private interests. Rather it complements private labor, diverting some "private" energy into social tasks while making citizenship mean more than the expression of preferences and the pulling of levers.

Whatever form they take—and they can be organized at the national level (as in the universal citizen service, discussed below) as well as at the local level—programs of common work are valuable

54. Punitive poorhouse and workhouse ideas borrowed from the nineteenth century have tainted what is potentially a good idea. In fact, a great many citizens are on welfare because they cannot work due to illness, disability, or parental responsibilities. And work assignments resting on makeshift or featherbedded projects are clearly not in the public interest. Nevertheless, offering work rather than welfare to those able to work obviously serves both individual dignity and public goods.

both to participants and to the communities they serve. They make communities more self-sufficient and thus more self-governing and build a genuine sense of community in the neighborhood. Such programs thereby lower the pressure on central government to monopolize the governing and administering functions. By addressing residents as citizens rather than as clients or wards, these programs also cultivate civic ideals of service and direct attention away from fractious private interests. They provide dignifying work for those who in the present economy are disqualified by age or race or training from succeeding in the private sector. And they confront every kind of dependency with the discipline of self-help and thus lay the foundation for self-government in individuals as well as communities. Finally, by completing the cycle of citizenship begun with common deliberation and common legislation, these projects provide a complete institutional framework for civic action and civic responsibility at the national level—where participation is harder but the stakes are much higher.

There is a growing resentment of government's efforts to redistribute income by fiat; those from whom the government takes may not deserve what they have, but neither do those to whom the government gives earn what they get—nor, indeed, are they allowed to earn it. Forced to give and forced to take, citizens of Western democracies are allowed neither to contribute nor to earn. They are treated as exploited or exploiters, to be coddled or scolded by an avuncular bureaucracy, but rarely as citizens responsible for their own destinies. They in turn disparage their government as a grasping Scrooge or as a foolish spendthrift, dissociating themselves from its pathologies—which, they prefer not to realize, only mirror their own. Common work earns for each a common share and helps to justify the redistribution by which a society assures that shares will be held justly and in common. It permits giving and legitimates taking; indeed, it shows that these are but the economic reflection of duties and rights, which are the two sides of citizenship, just as it forces citizens to see their own faces, for better or for worse, in the fragile mirror of their government.

The key to politics as its own epistemology is, then, the idea of public seeing and public doing. Action in common is the unique province of citizens. Democracy is neither government by the majority nor representative rule: it is citizen self-government. Without citizens there can be only elite/mass politics. "Create citizens," cried

Rousseau, "and you will have everything you need."[55] Politics in the participatory mode relies in the final instance on a strong conception of the citizen. It makes citizenship not a condition of participation but one of participation's richest fruits.

Every argument advanced in this chapter has pointed to a conception of the citizen. It is to that conception of the citizen and to the idea of the civic community that we will now turn our full attention.

55. Jean-Jacques Rousseau, "A Discourse on Political Economy," in *Social Contract and Discourses* (London: Dent, 1913), p. 251.

Chapter Nine

Citizenship and Community:
Politics as Social Being

There can be no patriotism without liberty; no liberty without virtue; no virtue without citizens; create citizens and you will have everything you need; without them, you will have nothing but debased slaves, from the rulers of the state downwards.

(Jean-Jacques Rousseau)

But what is government itself but the greatest of all reflections on human nature?

(James Madison)

The State of Civil Society is a state of nature. . . . Man's nature is Art.

(Edmund Burke)

If government is but the greatest of all reflections on human nature and if, in Rousseau's inversion of Madison's claim, a people can be "no other than the nature of its government," then there is no better way to elucidate the difference between strong democracy and liberal democracy than by comparing how they portray human nature.[1] In Chapter 4 we examined the liberal portrait of human nature, which construed the human essence as radically individual and solitary, as hedonistic and prudential, and as social only to the extent required by the quest for preservation and liberty in an adversary world of scarcity.

1. Jean-Jacques Rousseau, *Confessions*, book 9. The full quotation reads: "I had come to see that everything was radically connected with politics, and that however one proceeded, no people would be other than the nature of its government."

This conception presented human behavior as necessarily self-seeking, albeit in a premoral way. People entered into social relations only in order to exploit them for their own individual ends. Because modern liberal democracy is an accretion of democracy on a liberal philosophical base, American democratic theory has from its beginnings been weighted down by radical individualism. This association has created tensions within liberal democracy that, because they are rooted in conflicting notions of the human essence, cannot easily be resolved by politics. Marx took note of these tensions in the aftermath of the French Revolution. Rather than resurrecting freedom, he remarked, it produced a profound cleavage between man conceived as an individual member of civil society pursuing his private aims in conflict with others and man conceived as a citizen cooperating in "illusory" universals—namely, the "political state."[2]

In the *Grundrisse*, Marx offered an alternative construction of human nature as socially determined, a construction that links Aristotle to the modern sociological conception. "The human being," Marx wrote, "is in the most liberal sense a *zoön politikon*, not merely a gregarious [*geselliges*] animal, but an animal that can individuate itself only in the midst of society."[3]

The social construction of man is not, however, simply the antithesis of the individual construction formed in social-contract theory. It is dialectical, for it perceives an ongoing interaction by which world and man together shape each other.[4] Peter Berger and Thomas Luckmann capture the dialectic perfectly in this post-Marx-

2. In *On the Jewish Question*, Marx writes:

Where the political state has attained to its full development, man leads . . . a double existence—celestial and terrestrial. He lives in the *political community*, where he regards himself as a *communal being*, and in *civil society* where he acts simply as a *private individual*, treats other men as means, degrades himself to the role of a mere means, and becomes the plaything of alien powers. . . . Man . . . in civil society, is a profane being. . . . In the state, on the contrary, where he is regarded as a species-being, man is the imaginary member of an imaginary sovereignty, divested of his real, individual life, and infused with an unreal universality. (In Robert C. Tucker, ed., *The Marx-Engels Reader* [New York: Norton, 1972], p. 32)

3. Karl Marx, *Grundrisse: Foundations of the Critique of Political Economy*, trans. M. Nicolaus (New York: Vintage Books, 1973), p. 84. In the better-known *Sixth Thesis on Feuerbach*, Marx and Engels wrote that "the human essence is no abstraction inherent in each single individual. In its reality it is the ensemble of social relations" (in Tucker, ed., *Reader, Theses on Feuerbach*, p. 109).

4. Continental existentialists typically commence the confrontation with human existence by presenting man as a "being-in-the-world," which makes a much more useful starting point for political reflection. Heidegger's *Being at Time* thus explicitly associates the hyphenated man-in-the-world with the inescapable dialectic that links particular human nature to the character of being in general.

ist depiction of man's social nature: "Man is biologically predestined to construct and inhabit a world with others. This world becomes for him the dominant and definitive reality. Its limits are set by nature, but once constructed, this world acts back upon nature. In the dialectic between nature and the socially constructed world the human organism itself is transformed. In this same dialectic, man produces reality and thereby produces himself."[5]

Strong democratic theory posits the social nature of human beings in the world and the dialectical interdependence of man and his government. As a consequence, it places human self-realization through mutual transformation at the center of the democratic process. Like the social reality it refracts, human nature is compound; it is potentially both benign and malevolent, both cooperative and antagonistic. Certain qualities enjoin a "degree of circumspection and distrust," as Madison prudently notes in *The Federalist Papers*; others may "justify a certain portion of esteem and confidence."[6] But all these qualities may be transformed by legitimate and illegitimate social and political forces. For man is a developmental animal—a creature with a compound and evolving telos whose ultimate destiny depends on how he interacts with those who share the same destiny. Such creatures possess neither fixed natures nor absolute, independently grounded notions of reality and right. They seem rather to follow what Alexander Bickel has called the Whig model of political life. This model posits that human nature is "flexible, pragmatic, slow-moving, and highly political" and therefore that politics will be a process of "untidy accommodation."[7]

5. Peter L. Berger and Thomas Luckmann, *The Social Construction of Reality* (New York: Doubleday, 1966), p. 183. In his classic study *Community*, Robert MacIver makes the simple assertion: "Every individual is born into community and owes its life to community, . . . community is always there" ([London: Macmillan, 1917], p. 204).

6. James Madison et al., *Federalist Papers*, no. 55 (New York: Random House, 1937), p. 365. Hanna Pitkin offers a characterization of man that is completely in the spirit of the following discussion:

> Man is neither a species of organic being whose behavior is causally determined, like that of a river, nor an angel who always does what is right because it is right, independently of any needs, fears, or feelings. Politics is neither the greedy machinations of selfish power seekers nor the selfless pursuit of a higher good unrelated to purposes. Nor does the truth lie "somewhere in between." We are creatures who can be seen in . . . both of these seemingly incompatible ways; we are engaged in the continual, endless transformation of organic into moral, of instinct into authority . . . a continual translating of partial interest and private need into public decisions and authoritative structures. ("Inhuman Conduct and Unpolitical Theory," *Political Theory* 4, 3 [August 1976]: 316)

7. Alexander Bickel, *The Morality of Consent* (New Haven: Yale University Press, 1975), p. 4.

Political animals interact socially in ways that abstract morals and metaphysics cannot account for. Their virtue is of another order, although the theorists who have defended this claim have been called everything from realists to immoralists for their trouble. Yet Montaigne caught the very spirit of social man when he wrote, "the virtue assigned to the affairs of the world is a virtue with many bends, angles, and elbows, so as to join and adapt itself to human weakness; mixed and artificial, not straight, clean, constant or purely innocent."[8]

If the human essence is social, then men and women have to choose not between independence or dependence but between citizenship or slavery. Without citizens, Rousseau warns, there will be neither free natural men nor satisfied solitaries—there will be "nothing but debased slaves, from the rulers of the state downwards."

To a strong democrat, Rousseau's assertion at the opening of his *Social Contract* that man is born free yet is everywhere in chains does not mean that man is free by nature but society enchains him.[9] It means rather that natural freedom is an abstraction, whereas dependency is the concrete human reality, and that the aim of politics must therefore be not to rescue natural freedom from politics but to invent and pursue artificial freedom within and through politics. Strong democracy aims not to disenthrall men but to legitimate their dependency by means of citizenship and to establish their political freedom by means of the democratic community.

In *Emile*, Rousseau wrote: "We are born weak, we need strength; we are born totally unprovided, we need aid; we are born stupid, we need judgment. Everything we do not have at our birth and which we need when we are grown is given us by education."[10] The corresponding political assertion would be: "We are born insufficient, we need cooperation; we are born with potential natures, we require society to realize them; we are born unequal, we need politics to make us equal; we are born part slave, part free, we can secure full liberty only through democratic community."

Citizenship and community are two aspects of a single political reality: men can only overcome their insufficiency and legitimize

8. Montaigne, "Of Vanity," in Donald M. Frame, ed., *The Complete Essays of Montaigne* (Stanford: Stanford University Press, 1965), p. 758.
9. Jean-Jacques Rousseau, *The Social Contract*, book 1, chap. 1.
10. Jean-Jacques Rousseau, *Emile, or Education*, trans. Allan Bloom (New York: Basic Books, 1979), p. 38.

their dependency by forging a common consciousness. The road to autonomy leads through not around commonality. As George Bernard Shaw wrote: "When a man is at last brought face to face with himself by a brave individualism, he finds himself face to face, not with an individual, but with a species, and knows that to save himself he must save the race. He can have no life except a share in the life of the community."[11]

In this chapter we will examine both aspects of the civic relationship: (1) the democratic community, defined by the participation of free, active, self-governing citizens in the creation of their common future in the absence of independent grounds and (2) the democratic citizen as the participant in a self-governing democratic community. Then we will look at both the conditions that facilitate strong democratic citizenship and the limits that constrain it. The facilitating conditions include civic education, leadership, religion, and patriotism; the limits include the problem of scale, structural inequality, rights, and the ultimate uncertainty of all human vision—and of public vision in particular—in a world where no knowledge is certain, no grounds absolute, and no political decision irrevocable.

CITIZENSHIP

If we accept the postulate that humans are social by nature, then we cannot regard citizenship as merely one among many artificial social roles that can be grafted onto man's natural solitariness. It is rather the only legitimate form that man's natural dependency can take. The civic bond is the sole legitimator of the indissoluble natural bond: it makes *voluntary* those ties that cannot in any case be undone, and it makes *common* and susceptible to mutuality the fate that is in any case shared by all men. As Aristotle noticed long ago, the civic bond is in fact the one bond that orders and governs all others—the bond that creates the public structure within which other, more personal and private social relationships can flourish.

We can expand on these rather general considerations, first by relating them to the several types of citizenship distinguished in Chapter 7 and then by seeing how the various forms of democracy answer the three questions that can be put to any theory of citizen-

11. George Bernard Shaw, "Commentary on Ibsen's *Little Eyolf*," in Shaw, *The Quintessence of Ibsenism* (New York: Hill and Wang, 1957), p. 130.

ship: what is the basis or grounds of citizenship? What are the character and the quality of the civic bond? And where does one place the boundaries of citizenship? The answers to these three questions will reveal how representative, unitary, and strong democracy view the origin, the nature, and the extent of the civic tie and will permit us to elucidate in full the strong democratic theory of citizenship.

The Grounds of Citizenship. In modern states, territory is generally regarded as the primary ground of citizenship. Nonetheless, a number of alternative grounds can also be extrapolated from the history of civic identity in the West. Among these are blood (as in the clan or tribe); personal fealty (as in early feudalism); proprietary jurisdiction (as in the feudalism of the High Middle Ages); common belief (as in early Christian communities or Augustine's City of God); economic contract (as in the Renaissance economic association [*Genossenschaft*] or Robert Nozick's "protective association"); political contract (as in the Mayflower Compact); and a commitment to common processes and common ends (as in such traditional face-to-face communes as the Alpine *Gemeinde* or the New England town).

The three kinds of modern democracy distinguished in Chapter 7 (representative, unitary, and strong) are all territorial in the fundamental legal sense, but each one is also inclined to accept a secondary and distinctive ground for civic identity (see Figure 3). Thus representative or thin democracy conceives the civic bond as an original contract that authorizes the sovereign to govern individuals, on their behalf and in their name. This citizenship is a function of an original and abstract authorship of the regime and consequently has a watchdog quality: it is passive rather than active, and it implies potentiality (abstract legal status) rather than actuality (concrete political status). To be a citizen is to be a party to the social contract and thus to be a legal person.

Unitary democracy scoffs at legal personhood as a lifeless fiction. It prefers to root citizenship in the much more vivid idea of blood: citizens are blood brothers united by a genetic (rather than a generic) consensus and bound together almost preternaturally—certainly not by choice or will. Pan-Slavism or Aryan nationalism or even Zionism may be taken as an example of such civic ideologies rooted in blood, where territory follows rather than precedes civic identity. (Modern Israel faces a civic quandary precisely because its Zionist tendencies are at odds with its secular, territorial tendencies, so that

FIGURE 3 *Forms of Citizenship*

	Representative Democracy	Unitary Democracy	Strong Democracy
Citizens Conceived	legal persons	brothers	neighbors
Bound Together by	contract	blood	common participatory activity
Related to Government as	sovereign but also subject	corporate body	active participants
By Ties That Are	vertical (citizen to government	horizontal (citizen to citizen)	dialectical ("levels" vanish)
Political Style	distrustful, passive	self-abnegating, submissive	cooperative, active
Civic Virtue	accountability (reciprocal control)	fraternity (reciprocal love and fear)	civility (reciprocal empathy and respect)
Status of Citizenship (vis à vis other social identities)	discretionary (one among many)	omincompetent (the only permissible one)	sovereign (the first among equals)
Ideal Ground (actual ground) is territory)	common contract (generic consensus)	common beliefs, values, ends, identity (substantive consensus)	common talk, decision, work (creative consensus)

the Israeli citizen is torn between the competing claims of Jewish birth and mission and the Israeli constitution and laws.)

Strong democracy places the democratic process itself at the center of its definition of citizenship. In this perspective, voluntary will is an active and continuing function of politics that becomes critical to the civic tie. Citizens are neighbors bound together neither by blood nor by contract but by their common concerns and common participation in the search for common solutions to common conflicts.

In actual democratic states, as one might expect, a compound notion of citizenship is at work: territory and birth are the condition of citizenship, whereas contract (the basis of governmental legitimacy), blood (the sense of a national culture), and common activity (practical politics as a process) give it its concrete character. Nevertheless, each form of democracy emphasizes a particular ideal ground and thereby endows its view of citizenship with a particular character. This point becomes increasingly convincing when we look more closely at the nature (as opposed to the grounds) of the civic tie.

The Character and Quality of the Civic Bond. As Figure 3 suggests, the three forms of democracy differ most sharply in their evaluations of the quality of the civic bond. From these differences emerge others that account for the forms' varying interpretations of ties to government, political style, civic virtue, and citizen relations.

In representative democracies such as the United States, citizens define themselves as legal persons and as autonomous parties to a sovereign compact. Their civic identities tie them not to one another but to the government, first as sovereign contracting parties, second as subjects or beneficiaries. The citizen is a citizen exclusively by virtue of his relationship to the government, of which he is both author and subject. His relations with his fellow citizens are entirely private and have nothing of the civic about them. This privatization helps to explain the fearsome civic anomie that has bereaved the Western democracies of almost all civility and has made representative democracy so hostile to the idea of communitarian ties among citizens.

It may also explain the civic climate—the political style—of passive distrust that has made America at once a bastion of private rights and a graveyard of public action. When the citizenry is a watchdog that waits with millennial patience for its government to make a false move but that submits passively to all other legitimate governmental activity, citizenship very quickly deteriorates into a latent function. Civic virtue remains, but it is a civic virtue that is defined by reciprocal control or *accountability*. Government is responsible to and for the body of citizens but is in no way comprised of that body. The chief device of accountability is representation itself, an institution that permits public watchdogs to spend most of their time pursuing their private business while functionaries and hirelings (delegates and representatives) minister to the public business.

Understood in this fashion, citizenship is only one of many roles available to individuals who live in a pluralistic society that assumes that all roles are roughly equal. "Citizen" becomes an identity on a par with "worker," "parent," "Catholic," or "commuter." It loses its ordering function (its "sovereignty") and its association with commonality and becomes synonymous with particularistic and mostly client-style roles, such as taxpayer, welfare recipient, special-interest advocate, or constituent. The very term *constituent* has been transmogrified from a noble word signifying constitutional author into a term for voter and thence into an almost derisive synonym for *client*—for the individual whom representatives must please and pacify in order to retain their offices.

Constituents of thin democracies are normally stirred into action only by constitutional crises and governmental defalcations; otherwise, they are content to leave the governing to others and to reserve their energies for the boundless private sphere. Aside from the occasional election, the infrequent letter to a Congressperson, or the biennial media event of a political scandal, citizenship reduces to either an exercise in client relations or a political insurance policy—a powerful fire extinguisher that reads, "To be used only in cases of constitutional conflagration."

Unitary democracy has a quite different character. It manages to remedy (or to avoid) many of the weaknesses and defects of thin democracy, but its version of democratic citizenship introduces new and more alarming problems. Because citizens in a unitary state are bound together by powerful "personal" ties that, at least metaphorically, are "blood ties," they understand their citizenship as a function of their relations with their fellow citizens. The government embodies the unitary community created by these strong lateral ties—the citizen is the community, which is the state—and thus functions directly in the name of the citizenry. "I am Germany," Hitler might have said, "and Germany is the community of pure-blooded Aryans, so that when I act, Germany acts, which is to say each and every Aryan acts." The point is not that Hitler *represents* Germany or the Aryan community, but that he *is* Germany; for it is precisely the aim of unitary communities to bridge the chasm between individuals and to forge out of single persons one organic whole—the people or the nation or the Collective Will.

Where thin democracy makes accountability its primary virtue, unitary democracy celebrates the more active and inspirational ideal of fraternity as its primary virtue. This is perfectly in keeping with the lateral ties that characterize unitary civic relations. Under the best of conditions, fraternity enjoins mutual love and respect; under the conditions of mass or totalistic society, however, it may motivate only through fear. Fraternity is certainly associated with a submissive political style, with a form of civic obligation that demands self-abnegation. The sociologist Durkheim thus cannot avoid concluding that in order for society to establish the rule of morals, the individual must "yield" to an authority higher than himself.[12] Goebbels, pursuing a much purer form of unitary community, proclaimed: "To be socialist is to submit the I to the thou; socialism is sacrificing the individual to the whole."[13] There is no Rousseauian dialectic here, in which by obeying others we obey only ourselves. Autonomy is sublimated; the political mode that results is sacrificial.

Associated with the political style of self-abnegation is the omnicompetence of the civic role. Whereas in thin democracy, citizenship is only one among many coequal social roles, in unitary democracy it is the only legitimate role. Other identities are not merely subordinate to it but utterly inconsequential compared to it. Thus can parents turn in their children as "traitors" in a unitary regime (that has democratic pretensions) such as Khomeini's Iran; thus are religion and art made to serve higher community goals in a revolutionary monolith such as the France of 1792; thus can money-making and childbearing be declared impious by a unitary sect such as the Shakers, where the religious-civic role is omnicompetent. In primitive unitary communities there is little need for actual force, because consensus is natural and the fraternal tie uncontested. But in larger, modern societies that have had some experience with multiple social identities and cleavages of interest, force becomes a necessary concomitant of civic omnicompetence.

Citizens in a unitary democracy need not fear the civic languor typical of thin democracy; but they face the still greater danger of an activist totalism. Where politics means too little to the privatized denizens of the representative system, it means far too much to the blood brothers of the organic community. On these latter, politics exerts a relentless pressure, and it leaves little of them behind as individuals. Such forms of politics are rightly feared by those who cherish liberty no less than community and who seek a form of public being that can preserve and enhance the autonomy of the participants.

12. Emile Durkheim, *Moral Education* (Glencoe: Free Press, 1961), p. 34.
13. Joseph Goebbels, cited in Erich Fromm, *Escape from Freedom* (New York: Rinehart, 1941), p. 223.

Somewhere between the wan residualism of instrumentalist democracy and the omnicompetent totalism of unitary democracy lies the public realm of strong democratic politics. In this realm, citizenship is a dynamic relationship among strangers who are transformed into neighbors, whose commonality derives from expanding consciousness rather than geographical proximity. Because the sharp distinction that separates government and citizenry in representative systems is missing, the civic bond under strong democracy is neither vertical nor lateral but circular and dialectical. Individuals become involved in government by participating in the common institutions of self-government and become involved with one another by virtue of their common engagement in politics. They are united by the ties of common activity and common consciousness— ties that are willed rather than given by blood or heritage or prior consensus on beliefs and that thus depend for their preservation and growth on constant commitment and ongoing political activity. Such latent virtues as accountability permit common ties to wither, whereas virtues as powerful and unitary as fraternity make ties rigid and immutable and place them beyond the pale of individual volition.

The political style that emerges from this dialectic of common association is one of activity and cooperation, and the civic virtue that distinguishes that style from other styles is civility itself. Strong democracy promotes reciprocal empathy and mutual respect, whereas unitary democracy promotes reciprocal love and fear and thin democracy promotes reciprocal control. Civility is rooted in the idea that consciousness is a socially conditioned intelligence that takes into account the reality of other consciousnesses operating in a shared world. As Michael Oakeshott has suggested, civility assumes free agents who are roughly equal, not necessarily by nature or right but by virtue of their shared consciousness. Oakeshott writes of citizens: "*Cives* are not neurophysiological organisms, genetic characters, psychological egos or components of a 'social process,' but 'free' agents whose responses to one another's actions and utterances is one of understanding; and civil association is not an organic, evolutionary, teleological, functional, or syndromic relationship but an understood relationship of intelligent agents."[14]

14. Michael Oakeshott, *On Human Conduct* (Oxford: Clarendon Press, 1975), p. 112. It is ironic that conservative thinkers such as Oakeshott have developed the idea of civility with considerably more conviction than have democrats—who one might think would benefit from this line of thinking.

It is neither in time nor in space but in the imagination that strong democratic citizens become "neighbors." Theirs is the neighborhood of creative consciousness struggling with material conflicts, in which the necessity that outcomes be commonly conceived disciplines the adversary competition of the divided and plural present.

The civic role here is not omnicompetent or exclusionary, but neither is it merely one among many roles. It is primus inter pares. Citizenship is not necessarily the highest or the best identity that an individual may assume, but it is the moral identity par excellence. For it is as citizen that the individual confronts the Other and adjusts his own life plans to the dictates of a shared world. *I* am a creature of need and want; *we* are a moral body whose existence depends on the common ordering of individual needs and wants into a single vision of the future in which all can share. The citizen does not define civic wants and needs; he develops common measures by which private wants and needs can be transformed into public goods and ends.

To return to the point from which we started: the ideal ground of thin democracy is *generic consensus*—a common contract that authorizes a sovereign, who is accountable to the contractees, to provide for their interests. James Buchanan thus describes democratic government as an efficient means of achieving our individual objectives.[15] The ideal ground of unitary democracy is *substantive consensus*—common beliefs, values, and ends that precede government and predefine the community in and through which individuals can realize themselves (these selves being defined by the community). And the ideal ground of strong democracy is *creative consensus*—an agreement that arises out of common talk, common decision, and common work but that is premised on citizens' active and perennial participation in the transformation of conflict through the creation of common consciousness and political judgment.

Evidently, the fact that all modern democratic regimes base their definition of citizenship on territory is of little consequence when set against these remarkable differences in their conceptions of civic

15. A democratic approach, Buchanan writes, "is merely a variant on the definitional norm for individualism. Each man counts for one, and that is that. . . . A situation is judged 'good' to the extent that it allows individuals to get what they want to get, whatsoever this might be, limited only by the principle of mutual agreement. Individual freedom becomes the overriding objective for social policy" (*The Limits of Liberty: Between Anarchy and Leviathan* [Chicago: University of Chicago Press, 1975], p. 2).

relations, ideal grounds, civic virtue, and political style. These differences, of course, do little more than reflect and enhance the sharp fundamental differences between the three types of democracy.

The Boundaries of Citizenship. If territoriality seems the obvious common ground of all modern forms of democratic citizenship, then universality appears to be the obvious common response to the question of the extent or boundaries of citizenship in modern democracies. It is indeed true that every modern form of democracy claims to extend the civic franchise to "all" or to "all human beings" or to "all members of the community." Yet that "all" is always conditional, and "universal" always refers to some particular universe with its own presumptive boundaries. There was a sense in which Aristotle endorsed universal citizenship for the entire human community—for each and every *zoön politikon* resident in the polis. But of course Aristotle did not count women, or slaves, or barbarians as fully human. Because they were incomplete, something less than *zoön politikon*, Aristotle could bar these individuals from the polis without compromising the ideal of "universal citizenship." Few tyrannies that have wanted to march under the banner of democracy have been unable to reconcile theoretical universality with the most arbitrarily restrictive civic practices—simply by ruling women or blacks or Jews or even the poor (Locke's "quarrelsome and contentious") out of the human race.[16]

Moreover, even those who most zealously honor the principle of universality find themselves bending the abstract boundaries of the biological species when dealing with the civic role of children, criminals, the insane, and "foreigners." Boundaries also tend to give way when one tries to sort out competing levels of citizenship (federal versus state versus local, for example) or overlapping civic responsibilities (national versus international obligations, for example).

The principle of universality conceals more than it reveals about the boundaries of citizenship. Apparently, a more precise and pertinent test must be found, one that will determine *how* boundaries are drawn rather than *where* they are drawn; for how boundaries are

16. Commentators from Rousseau to C. B. Macpherson have pointed to the inegalitarian implications of Locke's distinction between the "Industrious and the Rational," for whose use God gave the world, and the "Quarrelsome and Contentious" who—it would seem to follow—are entitled neither to property nor to citizenship (in chap. 5 ["On Property"] of the *Second Treatise of Civil Government*).

drawn affects not only where they are drawn but also how flexible or rigid, how reasonable or arbitrary, and how self-governing or independently grounded they are.

When one begins to ask how boundaries are determined instead of what those boundaries are, important distinctions become apparent. Representative democracy seems to posit a generic standard embodied in a fixed constitution; unitary democracy seems to posit a substantive standard embodied in a fixed identity; and strong democracy seems to posit a procedural standard embodied in a notion of dynamic activity. In other words, in representative systems the extent of citizenship is a function of *what we agree to* and thus a matter of contract; in unitary systems it is a function of *what or who we are* and thus a matter of identity; and in strong democratic systems it is a function of *what we do* and thus a matter of activity. In the third case the point is not that those who are citizens participate in self-governance but that those who participate in self-governance are citizens of a polity in which participation is open, access to self-governance is unobstructed, and participatory institutions are generally available. Of the three, this alternative would seem to be the least exclusionary, although it is also the most prone to ambiguity and thus to perversion and abuse.

Constitutional definitions of citizenship that are based on generic consensus can exclude from participation as many kinds of people (women or slaves or non–property owners, for example) as the consensus chooses to proscribe, but those who do count as parties to the contract receive firm guarantees of a permanent and inviolable citizenship, regardless of performance, as it were. The standard is inflexible and may in its origin be discriminatory, but it is unimpeachable. Unitary democracy is also capable of generic exclusion—of excluding those who do not fit into the substantive community or *volk* or tribe identity that is the basis of citizenship. ("All Aryans are members of the German Nation and thus citizens of the National Socialist State, therefore Jews cannot be German citizens.") But unitary democracy also guarantees a certain and irrevocable citizenship to those with the correct identity. In both representative and unitary democracy, the independent ground that allegedly gives politics an incorrigible, nonpolitical base also legitimates the drawing of civic boundaries.

Eschewing all independent grounds, strong democracy cannot develop arguments that exclude particular sets or classes of human beings from potential membership in the polity because they do not conform to a prior standard (such as a contract rooted in right and the binding character of all promises). The scope of citizenship itself becomes a subject for ongoing democratic discussion and review, and one's participation in such discussion becomes a brief for inclusion. This procedural conception has a welcome openness and dynamism, but it introduces dangers of a kind to which both representative and unitary democracy are immune. For instance, if activity is a measure of citizenship, will the lethargic, the apathetic, and the alienated be excluded, as Hannah Arendt seems to believe? Or do they exclude themselves and suffer defacto servitude even where their civic identity is constitutionally certified or unconditionally attested to by the blood that runs in their veins?

If citizenship is not a constant but instead a function of changing attitudes and historical activity, would not transient majorities, made powerful and intolerant precisely by the aggressive activity that signifies their civic legitimacy, have limitless opportunities to exclude the weak and disadvantaged? Because activity is power, the powerful will always have a special claim on activity. If the idea of open citizenship is not to become a one-way door through which undesirables are continuously ejected, it must be conditioned by the premise of biological universality. This concept maintains that every biological human being is potentially a citizen and that, consequently, the burden of proof must always be on the would-be excluders rather than on those who favor inclusion. Moreover, an excluded individual or class must automatically be reincluded in the absence of a conscious and determinate renewal of the exclusion (i.e., a "sunset" provision that limits every temporary exclusion).

Given the importance of active participation to the definition of citizenship itself, the autonomous individual would seem to enjoy a "right" of citizenship that he can forfeit only by his own action—which is to say, by his own inaction—and then only temporarily. This "right" is political rather than natural; it is created by the polity rather than prior to it. Children may be incapable of political action and so disqualified from citizenship, but they remain potential citizens and need only await the awakening of their political senses to claim their "rights." Criminals, as criminals, forfeit their citizenship not because they revert to the "state of nature" where any man may kill them (Hobbes), or because they shed their tribal identity by contravening the mores of the tribe (the true Aryan will not steal from the Fatherland), but because they have ceased to engage in talk, deliberation, and common action and have substituted private force for public thinking. If this definition enlarges the pale of criminality, it nonetheless displays a beneficence toward the criminal, who may reclaim his civic identity (if not necessarily his freedom from incarceration) merely by forswearing force and reengaging in dialogue. By the same token, immigrants in a strong democratic regime acquire the right to vote as they acquire the ability and will to participate.

This discussion should make it evident that the American idea of citizenship incorporates elements of each of the three civic formulas. A contractual element informs the legal conception of citizenship (the American as a person at law); a communal element lies behind the national conception of citizenship (the American as a native-born Yankee); and an activist element supports the civic conception of citizenship used in devising standards for "new" citizens (the American as a literate, participating actor). Consequently, the argument for strong democracy suggests not that we substitute civic participation for the traditional legal and national definitions of citizenship but that we give greater prominence to the role of civic activity. Measured by national identity and by the standard of the Constitution, there are more than a hundred million American citizens. Of these, however, most are passive, apathetic, inactive, and generally uninterested in things public. As Robert Lane has pointed out, a great majority of Americans count government (and the civic identity it entails) as a very small part of their "life satisfaction"—Lane's figure is 5 percent. Indeed, according to Lane, "Most people are unable to state how government affects their lives at all."[17] In the language of this book, this finding means that most people have no sense of themselves as citizens.

Definitions of citizenship that do not include a measure of political activity may seem wan and unconvincing; the citizen who does not engage in civic activity is at best a citizen *in posse*—the watchdog we have learned to know so well from thin democracy's prudent obsession with accountability and control. Unfortunately, the legal and communal definitions of citizenship have let sovereignty fall away from the American idea of civic identity and have replaced it with a sociological pluralism that makes every identity—the civic one in-

17. Robert Lane, "Government and Self-Esteem," *Political Theory* 10, 1 (February 1982): 7–8.

cluded—the competitive equal of every other. But civic activity, though omnicompetent only in unitary democracy, stands in lexical priority to all social activities in strong democracy. Because it is public it orders and guides all forms of private activity. These private forms may be more valuable and precious than civic activity, but they are nonetheless only possible in a framework of public seeing and within a workable public order.

If to make the civic role sovereign over other forms of identity resolves the problem of the relationship of public to private, it leaves open—indeed, it complicates—the problem of the relationship among the various levels of "public" activity. How do we rank neighborhood and national citizenship? Aristotle's principle of "the higher, the more sovereign" would suggest that national takes priority over municipal. But the fact that concrete local participation is greater and more intense than abstract national participation might suggest an inversion of those priorities. Certainly in practice the two levels seem to be in competition—at least as to how each would handle many particular political issues such as taxation, economic redistribution, educational opportunity, and so forth. The ideal solution is to bring the intimacy and intensity of local political engagement to the highest level of association while bringing some of the power of central government down to the neighborhood level. Some of the institutions portrayed in the next chapter aspire to do just this. In practice, however, the tension will remain and the commitment to intense engagement and vigorous participation will yield a more local and restricted measure for ideal citizenship than the commitment to sovereignty and to the all-seeing character of true public vision. As with telescopes, the higher the level of magnification, the dimmer the vision: as the compass of the public enlarges, our capacity to see publicly is diminished. The ideal of the world citizen is a splendid one, but the world citizen reaches the limits of public vision and seems to vanish beyond the pale into darkness. Finally, this is the problem of scale, which we shall review shortly as one of the several limits on strong democracy.

STRONG DEMOCRATIC COMMUNITY

If we were trying here only to construct a typology, we might advance the discussion of strong democratic community by proceeding analytically (enumerating key conceptual distinctions) or by listing ideal types (identifying clusters of concepts around logical or historical archetypes). We could use the analytic category of hierarchy to distinguish hegemonic from egalitarian communities; of ascriptive identity to distinguish status-ordered from voluntaristic communities; of mutability over time to distinguish static from dynamic communities; of scale to distinguish small-scale or face-to-face communities from large or impersonal communities; of jurisdiction to distinguish personal from territorial communities; and of grounding values or beliefs to distinguish spiritual from secular communities. Each of these contrasts suggests the dimensions along which the communal character of particular societies might be measured. Thus, the Swiss town of Glarus in the fourteenth century would appear as predominantly egalitarian, voluntaristic, dynamic, small-scale, territorial, and secular. The Holy Roman Empire of the German nation would look hegemonic, ascriptive, static, large-scale, personal, and ecclesiastic.

Historians and political anthropologists more often approach a subject by seeking clusters of characteristics that define types or ideal types, because such types correspond more readily with historical experience and its organizing categories. The "feudal corporation," the "tribal society," the "Renaissance city," the "community of true believers," the "modern bureaucratic state," or Ferdinand Tonnies's *Gemeinschaft* and *Gesellschaft* are not simply examples of clusters of communal traits; they are recurring archetypes in the history of man's social organization and of his theories about that organization.

But typology is not the aim here. Rather, we are attempting to clarify the notion of community as an aspect of the representative, the unitary, and the strong theories of democracy and of the forms of citizenship we have associated with these theories. It quickly becomes apparent that as when they discuss democracy itself, democratic theorists too often see community in terms of neat antitheses. On the one hand, the liberal democrat's purely voluntaristic community is an aggregate of interest-seeking individuals. These make up at best (in de Tocqueville's phrase) "a motly multitude" that pays for equality with conformity and mediocrity and that is free only because it is anomic and tied together by no significant social bonds whatsoever. On the other hand, the traditionalist's consensual community is bound together, in Robert Nisbet's words, by "affection, friendship, prestige and recognition" and nourished by "work, love, prayer, devotion to freedom and order."[18] This conservative notion of community, favored by sociologists who wear the Burkean mantle, makes the radically antidemocratic claim that "inquality is the essence of the social bond."[19] This claim not only polarizes egalitarianism and communitarianism but also explodes the integral notion of democracy itself as a theory of citizenship.

Thus the radically individualist community is populated by competitors whose commonality is understood as nothing more than an "efficient means of achieving individual objectives,"[20] whereas in the organic community of status and hierarchy the individual is altogether sublimated. These two rough caricatures in fact can serve nicely as models of the archetypical thin democratic community and of the archetypical unitary democratic community. The middle ground (strong democracy) is omitted. In the first case, the community of citizens results wholly from a social contract and owes its existence and its legitimacy to the voluntary consent of a self-constituted aggregation of individuals seeking the preservation of their lives, liberties, properties, and happiness. In the second case, the community is bound together by existential ties that define and limit the individual members no less than the community to which they belong. These ties, because they are primarily affective, historical, and unchosen, create a structure that can be hegemonic and inegalitarian. Although it does guarantee a place to every member, such a community often subverts equality.

Neither of these two alternatives offers a satisfactory picture of democratic community. The first commits the fallacy of aggregation, presupposing that a community represents *only* the characteristics of its constitutent parts. The second commits the fallacy of organicism, presupposing that a community represents *none* of the characteristics of its constituent parts. Thus, the thin liberal community lacks any semblance of public character and might better be called a multilateral bargaining association, a buyer-seller cooperative, or a life-insurance society. It eschews every advantage of affect, historical continuity, and common vision; it is, in typical reductionist fashion, a collection rather than a collectivity. By contrast, the traditional hegemonic community achieves the integral and public character

18. Robert A. Nisbet, *The Quest for Community* (Oxford: Oxford University Press, 1953), p. 50.
19. Robert A. Nisbet, *The Twilight of Authority* (New York: Oxford University Press, 1975), p. 217.
20. Buchanan, *Limits*, p. 2.

missing in thin democratic communities—but only by bartering away autonomy and equality. The vision of self-government by a community of equals is not well served by either of these versions of community.

In a strong democratic community, our third alternative, the individual members are transformed, through their participation in common seeing and common work, into citizens. Citizens are autonomous persons whom participation endows with a capacity for common vision. A community of citizens owes the character of its existence to what its constituent members have in common and therefore cannot be treated as a mere aggregation of individuals. The strong democratic community is not (at least initially) an association of friends, because the civic tie is a product of conflict and inadequacy rather than of consensus. But that community cannot remain an association of strangers because its activities transform men and their interests.

What is crucial about democratic community is that, as Rousseau understood, it "produces a remarkable change in man"; that is to say, through participation in it, man's "faculties are exercised and developed, his ideas broadened, his feelings ennobled, and his whole soul elevated."[21] Thin democratic community leaves men as it finds them, because it demands of men only the self-interested bargain and of community only that it provide and protect market mechanisms. Unitary community creates a common force, but it does so by destroying autonomy and individuality altogether. In the first instance, individuals are left alone; in the second, they are extirpated. Only in strong democratic community are individuals transformed. Their autonomy is preserved because their vision of their own freedom and interest has been enlarged to include others; and their obedience to the common force is rendered legitimate because their enlarged vision enables them to perceive in the common force the working of their own wills.

The perspective of the citizen and of the community, joined in Rousseau's account, are nonetheless distinct. Each serves the other, but conditions independent of the individual have a great effect on citizenship. Traditional democratic theorists have devoted much attention to these conditions, and with good reason. Some of the conditions support democracy, or are even prerequisites to it; these can be called *facilitating* conditions. Others are obstructive or *limiting*

21. Jean-Jacques Rousseau, *The Social Contract*, book 1, chap. 8.

conditions. Among the former are civic education, leadership, and *moeurs*, which lend institutional support to integrative and affective values that issue naturally from patriotism, public culture, philosophy, and religion and that are indispensable to the creation and survival of cohesive communities. Among the limiting conditions are the problem of scale, the persistence of structural socioeconomic inequality, and the ultimate uncertainty of public vision.

THE FACILITATING CONDITIONS OF CITIZENSHIP

Given the intractability of dissensus and the problematic character of even the strongest democratic institutions, most theorists have sought support for democracy in second-order facilitating institutions. The challenge they have faced is how to contrive institutions that facilitate democracy without supplanting it and that enhance participation without making it unnecessary.[22] The danger is that the nurturing of affective ties will impede genuine cognitive debate and that the enhancement of empathetic imagination will corrupt the capacity for moral autonomy. Thus a civil religion that is too powerful will impose consensus on individuals before they have time to perceive and assess their individuality and to identify the legitimate claims that arise out of it. Or a binding set of values encapsulated as patriotism can forge a people so uniform in their interests that conflict or dissent of any kind becomes tantamount to treason. Leadership that arouses popular feelings but preempts civic activity suffocates participation. The challenge facing strong democratic theory is to elaborate institutions that can catalyze community without undermining citizenship. With this goal in mind, we will survey typical supporting institutions, starting with civic education.

Civic Education. Civic education for democracy can take at least three pertinent forms: formal pedagogy (institutional schooling in civics, history, and citizenship); private-sphere social activity; and participatory politics itself.[23]

22. This is the problem Rousseau faces in books 3 and 4 of *The Social Contract*. He tries to give the procedural devices of the General Will the support of customs and mores, but these customs and mores suggest a form of unitary consensus that is inimical to genuine democratic politics.

23. I am concerned here with conscious forms of learning and of political experience rather than with "political socialization"—a phrase preferred by many political scientists but that I find both too general and too biased in favor of environmentalist answers to crucial questions of will.

Formal pedagogy, understood as formal socialization into the political community, is probably most useful as a training device for unitary democracy and least useful for strong democracy. A basic knowledge of the nation's constitution and legal system, of its political history and institutions, and of its culture and political practice is obviously indispensable to democracy in any form. But there is no necessary correlation between educational training and political or moral judgment, although there is a connection between knowledge and civic aptitude. The American system takes some responsibility for the procedural aspects of civic education through its election laws, equal-time provisions for the media, and enforcement of the Bill of Rights; but it seems little concerned to provide education on substantive issues. Like most other public responsibilities, this crucial function is left largely in private hands.

Strong democracy, in any case, relies less on formal civic education: knowing your rights and knowing the law are concomitants first of all of minimalist or weak democratic politics. In the strong democratic perspective, knowledge and the quest for knowledge tend to follow rather than to precede political engagement: give people some significant power and they will quickly appreciate the need for knowledge, but foist knowledge on them without giving them responsibility and they will display only indifference.

Local public or small-scale private activity seems to be vital to civic education in all three forms of modern democracy. It promotes affective links that support unitary democracy, measures of judgment useful to representative institutions, and forms of public thinking essential to strong democracy. De Tocqueville saw in local institutions and voluntary associations a key to national democracy in America: "Municipal institutions constitute the strength of free nations. Town meetings are to liberty what primary schools are to science; they bring it within the people's reach, they teach men how to use and enjoy it. A nation may establish a free government, but without municipal institutions it cannot have the spirit of liberty."[24]

Like de Tocqueville, many modern advocates of "mediating structures" and intermediate associations argue that voluntary associa-

24. Alexis de Tocqueville, *Democracy in America* (New York: Vintage Books, 1960), vol. 1, p. 63. Elsewhere in his classic study, he argues: "Civil associations, therefore, facilitate political association. . . . [A] political association draws a number of individuals at the same time out of their own circle; however they may be naturally kept asunder by age, mind, and fortune, it places them nearer together and brings them into contact" (vol. 2, pp. 123–24).

tions, church groups, and the family have an important democratic effect in guiding the elephantine nation-state and in giving a palpable local expression to the idea of national citizenship. Peter Berger and Richard Neuhaus see in such mediating institutions the only instruments of "empowerment" that can oppose the pervasive alienating effect of modern centrist politics.[25]

Local institutions can indeed be a crucial training ground for democracy. But to the extent that they are privatistic, or parochial, or particularistic, they will also undermine democracy. Parochialism enhances the immediate tie between neighbors by separating them from alien "others," but it thereby subverts the wider ties required by democracy—ties that can be nurtured only by an expanding imagination bound to no particular sect or fraternity.

Strong democracy creates a continuum of activity that stretches from the neighborhood to the nation—from private to public—and along which the consciousness of participating citizens can expand. "As soon as you are obliged to see with another's eyes," wrote Rousseau in *Emile*, "you must will what he wills."[26] The circle of common volition is only as wide as the circle of common perception; if perception and imagination can be made to grow progressively as the result of common activities, parochialism can be overcome. Participants who are active simultaneously in a local church, a municipal community board, a national service corps, a grass-roots political organization, and a national referendum campaign are more likely than a church deacon or a senator to perceive their activities as overlapping and mutually reinforcing.

Finally, however, only direct political participation—activity that is explicitly public—is a completely successful form of civic education for democracy. The politically edifying influence of participation has been noted a thousand times since first Rousseau and then Mill and de Tocqueville suggested that democracy was best taught by practicing it. De Tocqueville argued that participation could at a single stroke solve two problems. It could interest people in citizen-

25. "One of the most debilitating results of modernization is a feeling of powerlessness in the face of institutions controlled by those whom we do not know and whose values we often do not share. . . . [T]he mediating structures under discussion here are the principal expressions of the real values and the real needs of people in our society. . . . [P]ublic policy should recognize, respect, and, where possible, empower these institutions" (Peter L. Berger and Richard John Neuhaus, *To Empower People: The Role of Mediating Structures in Public Policy* [Washington, D.C.: American Enterprise Institute, 1977], p. 7).

26. Rousseau, *Emile*, book 2.

ship even though liberty demanded such an "arduous" apprentice-ship, and it could educate them to prudent self-government even when they comprised an "unfit multitude." Of the first problem—made famous by Oscar Wilde's complaint about the number of free evenings that could be taken up in the quest to become a good so-cialist—de Tocqueville wrote: "I maintain that the most powerful and perhaps the only means that we still possess of interesting men in the welfare of their country is to make them partakers in the gov-ernment. . . . civic zeal seems to me to be inseparable from the ex-ercise of political right."[27] Too often liberals have had it both ways: life is supposed to be a "ceaseless search for power after power unto death," yet men for the most part supposedly have little interest in civic participation. Of course when participation is neutered by being separated from power, then civic action will be only a game and its rewards will seem childish to women and men of the world; they will prefer to spend their time in the "real" pursuit of private interests. But, as the Hobbesian phrase suggests, most citizens will care for participation because it alone gives them power over their lives.

In addressing the problem of motivation, de Tocqueville also re-sponds to the question of motive. The most frequent complaint lodged against democracy has been the unfitness of the masses to rule. De Tocqueville acknowledges the point: "It is incontestable," he begins, "that the people frequently conduct public business very badly." Yet he continues: "It is impossible that the lower orders should take a part in public business without extending the circles of their ideas and quitting the ordinary routines of their thoughts. The humblest individual who cooperates in the government of so-ciety acquires a certain degree of self-respect . . . he is canvassed by a multitude of applicants and in seeking to deceive him in a thou-sand ways, they really enlighten him."[28]

False consciousness appears here as the road to political con-sciousness, because those who attempt to manipulate the popular will in fact help to inform it. As the Age of Populism proved, the rhetoric of self-government is hard to contain. And once implanted, self-respect is difficult to "use," because self-respect entails a new way of seeing oneself and the world. Lawrence Goodwyn, in his brilliant portrait of American populism, writes: "Populism is the

27. De Tocqueville, *Democracy*, vol. 1, p. 252.
28. Ibid., pp. 260–61.

story of how a large number of people, through a gradual process of
self-education that grew out of their cooperative efforts, developed
a new interpretation of their society and new political institutions to
give expression to these interpretations. Their new ideas grew out
of their new self-respect."[29]

It has generally been recognized that the political wisdom of representative statesmen and politicians is determined in large part by
the extent of their political experience. Why should it be different
with citizens? To rule well they need first to rule. To exercise responsibility prudently they must be given responsibility. Faith in democracy requires a belief neither in the benevolence of abstract human
character nor in the historical altruism of democratic man. Altruists
do not need government. What is required is nothing more than a
faith in the democratizing effects that political participation has on
men, a faith not in what men are but in what democracy makes
them. Strong democrats need be no more sanguine about man's *natural* capacity for self-government than was the skeptical Madison.
Unlike Madison, however, they suspect that empowerment renders
men artificially responsible, just as the art of politics makes them
artfully prudent—particularly when politics means confrontation
with the myriad others with whom a common world must be
shared.

Liberal democracy makes government accountable, but it does
not make women and men powerful. It thrusts latent responsibilities on them while at the same time insisting that they keep a wholly
passive watch over their treasured rights. For this self-contradictory
form of popular government there can be no adequate preparation
and no fit education. Strong democracy alone seems capable of
educating by practice and thus of preserving and enhancing
democracy.

Leadership. The role of leadership is as obvious in representative
democracy as it is problematic in strong democracy. In representative systems there are only leaders and followers; the efficacy of representation depends on this clear delineation of functions. "Lead or
follow or get the hell out of the way" reads a popular corporate desk
sign. Madison's benign view was that representative institutions are

29. Lawrence Goodwyn, *Democratic Promise: The Populist Movement in America*
(New York: Oxford University Press, 1976), p. 88. Peter Dennis Bathory draws out
the implications that Goodwyn's and de Tocqueville's arguments have for leadership
in his *Leadership in America* (New York: Longman, 1978), pp. 39–59.

the filter through which public opinion can be refined and corrected by a prudent leadership. In short, liberal democracy sees strong leadership as the sine qua non of effective government.

In unitary systems, even the more charismatic and overbearing forms of leadership—those that border on tyranny—have their proper place. Where the object is unity and cohesion, such leadership becomes indispensable.

It is only in systems where self-government and vigorous individual participation are central that leadership takes on a problematic character. On its face, leadership is opposed to participatory self-government; it acts in place of or to some degree encroaches on the autonomy of individual actors. The statesmanship of a leader such as Churchill may stultify the liberty of an admiring but passive followership no less than might the charisma of a Hitler. As a consequence, one might wish to say that in the ideal participatory system leadership vanishes totally. Complete self-government by an active citizenry would leave no room for leaders or followers. "Pity the country that has no heroes," says a character in Brecht's *Galileo*; "No, pity the country that *needs* heroes," replies another. It is the country that desperately needs leaders that the strong democrat worries over and pities. As the Mexican revolutionary leader Zapata is reputed to have said, strong leaders make a weak people.

Yet for all of this, actual participatory systems—either those in transition or those more familiar composite forms that mix participation with representation—are clearly burdened with the need for leadership. Among the factors that create this situation, the following are noteworthy:

1. The need for *transitional leadership* of the kind familiar in representative systems, to guide a people toward greater self-government.

2. The inescapability of *natural leadership*, which is rooted in the fact that legally equal citizens differ naturally in articulateness, will power, experience, personality, and other characteristics that affect the intensity and efficacy of participation even in the most egalitarian communities.

3. The importance of *facilitating leadership*, which makes participatory institutions work well despite the skewing effects of natural leadership.

4. The indispensability of *moral leadership*, which promotes social

cohesion and community and celebrates the freedom and individual dignity on which democracy depends.

The factors listed above suggest that three special kinds of leadership are pertinent to strong democracy: transitional leadership on the model of the founder; facilitating leadership as a foil for natural hierarchy and a guarantor of participatory institutions; and moral leadership as a source of community.

The process of transition calls for leadership in the tradition of the republican founding—for what traditional political theory calls the Legislator. The transitional leadership must invent participatory institutions that can support strong democracy without destroying or going to war with liberal institutions; then, like a founding leadership, it must fade away. Leaders who linger on into the operational period have failed: to be successful is to make oneself superfluous. The task of these leaders is not to dictate solutions of their own but to offer mechanisms for the participatory resolution of conflict, to contrive devices by which private sympathies can be extended and individual imaginations enhanced. Transitional leaders have no special capacity for measuring the public character of a democratic will; they possess no hierarchy of values by which the decisions of common institutions can be judged. They are originators, generic facilitators, who must themselves never govern.

It is easy to say what the limits on transitional leadership should be but much more difficult to ensure that men and women capable of leading will actually relinquish their leadership roles. This problem points to the second and more troublesome dilemma of strong democracy: How to deal with natural leadership and with the natural inequality it creates within participatory systems? The talents and capabilities that generate the sort of political skills needed by founders or by conscientious facilitators in a direct democracy are unequally distributed among citizens. Rationality, rhetorical finesse, imagination, persuasiveness, and articulateness are essential not only to leadership but to effective participation in common deliberation and common action. Traditional theory from Aristotle to Rousseau argues that the citizen is at once the author and the subject of laws. Yet common lawmaking in a strong democracy may make authors of some persons and subjects of others—depending upon the distribution of talent. Although each has a voice and a vote, trailer-park welfare clients in a rural Vermont town, for example, are likely to feel much less like the authors of their town meeting's business than the articulate lawyers and schoolteachers of the town who make their living with informed talk and persuasive argument.[30] Likewise, the personally appealing town altruist may attract more votes for a weak public position than the argumentative town misanthrope will attract for a strong public position. These factors operate even where economic and social inequities have been removed. How much eloquence can a common meeting tolerate? Is the heroic citizen too big for the democratic community? The Greek practice of ostracism tried to combat natural superiority, although it did so at a cost to leadership and to the competence (*aretē* or *virtū*) of elites.

For strong democracy, the fairest response to such problems is *facilitating leadership*. Every competent classroom teacher must learn the subtle techniques that can keep expressive and articulate students from dominating classroom debate at the expense of their more timid or inarticulate classmates while preserving the right of the articulate to speak and to grow. Every competent trial judge must learn how to instruct and guide jurors in the technicalities and possibilities of the law without encroaching on their ultimate right to reach an autonomous verdict. In strong democracy, offices rather than persons function to attenuate the effects of natural inequality and to counteract the skewing influence of natural leaders.

Like the teacher and the judge, the facilitator is responsible to a process rather than to specific outcomes—to the integrity of the community rather than to the needs of particular individuals. He is an ombudsman for the community who protects individuals only in the name of the community's interests. Listeners must be protected no less than speakers. Like speech, silence has its rights, which usually turn out to be the rights of the reticent, who need time and quiet and an absence of competitive talk to find their own voices. There is no final way to equalize energy and ambition in human beings, but some of the more inequitable effects of their maldistribution in a

30. Jane J. Mansbridge, in her perceptive study of alternative forms of democracy, investigated such a small Vermont town. She found that there, "as in many face to face democracies, the fear of making a fool of oneself, of losing control, of criticism and of making enemies, all contribute to the tension that arises in the settlement of disputes." Even more to the point, she remarks that "removing the legal barriers to influence, even in the open town meeting democracy, will not by itself produce either the political equality theoretically required by adversary democracy or the widespread participation and equal respect that sustain unitary democracy" (*Beyond Adversary Democracy* [New York: Basic Books, 1980], pp. 149, 125).

given community can be offset by effective facilitating leadership and commensurate institutions (see Chapter 10).

Transitional leaders who vanish, facilitating leaders who are politically neuter and who play no substantive role in the discussions and decisions they guide suggest strong democracy's skepticism toward leadership. Yet if democracy requires community, it also requires forms of moral and inspirational leadership that create and hold together a community. Yet in many ways these are the most dangerous forms of leadership. To embody and catalyze public loyalty, fraternity, and the spirit of common commitment to values beyond the selfish individual, democracy needs symbolic leaders of great spiritual stature—leaders whose stature can become a rebuke to men of merely average courage and conventional vision.

In the ideal participatory community, moral leadership must therefore be exercised *outside* the political arena, in a public but nonpolitical fashion that is conducive to fraternal affection and common values yet hostile to conformity. Otherwise, when moral and political leadership overlap, the need for social cohesion becomes confused with the disposition toward political unanimity, and inspirational persuasion by example becomes charismatic aggression by manipulation. The moral leader who incarnates the spirit of a community, and who thereby encourages a mutualist and cooperative approach to its conflicts and divisions, strengthens strong democracy. The moral leader who imposes his vision directly on the political realm, substituting his own perspective for political debate and deliberation, short-circuits politics and curtails democratic participation. Christ, Gandhi, and Martin Luther King were moral leaders who induced women and men to take control of their own lives in the name of principles greater than their own lives. Like founding leadership, moral leadership is self-liquidating. Such leaders are not like Ibsen's fanatic preacher Brand, who led his people up the mountain and then, when they could go no further, went on without them. They are more like Gandhi, who aspired to induce in his people a will to freedom that would enable them to go on without him. "Excuse me," Gandhi once said to a reporter, "but I must catch up to my followers."

Julius Caesar in Rome's faltering republic, Winston Churchill in wartime England, John F. Kennedy on America's dangerous new frontier were powerful leaders, but they led for their people and in place of them and ultimately diminished the popular capacity for self-government and thus for self-cure.[31] Eugene Debs went to the heart of this crucial distinction: "Too long have the workers of the world waited for some Moses to lead them out of bondage. He has not come; he will never come. I would not lead you out if I could; for *if you could be led out, you could be led back again.*"[32] To create a community in which men lead themselves, in which they can be moved only by the common will in which they participate—that is the challenge of moral leadership.

Morals and Values. The problem of how to exercise moral leadership in a strong democratic system, when reformulated as the problem of how to secure morals and values, is even more troublesome. As Rousseau expressed it, the problem is that individuals cohere into a community through the process of communally resolving conflict but that, at the same time, the ability to resolve conflict seems to depend on the community's prior cohesion and on a generic commitment to common values.

Without loyalty, fraternity, patriotism, neighborliness, bonding, tradition, mutual affection, and common belief, participatory democracy is reduced to crass proceduralism; it becomes hardly less mechanistic than the self-interested contractualism of the liberal state it purports to supplant. If a community is no more than an arbitrary collection of radically disparate individuals, its chances of forging a common vision by which disputes and conflicts might be mediated would appear to be very slight. Yet by the same token, a community held together by bonds as powerful as those afforded by civil religion, national chauvinism, tribal kinship, or any other form of unattenuated consensualism would seem to lean toward a unitary rather than a strong form of democracy and to be achieving its cohesion at the expense of individual autonomy, social pluralism, and participatory activity.

In addressing this problem, democratic theorists have always shown a strong impulse to imitate Rousseau and burn the candle at both ends. At one end, they have designed procedures that will work in the most individualistic and pluralist (conflict-ridden) cir-

---

31. Gary Wills writes in his study of charismatic presidential powers, "We do the most damage under the Presidents we love most" (*The Kennedy Imprisonment: A Meditation on Power* [Boston: Little, Brown, 1982]). Wills's book is a case study of how charismatic presidential power undermines democracy. For a full discussion, see my "The Unmaking of the President," *London Review of Books* 4, 18 (7–20 October 1982).

32. Cited by Mark E. Kann, "Challenging Lockean Liberalism in America: The Case of Debs and Hillquit," *Political Theory* 8, 2 (May 1980): 214.

cumstances, where community is a peripheral byproduct of participation. At the other, they have designed procedures aimed at building community, procedures that mitigate conflict from the outset
and give to participatory activity the support of a prior consensus.
The idea of civil religion is an example of this latter approach. Rousseau, like de Tocqueville, perceives in it one of the great legacies of
the ancients. In *The Government of Poland* he notes that the three great
founders of antiquity, Moses, Lycurgus, and Numa, "sought ties
that would bind the citizens to the fatherland and to one another.
All three found what they were looking for in distinctive usages, in
religious ceremonies, . . . in games that brought citizens together
frequently, in exercises that caused them to grow in vigor and
strength and developed their pride and self-esteem; and in public
spectacles that stirred their hearts, set them on fire with the spirit of
emulation and tied them tightly to the fatherland".[33] Yet the more
effective such affective institutions are, the less need there will be
for democratic politics, and the more likely it is that a community
will take on the suffocating unitary character of totalistic states.

In principle there is no easy solution to this problem. In practice,
however, the fragmentation and pluralism of most contemporary
liberal democratic societies would seem to leave ample room for a
safe infusion of communitarian values—particularly if, as with
moral leadership, these values are largely nonpolitical. Neighborhood ties and the affective bonds that emerge out of common activity are obviously less risky than patriotism, which in modern times
has often meant chauvinism or jingoism, and less dangerous than
civil religion, which has often spawned a style of fundamentalist
zealotry incompatible with the separation of church and state and
with genuine pluralism. In "mass" societies, the healthy communitarian need for common foundations and for a certain minimal
homogeneity quickly becomes an unhealthy quest for uniformity.
The United States would seem to live to some degree in the worst of
both worlds. It is torn apart by cleavages of every kind and can
hardly offer a meaning for the word *public* (note that *Public Interest* is
a partisan political journal and Common Cause is a private interest
group), and yet it can be politically intolerant and conformist in its
political culture. Activity is private, passivity is public; the public
will is diseased by purposelessness even as private wills are cata-

33. Jean-Jacques Rousseau, *On the Government of Poland* (Indianapolis: Bobbs-Merrill, 1980), p. 8.

lyzed by private incentives; centrism and conformity are prized, but they are not permitted to express themselves as a common public voice.

Ultimately, strong democracy must hope to compensate for the absence of positive common values with post-hoc affections of the kind that grow out of common activity. A good deal of common bonding goes on in the process of politics itself. Like players on a team or soldiers at war, those who practice a common politics may come to feel ties that they never felt before they commenced their common activity. This sort of bonding, which emphasizes common procedures, common work, and a shared sense of what a community needs to succeed rather than monolithic purposes and ends, serves strong democracy most successfully. One of the mischiefs of representative government, which insists on governing for a citizenry to which it promises to be accountable, is that it robs individuals of common activities that could form a citizenry into a community. Even if a representative regime governs on behalf of its clients with efficiency, equitability, and due respect for popular liberty, it will impair rather than enhance the people's capacity for lateral public ties and community affection. John Stuart Mill seems aware of this impediment, as well as of the dangers of a too-vigorous leadership, when he notes in *On Liberty*:

The mischief begins when, instead of calling forth the activity and powers of individuals and bodies, [a government] substitutes its own activity for theirs; when, instead of informing, advising, and, upon occasion, denouncing, it makes them work in fetters, or bids them stand aside and does their work instead of them. . . . [A] State which dwarfs its men, in order that they may be more docile instruments in its hands even for beneficial purposes—will find that with small men no great thing can really be accomplished.[34]

Something like this statement ought to serve as a credo for the strong democratic approach to civic education, leadership, and common values.

34. J. S. Mill, *On Liberty* (London: Dent, n.d.), p. 170. A. V. Dicey makes the same point, although he has far more libertarian intentions. "The undeniable truth," Dicey writes, is "that State help kills self-help" (cited by Milton Friedman, *Capitalism and Freedom* [Chicago: University of Chicago Press, 1962], p. 201). That this kind of argument is abused by those who wish to emancipate corporate America from government control does not alter the nature of the relationship between a too-paternalistic government and a too-passive citizenry. The alternative to Big Government is neither Big Business nor privatism unleashed but rather active democracy and vitalized citizenship—viz., strong democracy.

THE LIMITING CONDITIONS OF CITIZENSHIP

I have argued that citizenship and community can flourish only where civility is reinforced by education, where leadership does not undermine public activity, and where morals and values abet commonality without destroying autonomy and plurality. But there are other conditions that obstruct and limit the realization of these goals. Such conditions can be manipulated and compensated for, but they cannot be altogether done away with. Consequently, they become absolute limiting conditions for strong democracy and a continuing testimony to the imperfectibility of man's political arrangements and to the corrigibility of his political ideals.

There are, goes the old joke, four insuperable barriers to communism: fall, winter, spring, and summer. There are at least three barriers to democracy, particularly in its strong form: mass society and the problem it raises of *scale*; capitalism and the problems it raises of *inequality* and *privatism*; and the absence of an independent ground and the problem that raises of ultimate *uncertainty*.

Each of these problems can be treated with ameliorative strategies, but generally speaking they are more easily overcome by liberal democratic (and, indeed, by unitary democratic) institutions than by strong democracy—for which, it must be conceded, they present a special challenge. Together they stand as a critical caveat, which once again underscores how much tolerance and prudent skepticism must accompany all political activity and all political ideals.

The Problem of Scale. Modern democratic theorists do not conceal their conviction that democracy—above all, participatory or communitarian democracy—is an anachronism. In the ancient and early modern world, democracy was preferred, when it was preferred at all, as the mode of politics only of small societies and face-to-face communities. For better or worse, both ancients and moderns have insisted that an imperial scale requires an imperial government, or that monarchy alone is suited to large-scale states. Neither Montesquieu nor Rousseau nor America's founding fathers believed that the participatory principle could succeed in "compound" republics with large, diversified populations and extended territory. America's founders attenuated their democratic hubris by a host of compromises. Representation, the electoral college, the separation of powers, federalism, and bicameralism were only the most salient of many constitutional innovations aimed at adapting democracy to the realities of a pluralistic, factionalized, economically diversified nation of continental proportions. Strong democracy, in criticizing the debilitating impact of such institutions as representation and party government, seems to attack the very devices by which the founders made the democratic spirit viable in the new large-scale world. This wariness about unfettered democracy, which has been endorsed in recent decades by social scientists of many different political persuasions, cannot go unanswered.[35]

Before seeking solutions for the dilemmas the problem of scale raises—and there will be no easy solutions—we should understand several pertinent aspects of that problem. First of all, like so many political yardsticks, political size is an ordinal rather than a cardinal measure. It is relative both to psychology and to technology. How big is a big country? How many people constitute a "mass"? In politics there are no absolute measures of size. In a romantic liaison three's a crowd. But a dozen neighbors venting a common hatred in a lynch mob may well constitute a "mass." A million anonymous New Yorkers riding out a blackout or a blizzard together may act like a community of neighbors, and a baseball pennant can make sisters and brothers of big-city strangers. But an adversary proceeding such as a commercial lawsuit can make implacable enemies of small-town kith and kin. When William James called for a "moral equivalent of war," he was seeking a way to promote nontoxic forms of peacetime bonding and thereby to diminish the impact of scale. In his oxymoron "the global village," Marshall McLuhan dramatized the capacity of television to transform a variegated mass audience into a single small-scale community united by common values and beliefs. Yet, so relative can scale be, we also talk about a "retribalized" America, which suggests the existence of endlessly individuated small-scale groups and subcultures within our mass-scale culture.[36]

If, in Aristotle's time, the self-governing polis could extend no further than the territory a man could traverse in a day (so that all men could attend any assembly), the ultimate permissible size of a polis is now as elastic as technology itself. Jefferson still worried about scale; he wondered how democracy would work in the West, where

35. More detailed and thoughtful but nonetheless typical of the serious social science literature is Robert A. Dahl and Edward R. Tufte, *Size and Democracy* (Stanford: Stanford University Press, 1973).

36. Marshall McLuhan, *Understanding Media* (New York: New American Library, 1964), pp. 268–94 ("Television").

distances were "too great for the good people and the industrious" and where only the "drunken loungers at and about the court-houses" would attend county meetings.[37] Yet by the middle of the nineteenth century, both literature and journalism were rife with portentous declarations that the new age of machines would make possible the "annihilation of space and time."[38] The elasticity of scale had become a reality of American life, one that was underlined over and over again during the late decades of the nineteenth century as the steam engine, the railway, electricity, the internal combustion engine, and finally the telephone broke upon the nation, shrinking its territory in a series of abrupt technological convulsions and thereby transforming a vast continent into a single political culture. Today the boundaries of the technological community push against global limits. The electronic communications systems of multinational corporations and of international banks tie millions of workers in dozens of countries together more efficiently than their intimate bonds once united the citizens of a nineteenth-century rural county.

Once it is understood that the problem of scale is susceptible to technological and institutional melioration and that political communities are human networks rooted in communication, scale becomes a tractable challenge rather than an insuperable barrier. Because strong democracy depends so crucially on direct communication, it is particularly vulnerable to the corruptions of scale. However, it is also particularly suited to coping with them, through empathetic imagination, common talk, and common action. Self-interested clients, competitive adversaries, and alienated subjects deteriorate into a "mass" far more quickly than do active citizens; neighbors are less easily deracinated than are strangers and can assemble in far greater numbers before losing their connectedness. Measures that enhance sympathetic communication—"interactive" television, discussed in Chapter 10, is one example—simultane-

37. Thomas Jefferson, "Letter to Joseph C. Cabell," 2 February 1816, in A. Koch and W. Peden, *The Life and Selected Writings of Thomas Jefferson* (New York: Random House, 1944), p. 661. This is the famous letter on ward government, in which Jefferson decries the "generalizing and concentrating of all cares and powers into one body" and issues an injunction to "divide the counties into wards." The federal principle is, as the following pages suggest, another way to treat the problem of scale.

38. In his remarkable book *The Machine in the Garden* (New York: Oxford University Press, 1964), Leo Marx writes: "No stock phrase in the entire lexicon of progress appears more often [in nineteenth-century literature] than the 'annihilation of space and time' " (p. 194).

ously counteract the problems of scale. Or, to put it more directly, the problem of scale *is* the problem of communication, and to deal with the second is to deal with the first. Scale produces alienation (the sociologists claim), but by the same token in overcoming alienation one overcomes scale—at least to a degree.

The relativity of scale has a second aspect that is subject to institutional remediation: the relationship between size and structure. A half-million souls whose commonality is defined only by a single vertical tie to a central organization will probably feel more estranged by scale than would several million whose commonality is filtered through several levels of organization where ties are lateral and where participation is initially "local." Decentralization, federalism, and other cellular social constructions—for which Jefferson's ward system is perhaps the ideal model—treat community as a collection of communities. Jefferson did not envision a fragmented nation, but he did believe that in the absence of wardlike structures— "these little republics," he called them—"liberty and the rights of man" could not survive.[39]

Here once again the democrat's devotion to locality and participation intersects with the conservative's commitment to immediacy. In Burke's words: "We begin our public affections in families. We pass on to our neighborhoods and our provincial connections. These are our inns and resting places. Such divisions of our country as have been formed by habit and not by a sudden jerk of authority are so many little images of the great country in which the heart has found something it could fill. The love to the whole is not extinguished by this subordinate partiality."[40]

The conservative looks to immediacy and to the lateral affections of family and neighbors to bring the mighty nation down to a size where civic fealty is possible. The democrat looks to parochial participation and local activity to give the individual citizen a stature that will enable him to feel part of the mighty nation. The conservative's appreciation of community and the democrat's attachment to participation meet in the strong democrat's idea of direct political activity, which commences with mediate and local forms of government. Representative government makes a small number of citizens the mediators between central government and the mass of constituents, thereby doing as much to separate as to unite citizens and

39. Jefferson, "Letter to Joseph C. Cabell," in Koch and Peden, *Life*, p. 661.
40. Edmund Burke, *Reflections on the Revolution in France* (London: Dent, 1910).

their communities. Strong democracy prefers to develop mediating institutions in which all citizens can participate, thereby strengthening both lateral and vertical ties.

The chief difficulty of the cellular or mediating approach to scale is parochialism. As we saw in our discussion of citizenship, the spirit of locality can conflict with the spirit of the greater community by playing on parochial feeling, insular self-sufficiency, and the tendency of small groups to spawn "us-them" psychologies of discrimination and exclusion.

Burke was too complacent when he wrote "the love to the whole is not extinguished by subordinate partiality." In reality, the political whole and its political parts have been at war since at least the Middle Ages, when the centripetal tendencies of kingship and the centrifugal tendencies of feudal structure produced five hundred years of conflict over issues of jurisdiction and fealty. In response to these difficulties we must recall that strong democratic bonding arises not out of substantive commonality but out of common deliberation, common work, common empathy, and common imagination. We should also remember that this sort of bonding is more elastic. The communal imagination is like a rubber balloon: the initial stretching is the hardest, but after that it stretches with increasing ease. The accelerating imagination, like a rolling ball, gains inertial momentum as it moves; making the initial move from the rest position requires the greatest effort. Thus the bigot who finally learns to see something of himself in his black fellow worker at the factory will find it much easier to learn to respect the Jew and the Catholic as well. Participation at local levels permits the insular and the bigoted to gain some momentum and facilitates their eventual approach to those who lie at greater imaginative distances (such as the foreigner or the "Communist").

Yet these arguments in favor of the relativity of scale and of the mitigating impact that federalism can have on centralism are fraught with difficulties. Why not accept the far simpler and historically more relevant argument for representative government? Did not the founders of America choose the representative principle itself as their primary means of accommodating to the scale of their new nation? And does that principle not, by addressing the dangers of anarchy and faction without falling prey to unaccountability and tyranny, give to democracy the only legitimacy it can hope to have under the circumstances of large-scale modern societies? This is, obviously, the argument of liberal democracy. And although it is an argument against citizenship and suffers from all of the deficiencies spelled out in Part I, it does seem to present representation as a particularly apt response to the challenge of scale. As such the argument demands an answer from the advocates of strong democracy.

For our purposes here, we can turn to the answer offered by Robert Michels at the beginning of the century. Surveying the democratic aspirations of French syndicalism, Michels concluded that the evolution of representative democracy was inherently unstable. It followed a parabolic course: it was democratic enough in its beginnings but inevitably oligarchical in its outcome. The "oligarchical and bureaucratic tendencies" of representation were for Michels a "matter of technical and practical necessity" because they were an "inevitable product of the very principle of organization."[41]

In the behavior of the French Left, Michels witnessed the typical weak democratic attempt to maintain popular sovereignty by "subordinating the delegates altogether to the will of the mass, by tying them hand and foot." Yet this form of mandate representation was a surrender to specialization, expertise, organization, bureaucracy, and leadership, so that even when "power issues from the people, it ends up by raising itself above the people."[42] From this, he could only conclude: "Under representative government the difference between democracy and monarchy, which are both rooted in the representative system, is altogether insignificant—a difference not in substance but in form. The sovereign people elects, in place of a king, a number of kinglets. Not possessing sufficient freedom and independence to direct the life of the state, it tamely allows itself to be despoiled of its fundamental rights."[43] Moreover, as Michels astutely foresaw, the problems posed by increasing scale were made worse rather than better by representation, the very device that was supposed to compensate for them. "It becomes more and more absurd to attempt to 'represent' a heteronomous mass in all the innumerable problems which arise out of the increasing differentiation of our political and economic life. To represent, in this sense, comes to mean that the purely individual desire masquerades and is accepted as the will of the mass."[44]

Modern presidents talk about representing the people's mandate

41. Robert Michels, *Political Parties: A Sociological Study of the Oligarchical Tendencies of Modern Democracy* (Glencoe, Ill.: Free Press, 1915; reprinted, 1949), p. 33.
42. Ibid., p. 38.
43. Ibid.
44. Ibid., p. 40.

or the national will, but their programs generally reflect special interests; and in those rare cases where they do not (such as the Carter energy program), they are apparently doomed to failure. Common will, depending on common talk and common seeing, cannot be represented. Rousseau said long ago that the moment a people permits itself to be represented it is no longer free. The principle of will depends on autonomy and activity, neither of which can be delegated without destroying their essential character. The representative principle is not the salvation of democracy under conditions of mass society: it is the surrender of democracy to mass society. If scale is to be overcome, it must be overcome by the extension of strong democracy itself.

The Problem of Inequality of Capitalism. The issue of the relationship between capitalism and democracy has been plagued with controversies for which there can be no decisive resolution here. The liberal and libertarian tradition represented by such economists as Frederick Hayek and Milton Friedman has made the defense of individual liberty and voluntary market relations into an argument for the inseparability of capitalism and democracy. Since political liberty depends upon economic liberty, they claim, the only legitimate role for a liberal democratic regime is as a "rule-maker and umpire" to "determine, arbitrate and enforce the rules of the game."[45] The game, of course, is the free market economy. Democratic socialists focus on equality rather than liberty and are concerned more with justice for consumers (distributive justice) than for producers ("rights"). They assume exactly the opposite position from the liberals. Capitalism and democracy, they say, are radically incompatible; capitalism makes a sham of democracy's pretensions to genuine self-government.[46] Still other observers follow Schumpeter and deny that there is any necessary connection at all between the two concepts. These thinkers claim that capitalism is in any case doomed by its own inner contradictions and that democracy is a form of elitism disguised as popular sovereignty.[47]

45. Friedman, *Capitalism and Freedom*, pp. 25, 27.
46. A variation on this argument, that capitalism is compatible with liberal democracy and responsible for its bourgeois possessive character, can be found in C. B. Macpherson, *The Real World of Democracy* (Oxford: Clarendon Press, 1966), and in Macpherson, *The Life and Times of Liberal Democracy* (Oxford: Oxford University Press, 1977).
47. Thus Joseph Schumpeter devotes the greater part of his *Capitalism, Socialism and Democracy* (London: Allen and Unwin, 1943) to showing that "there is inherent in the capitalist system a tendency towards self-destruction" (p. 162) and that democracy itself is an elite arrangement by which "individuals acquire the power to survive by means of a competitive struggle for the people's vote" (p. 269).

The dispute evidently turns on definitions—of *capitalism* and *socialism* but most particularly of *democracy* and of such prime democratic values as *freedom* and *equality*. If democracy is popular government in the name of and for the benefit of individual liberty (the classical Lockean formulation), collective coercion in matters political or economic will always appear as illegitimate. This is the argument that Robert Nozick makes in *Anarchy, State, and Utopia* and that Frederick Hayek makes in *Law, Legislation and Liberty*. On the other hand, if democracy is popular government in the name of equality and social justice, collective coercion will appear not only as a necessity but as an essential aspect of legitimacy. The legitimate common will will be manifested as the community in action, exerting itself as a decisive instrument in shaping the common future.

Each form of democracy (weak, unitary, and strong) would seem to have a distinctive relationship with capitalism. The market perspective certainly seems to share with representative democracy the liberal understanding of freedom as the absence of external constraints on individuals as well as the liberal understanding of equality as the commensurability of autonomous competitors. Similarly, the socialist perspective shares with unitary democracy a firm collectivism and a sense of the priority of the whole over the parts. Yet in both cases, and above all for the strong democrat, there is a necessary trade-off between the values of capitalism and socialism. The energetic entrepreneur offers a more inspiring model of self-governing citizenship than the terminally passive welfare client. Yet those seeking a paradigm of community are unlikely to accept the free marketeer's vision of society as an aggregation of acquisitive individuals thrown together in a Darwinian competition whose outcomes are wholly unrelated to justice.

If the simplistic definitions of traditional economic thought were relevant, one might posit a rough correlation between capitalism and liberal democracy and between socialism and unitary democracy. The truth is, however, that neither capitalism nor socialism has much to do with the economic realities of the modern world. If we wish to make such central values as freedom and equality the measure of democracy, then we must regard them as the products rather than the conditions of the political process—which is to say that politics precedes economics and therefore creates the central values of economy and society.

In this sense, strong democratic politics neither requires nor corresponds specifically with particular economic systems. Nonetheless, three important factors can cause the outlook and realities of modern monopoly capitalism to interfere with and finally jeopardize strong democracy: (1) the doctrine of economic determinism embraced by economists of capitalism on both the right and the left; (2) the privatistic character of economic individualism and the market approach; and (3) the giantism of the modern, monopolistic multinational corporation, which has been the liberty-corroding heir to the independent, small-scale firm.

Strong democracy's commitment to the autonomy of the political realm from independent grounds (see Chapter 7) obviously entails a rejection of economic determinism. The materialist ambience rather than the social structure of capitalism (and of Marxism) is what alienates strong democrats. To believe that property or class relations are prior to political and social relations, to think that politics is an instrument of private economic purposes, to make political power a derivative of economic power is in each case to reduce politics to a logical inference from some nonpolitical independent ground. As with Marxism, which derives its determinism from the same post-Enlightenment historicist sources as does capitalism, it is capitalist logic and epistemology that offends democracy rather than capitalist institutions or even capitalist values. To be understood democratically, politics cannot be treated as the necessary superstructure of some determinate economic base: the very self-regulating quality that makes politics democratic also severs or at least attenuates its dependence on the economic. In their wars over which contradictions are decisive, which institutions most conducive to productivity, and which classes most exploited or misunderstood, capitalists and their socialist critics have not noticed that they share one deterministic and antidemocratic assumption: namely, that communities are incapable of making their own histories through common talk and action.

This discussion points directly to the second feature of modern capitalist political thought that jeopardizes strong democracy: its pervasive privatism. The doctrine of the invisible hand—that public goods are served by the individual pursuit of private interests—has a negative corollary: that the conscious political pursuit of public goods by private actors (firms no less than individuals) is destructive of private rights and values. Milton Friedman is thus perfectly candid about his contempt for the arguments put forward by liberals about the "social responsibility of business." "There is one and only one social responsibility of business—to use its resources and engage in activities designed to increase its profits," Friedman states.[48] These activities may even include attempts to subvert the market itself through the creation of monopolies—because the ultimate standard is the absolute right of individuals to act and interact as they please in the name of their interests.[49]

The problem with this argument, from the point of view of democracy, is not that it asks men to be greedy or competitive but that it asks them to be *unimaginative*. It asks the bargainer not to second-guess his "adversary" with empathy, for that would corrupt the exchange between them. It asks the buyer not to consider whether the seller is getting a fair price for his goods as measured by (say) his needs or by what he deserves (rather than by the market), for that would throw a wrench into the machinery of the market (people might begin buying shoes in part because shoemakers are momentarily a disadvantaged class rather than solely because they need shoes—which behavior would be, economically speaking, utterly irrational).

Economic man as a calculator of self-interest imperils democracy not simply because, as nostalgic admirers of the ancient polis have suggested, he is a mean creature of household wants rather than a nobler member of the sovereign ("highest") political community. Nor is the issue whether the studiously self-interested seeker of self-advantage is amoral or immoral. The danger is rather that the self-interested competitor in the free market, robbed of his imagination and then told that lack of imagination is indispensable not only to his personal success but also to the virtue of the overall system, will

48. Friedman, *Capitalism and Freedom*, p. 133. Lest any think this is merely the conceit of free-market economists, compare Friedman's statement with this passage from Lester Thurow: "Western economics is at its heart an economics of the individual. . . . Group welfare is, if anything, only the algebraic summation of the individual welfare of the members of the group" (*The Zero-Sum Society* [New York: Basic Books, 1980], p. 172).

49. As Schumpeter notices, this logic is self-defeating. Although it depends on the free market, the competitive firm aims exclusively at maximizing its profits, which it accomplishes best by destroying competition and the free market—that is, by creating a monopoly. Writes Schumpeter: "The perfectly bureaucratized giant industrial unit not only ousts the small or medium-sized firm and 'expropriates' its owners, but in the end it also ousts the entrepreneur and expropriates the bourgeoisie as a class" (Schumpeter, *Capitalism*, p. 134).

Thurow makes a similar argument: "The ultimate aim of every firm is to establish a monopoly position so that it can earn more than the competitive rate of return" (*The Zero-Sum Society*, p. 153).

be deprived of the only faculties that make possible common willing and the creation of political communities. Individuals taught to think as isolated participants in the market are unlikely to be able to think as common participants in the polity. Liberal democracy makes of this limitation a virtue by treating politics as an arena of market competition that is indistinguishable from economics—"interest-group politics," as it is known.

The third capitalist reality that poses a challenge to strong democracy is, ironically, the obsolescence of the capitalist model itself—and the corresponding obsolescence of most of the language and rhetoric in which the debate is conducted. Smith and Ricardo regarded capitalism as a dynamic and evolving system. Marx described and deplored its destabilizing and self-destructive contradictions. And at least since the time of Veblen and Schumpeter, few have tried to put the case for capitalism in its pure, entrepreneurial, simple market form, although libertarians such as Robert Nozick and Milton Friedman still offer homage to the ideal and polemicists such as George Gilder still extoll the free market in litanies designed to legitimize supply-side ideology. But to pretend that the free market or the voluntary contract or the small firm have anything whatsoever to do with the activities of giant economic bureaucracies—which are aided and abetted (and regulated and controlled) by a still more giant political bureaucracy—is simply ludicrous. The elemental capitalism of entrepreneurial risk-taking, of saving and investment, and of gratification deferred in favor of long-term capital formation and enhanced productivity no longer exists (if it ever did). A description of individuals and small firms competing freely to attract roughly free and equal buyers to their goods and services so that the producers may earn profits and the buyers may satisfy needs fits the Western economic system about as accurately as Marx's description of post-historical "Communist" society fits the Soviet economic system. And of course, in the absence of the elemental system, all the rhetoric about freedom, rights, markets, individuals, and equality—as well as the counterrhetoric about class, exploitation, surplus value, labor power, and economic parasites—is an archaic jargon employed in desperate invocation of a reality long since vanished.[50]

50. The jargon of economic determinism is used by both right and left. The right ardently desires to prove that monopoly does not exist (other than in its technical or governmental manifestations), the left to prove that classes do exist. Both sides carry on as if our choice was between productive free-market firms or working-class revolution.

The actual relations between modern "capitalism" and modern "democracy" turn not on abstract questions of freedom, equality, and the proper functions of "public" and "private" sectors but on the strange new Leviathans of the modern economy: the multinational corporations, the international banks, and the cartels (such as OPEC). These gargantuan organizations, too large and bureaucratized and far-reaching to be private, too irresponsible and unaccountable to be public, have revolutionized the traditional debate about capitalism and democracy. While polemicists in the White House and the universities continue to spout the rhetoric of the frontier—to invoke visions of heroes, adventurers, risk-takers, volunteers, and entrepreneurs—corporate managers are developing a more pertinent language of order, security, organization, bureaucracy, and rationality. In contrast to George Gilder's depiction of businessmen as altruistic adventurers who take brave risks on behalf of a timid society, modern executives rank among the world's most conservative risk-avoiders. America has not socialized its industries, but it has been a pioneer in what the social scientist Theodore Lowi has dubbed the "socialization of risk." That is, it leaves the profits for the private sector and places all the risks on the public sector, spreading them judiciously across the backs of the taxpayers.[51] What remains of the distinction between the two sectors once this process is completed? What sense can the free marketeer's plea for "freedom from planning" have under these circumstances? Why should the democrat abandon all control over the economic dimensions of his common life to a market that does not exist? Why need he pretend that elephantine monopolies that use their profits primarily to fund utterly unproductive takeover bids and unnecessary (and illiberal) merger schemes are better guarantors of his freedom than a government over which he at least maintains formal control?

The relationship of capitalism to democracy may remain problematic and controversial, but the relationship of the multinational, monopolistic corporation to democracy involves no such mysteries.[52] The corporation is incompatible with freedom and equality, whether these are construed individually or socially. Like the night

---

51. Theodore Lowi, *The End of Liberalism*, 2d ed. (New York: Norton, 1979).
52. The modern corporation, writes Charles Lindbloom, "fits oddly into democratic theory and vision. Indeed, it does not fit at all" (*Politics and Markets* [New York: Basic Books, 1977], p. 356).

in which all cows are black, it obliterates the distinction between private and public. It leaves room for neither the self-governing citizen nor the voluntary contract. It smashes the small firm and displaces the very idea of autonomous activity with the idea of systemic rationality. It can accommodate neither the contractual relations of the liberal democrat nor the affective relations of the unitary democrat; and it sees the common talk and common action—the empathy and the imagination—of the strong democrat as a grave peril to its orderly world of clients, profits, and planning. It is an enemy of democracy in all its forms. While the arid debate about capitalism and socialism goes on, the corporation prospers. More than does the problem of scale, it threatens democracy at its vital center.

If the corporation is not to defeat democracy, then democracy must defeat the corporation—which is to say that the curbing of monopoly and the transformation of corporatism is a political, not an economic, task. Democracy proclaims the priority of the political over the economic; the modern corporation rebuts that claim by its very existence. But unitary democracy is too easily assimilated to the unitary aspects of corporatism, with possible results that can only be called fascistic. And liberal democracy is too vulnerable—its citizens too passive and its ideas of freedom and individualism too illusory—to recognize, let alone do battle with, the mammoth modern corporation that has assumed the identity and ideology of the traditional family firm.

Strong democracy has no qualms about inventing and transforming society in the name of a democratically achieved vision, and it may be able to engage the multinational corporation in a meaningful struggle. Yet the corporate society and the corporate mentality themselves stand in the way of the idea of active citizenship that is indispensable to strong democracy. That dilemma, too, will have to be confronted if democracy is to survive. And though through workers' participation, the democratization of workplaces, and other schemes the corporate monopoly can be loosened, the ultimate battle—if it is to be winnable—will have to be political. It will pit not only democratic society against monopolistic corporatism but autonomous politics against economic reductionism in both theory and practice. As the editors of the *Clarion* of Great Britain said long ago, we must build up a nation of democrats before socialism is possible.

The Problem of Uncertainty. Of all the dilemmas facing democracy, that of uncertainty is the most poignant. Although politics is a realm of contestability and conflict where no independent ground can provide solutions, it is also a realm of inevitable decision and necessary action. The uncertainty that is part of the definition of politics vanishes the moment an action is taken. Yet measured against the uncertainty, the action must always appear somewhat fortuitous and contingent. The creative element that belongs to democratic deliberation and to common imagination introduces a tone that, in strict moral terms, may even seem frivolous. How can our human fate be the product of an experimental vision? How can individuals be committed to future lives that are no more than the inventions of a collective artifice? Are not the minimalist politics of a Hayek or the skeptical politics of a Popper better suited to uncertainty than the imaginative visions of the strong democratic community?

The answer is, "Yes and no." Yes, because common political decisions appear to run into error more swiftly than do nondecisions. No, because strong democratic politics is informed with a spirit of transience and circumstantiality that encourages community self-reflection and favors its self-correction over time. Politics understood as the application of independently grounded principles to a changing world runs greater risks of institutionalizing error than does politics understood as the creation of a vision that can respond to and change with the changing world.

The problem of uncertainty is for politics very much what the problem of regret is to morals, at least as Stuart Hampshire conceives of the latter. Hampshire worries that a powerful moral intentionalism can create a monolithic moral world that will exclude contingency and possibility. To the moral rigidity of the individual whose "purposes may harden into habit and heedlessness when comparison and reflection die in him and his intentions are fixed [and are] always formulated in his own mind in the same narrow set of terms," Hampshire contrasts the idea of "morality as exploratory thinking, as an unresting awareness of that which [the moral actor] is neglecting in his intentions."[53] The danger for morals and politics alike is "a morality without perpetual regret, because it is without any sense of the many possibilities lost, unnoticed." What is wanted is a process in which "metaphysical deduction may be replaced by a study of the successive forms of social life, and of the typical pro-

53. Stuart Hampshire, *Thought and Action* (New York: Viking, 1959), pp. 241–42.

cesses by which one form of social life, [and] with it corresponding moral ideas, is typically transformed into another."[54]

Without decision and then action, the absence of an independent ground can only bring on the paralysis of skepticism. Without regret, decision and action may come to mean intolerance, uniformity, and the loss of freedom. The political question—the problem raised by uncertainty—is: How can we institutionalize regret without paralyzing common action? How can we, once we choose a road to take, keep on the horizon of our common imagination all the roads not taken? How can we keep possibility alive when we cannot avoid acting?

As an autonomous and self-regulating domain of common talk and common action, strong democracy *can* keep alive both action and possibility. The empathy and the imaginative reconstruction of self as other which are typical of strong democratic deliberation encourage an awareness of what might have been in the awareness of what will be. And the transitory character of every act and decision, each only one in a train of ongoing reflections and modifications intended to transform citizens and their communities over time, guarantees a certain impermanence in the decisional process and a certain mutability in the world of action that accommodates and even honors uncertainty. To declare that democratic politics *can* do this is not, however, to say that it will. If the necessary steps are to be taken, institutions as well as attitudes are required. Such institutions would give to regret a permanent political voice and would give all the lost opportunities an ongoing place as women and men deliberate about the shape of their own futures.

Regret puts to the common will a fearsome question: "But how do you know? Is it possible that you are wrong, that your vision of a common future omits contingencies or nurtures pathologies that will be *my* undoing? *Our* undoing?" And because there is no answer to this query—no answer, above all, for those who sever politics from all independent grounds—the strong democrat must do all he can to build into the system of common talk and common action certain governorlike mechanisms of regret. This limit to judgment, so easy to identify and so difficult to come to terms with, is ultimately the limit of all politics. It reminds us not of the right of individuals to some abstract autonomy but of the vulnerability of social animals to uncertainty and impotence. It is our incompleteness

54. Ibid., pp. 242–43.

rather than our self-sufficiency that demands the tribute of regret; it is our impermanence and frailty rather than our singularities that remind us of the hubris implicit in all human activity and all human willing, whether exercised in isolation or in common. Strong democratic thinking and strong democratic doing in fact require a special cautiousness. Where men walk together, the risk to those who may stumble and fall underfoot is all the more dire.

Chapter Ten

The Real Present:
Institutionalizing Strong Democracy
in the Modern World

Once a people permits itself to be represented, it is no longer free.
(Jean-Jacques Rousseau)

The majority of the plain people will day in and day out make fewer mistakes in governing themselves than any smaller body of men will make in trying to govern them.
(Theodore Roosevelt)

Making every citizen an acting member of the government, and in the offices nearest and most interesting to him, will attach him by his strongest feelings to the independence of his country, and its republican constitution.
(Thomas Jefferson)

Strong democracy requires unmediated self-government by an engaged citizenry. It requires institutions that will involve individuals at both the neighborhood and the national level in common talk, common decision-making and political judgment, and common action. Liberal democracy has many faults, but it also has a well-established and relatively successful practice. Strong democracy may derive from an attractive theoretical tradition, but it is without a convincing modern practice. Indeed, modernity is frequently regarded as its nemesis and the scale and technological character of modern society are often offered as insurmountable obstacles to its practical implementation.

Our task in this final chapter is to place strong democracy in an institutional framework where its realistic potential as a practice can be assessed. If these institutions are to bear witness to the viability and practicality as well as to the coherence of the theory, then they ought to meet the following criteria:

1. They should be realistic and workable. For all practical purposes, this means that they ought to be a product of actual political experience. Ideal and utopian institutions can clarify and embellish a theory (the inventions of Fourier come to mind), but they cannot be the test of a theory that claims to be of practical relevance.

2. They should complement and be compatible with the primary representative institutions of large-scale modern societies. Although there is necessarily a tension between the theories, strong democratic practice can only come as a modification of liberal democracy. Realistic strategies for change cannot be revolutionary if democracy is their object, and reform cannot await the razing of liberal society to the ground—even if that were desirable (which it obviously is not).

3. They should directly address liberal anxieties over such unitary propensities of participatory communities as irrationalism, prejudice, uniformity, and intolerance. This means they must offer safeguards for individuals, for minorities, and for the rights that majorities governing in the name of community may often abuse. The difference between autonomous participation and mere consensus, between ongoing talk and mere voting, and between political judgment and mere plebiscitary decision-making needs to be given institutional expression.

4. They should deal concretely with the obstacles that modernity appears to place in the way of participation: namely, scale, technology, complexity, and the paradox of parochialism (whereby participation is exercised in local institutions that sap national identity and power is exercised in centralized institutions that bar meaningful participation).

5. They should give expression to the special claims of strong democracy as a theory of talk, judgment, and public seeing by offering alternatives to representation, simple voting, and the rule of bureaucrats and experts. In other words, they should make possible a government of citizens in place of the government of professionals.

The innovative institutions described in this chapter should provide a concrete starting point for those who wish to reorient democracy toward participation. Yet strong democratic practice requires not just a political program but a political strategy. Neither ideas nor institutions are self-implementing. They demand a base: a political movement composed of committed democrats who understand themselves to have an interest in the realization of strong democracy. This fact means first of all that strong democracy must offer a systematic program of institutional reforms rather than a piecemeal package of particularistic, unrelated modifications.

The institutions depicted below are inseparable features of one integrated agenda—not a cafeteria menu from which items can be selected at whim but a dinner menu with a prix fixe that must be accepted in full. Historically, the great reform movements have been organized around a series of innovations whose radical character lay in their common vision and force. The Economic Opportunity Act of 1964 through which the progressive Democratic program for a Great Society was set in motion took the form of a great many individual programs, including Community Action, Head Start, the Jobs Corps, Legal Services, Vista, New Careers, Foster Grandparents, Upwardbound, and Followthrough. But the impact of these programs, which redirected the energies of both federal and local government toward the interrelated problems of poverty, unemployment, discrimination, health, and welfare, was measured by their combined effect. Much the same can be said of the New Deal or of such earlier programs of reform as the cooperative democracy movement of the 1920s and 1930s, the populist movement of the 1890s, and the syndicalist movement in Europe. Each of these movements defined itself by a set of related reforms that depended for their effect on the fact that they formed an integrated system and reflected one common vision of the political and economic world.

The institutions offered here cannot be addressed piecemeal. Taken one at a time, they become more vulnerable to abuse and less likely to succeed in reorienting the democratic system. Citizen service isolated from a general participatory movement becomes one more form of conscription and one more excuse for civic alienation. Referendum and initiative processes divorced from innovative programs for public talk and deliberation fall easy victims to plebiscitary abuses and to the manipulation by money and elites of popular prejudice. Television technology put to civic uses is beneficent only where it is one of many means of civic communication and political participation. Wise political judgments will not evolve from local participation in neighborhood assemblies and community organizations unless local participation is linked to central power and given the discipline of genuine responsibility. Common work projects uprooted from significant changes in patterns of political participation and economic opportunity will degenerate into surrogates for workfare and the poorhouse and will be of no civic benefit whatsoever. Voucher schemes undertaken in a climate of antigovernment privatism will only hasten the death of all public seeing and political judgment, enhancing the private power of individuals at the expense of a public vision of our common world.

In short, the potency of the reforms offered here lies almost entirely in their capacity for mutual reenforcement when implemented in concert. By the same token, many of the justifiable criticisms that can be leveled at them are pertinent only to individual innovations taken in isolation. Adopted piecemeal or partially, such innovations will at best only be assimilated into the representative adversary system and used to further privatize, alienate, and disenfranchise citizens. At worst, they may even undermine the safeguards of liberal democracy without achieving any of the benefits of participation. They must be adopted together or not at all—and this stipulation should be in the forefront of every reader's mind in contemplating them.

For this reason, it is imperative that we adopt a programmatic approach in outlining a political strategy for strong democracy. There are a number of constituencies already mobilized that might take an interest in a systematic program of participatory reform. These include public-interest pressure groups that, while they have assumed the posture and tactics of special-interest lobbies, are distinctively radical in their concern for public thinking and common values—for the public good; local community action and neighborhood groups and the umbrella organizations that have sprung up to give them a common forum;[1] citizen movements such as those that

1. Local neighborhood groups and community action organizations have sprung up throughout the nation, often to fight city hall but also to give a voice to otherwise powerless local communities. These groups have in turn joined together for mutual support in such regional and national organizations as the National Association of Neighborhoods, the Center for Community Change, the Conference on Alternative State and Local Policies, the Center for Community Economic Development, the Movement for Economic Justice, the National Center for Urban Ethnic Affairs, the National Congress of Neighborhood Women, Rural America, the Youth Project,

created the Green Party in the Federal Republic of Germany and that have spontaneously formed around the issue of a nuclear-weapons freeze; neighborhood government enthusiasts inspired by the model of the New England town meeting; and followers of such recent theorists of small-scale economics and neighborhood government as Milton Kotler, Karl Hess, and E. F. Schumacher.[2]

Yet although these groups play an increasingly important role in the political process, the public at large has no specified constituency in America's pluralist politics—where the private character of an interest remains its passport to political respectability. Individuals living under the spell of elite/mass politics tend to see themselves in terms of their economic, social, or ethnic interests and to mobilize solely in the name of those interests. Those who are powerless in the system fail to mobilize at all and fall away largely unnoticed.[3]

How then can we expect either the self-interested or the apathetic to identify with a program of participation and civic renewal in which their most immediate interests would be ignored, at least in the short run? Through persuasion, through the self-education yielded by democratic participation itself, and through the logic of political priority, which demonstrates that even in a privatistic politics dominated by economic interests, it is only the autonomy of politics and the rights of citizens that give modern women and men the real power to shape their common lives. The taste for participation is whetted by participation: democracy breeds democracy. In each

and—perhaps the best known—the Association of Community Organizations for Reform Now (ACORN). These groups and many others like them are part of what Harry C. Boyte has called the "new citizen movement" in his important study, *The Backyard Revolution: Understanding the New Citizen Movement* (Philadelphia: Temple University Press, 1981).

2. See for example Milton Kotler, *Neighborhood Government: The Local Foundations of Political Life* (Indianapolis: Bobbs-Merrill, 1960); David Morris and Karl Hess, *Neighborhood Power: The New Localism* (Boston: Beacon Press, 1975); and E. F. Schumacher, *Small Is Beautiful* (New York: Harper Torchbooks, 1973). Other seminal works include Saul Alinksy, *Reveille for Radicals* (New York: Vintage Books, 1969); Paul and Percival Goodman, *Communitas* (New York: Vintage Books, 1960); and Murray Bookchin, *Post-Scarcity Anarchism* (Berkeley: Ramparts Press, 1971).

3. Frances Fox Piven and Richard A. Cloward have given a convincing account of the relationship between community action and welfare in their study of the welfare protest movement of the 1960s (*Regulating the Poor: The Functions of Public Welfare* [New York: Vintage Books, 1971]). They take up the normative question of mobilizing the poor for political action in *The Politics of Turmoil: Poverty, Race, and the Urban Crisis* (New York: Vintage Books, 1975). The relationship between policy and community in general is treated in an imaginative, democratic fashion by David E. Price, *The "Quest for Community" and Public Policy* (Bloomington, Ind.: The Poynter Foundation, 1977).

of the great American movements of political reform, from populism and progressivism to the civil-rights movement, a little experience with self-government and political action inspired a desire for
a great deal more. Surveys and polls suggest over and over again
that while citizens distrust politics in the abstract, they desire concrete participation and work to enlarge the scope of that participation when they have once experienced it.[4]

Strong democracy can have no special-interest partisans, but it is
a cause that, like the original movement for suffrage, makes potential supporters of every citizen. We have become accustomed to
thinking that men will fight fiercely only for private right and economic advantage, but historically they have fought fiercely for political right as well. Strong democracy looks to wage a second war for
suffrage, a second campaign to win the substance of citizenship
promised but never achieved by the winning of the vote. We have
the same interest in a substantive victory that we had in the original
formal victory: the liberation of women and men from bondage to
others, and to privatism, through the legitimation of participatory
self-government and the democratic creation of a common good. In
this struggle, politics is always prior to economics, for it remains the
sovereign realm in which the ordering of human priorities takes
place. The victory of man over bondage will occur there, or not at
all.

In order to give some system to the following presentation of institutional reforms, I have organized them around the categories
precipitated by the theory of strong democracy: namely, strong
democratic talk (deliberation, agenda-setting, listening, empathy);
strong democratic decision-making (public decision, political judgment, common policy-making); and strong democratic action (common work, community action, citizen service). Because a number of
the reforms serve several functions at once, none rests altogether
satisfactorily in its slot. But as the three categories themselves over-

4. For example, in 1977 the Exploratory Project for Economic Alternatives released
a report entitled "Strengthening Citizen Access and Governmental Accountability."
Having canvassed citizen involvement in government, the researchers reported that
"contrary to popular myth . . . citizens do not want less government involvement in
the economy. They strongly support public responsibility, but under a modern banner which could well read, 'No regulation without citizen representation.' They are
demanding a direct role in the administrative and judicial processes which have
largely excluded them" (Quoted in *The New York Times*, 3 July 1977).

lap, this characteristic ought not to occasion any great surprise or difficulty.

My classification is also alive to the differences between reforms aimed primarily at promoting local participation and those that envision participation at higher and thus more power-centered levels of government. I have insisted that strong democracy entails both the intimacy and the feasibility of local participation *and* the power and responsibility of regional and national participation, and the reforms offered here are geared to both levels. This is not to say that strong democracy aspires to civic participation and self-government on all issues at all times in every phase of government, both national and local. Rather, it projects some participation some of the time on selected issues on both national and local levels of power. If all of the people can participate some of the time in some of the responsibilities of governing, then strong democracy will have realized its aspirations.

INSTITUTIONALIZING STRONG DEMOCRATIC TALK

1. *Neighborhood Assemblies*. Hannah Arendt begins her discussion of revolution by reminding us that Jefferson "had at least a foreboding of how dangerous it might be to allow a people a share in public power without providing them at the same time with more public space than the ballot box and more opportunity to make their own voices heard in public than election day."[5] Citizens of Western democracies can vote for those who will govern them but rarely for the policies by which they are governed; more rarely still are they provided the opportunity to create their own agendas through permanent public discourse.

Every democracy rests on what de Tocqueville called the local spirit of liberty, and every democratic revolution has begun with a commitment to pervasive local participation—in town meetings or communes or revolutionary societies or committees of correspondence or soviets. The township may not have come "directly from the hand of God," as de Tocqueville liked to say, but it has always been the basic building block of democratic societies, the indispensable local forum that made talk possible. Without talk, there can be no democracy. Whether in a marketplace, a public square (like the ancient Greek agora), a country store, a barber shop, a school board,

5. Hannah Arendt, *On Revolution* (New York: Viking Books, 1965), p. 256.

or a town meeting, democracy must have its local talk shop, its neighborhood parliament. The objective is not yet to exercise power or make policy: it is to create the conditions for the exercise of power—to instill civic competence.

It is one of the ironies of the American form of government that no uniform nationwide system of local participation has ever been instituted or even considered. Jefferson outlined a plan for ward government throughout the young nation that might have given it a participatory infrastructure from the outset—"Divide the country into wards!" was for a time his motto. But most of the founders concurred with Madison in his distrust of direct participation and hastened to insulate the republic against its tumultuous populace by means of representation. Today there are direct democratic assemblies only in a handful of Northeastern states—thirteen in all—and only the town meetings of Vermont, Massachusetts, and Connecticut continue to play a significant role in local government and in the nation's democratic imagery.[6] Where they persist, these spirited local institutions are still cherished.[7] The last time a town in Massachusetts yielded its assembly form of government was in 1922. And even where, as in Connecticut, the town meeting lacks inherent powers, its competences remain far-reaching in a surprising number of areas.[8]

Urban areas outside of the Northeast have not enjoyed town-meeting government but they have in recent decades developed surrogate forms of local participation, both as a consequence of antigovernment community-action groups and of governmental policies of decentralization.[9] City charters increasingly rely on commu-

6. According to the *Municipal Yearbook for 1981* (Washington, D.C.: International City Management Association, 1981), fewer than one thousand towns today hold such meetings, a number of which are representative town meetings with citizens participating only via selected delegates. The town meetings are concentrated in Massachusetts, Vermont, Connecticut, New Hampshire, New York, Rhode Island, New Jersey, and Maine.

7. Frank M. Bryan reports that there is "overwhelming support for the town meetings around the state" in Vermont in his "Town Meeting Government Still Supported in Vermont," *National Civic Review* no. 6 (July 1972): 349.

8. Max R. White notes that the state of Connecticut has delegated to its town meetings powers over local ordinances, fines, liquor laws, motorboats, sidewalks, blue laws, movies, traffic, local school matters, elections, health and sanitation, highways and streets, libraries, graveyards, planning and zoning, parks, trees, water, welfare, recreation, and local police and judicial functions (*The Connecticut Town Meeting* [Storrs, Conn.: University of Connecticut Press, 1951]).

9. Decentralization and neighborhood control were introduced in Newton, Massachusetts, in 1971; in Honolulu, Hawaii, in 1972; in Detroit in 1973; and in Pittsburgh and in Washington, D.C., thereafter. Anchorage, Alaska, now has a "community

nity boards, neighborhood councils, little town halls, local zoning and school boards, and other similar instruments of civic participation at the block or neighborhood level. Extragovernmental bodies have also sprung up in middle-class urban neighborhoods; these block and neighborhood associations often originate in a concern over crime but quickly burgeon into full-fledged community organizations. The local-option groups organized to defend local interests in poorer neighborhoods have also gained some momentum, although the withdrawal of federal funding from central city areas in recent years has exacted a price.

Rural America (outside of the Northeast) has had its granges and its fraternal associations, and it still carries the seeds of the civic potential that once burst forth in the populist and progressive movements. The absence of palpable institutions is the primary obstacle today to greater local activity in the Plains states and the Southwest.

Yet for all the spirit of localism, America still has no nationwide system of local civic participation. For this reason, the first and most important reform in a strong democratic platform must be the introduction of a national system of *neighborhood assemblies* in every rural, suburban, and urban district in America. Political consciousness begins in the neighborhood. As Milton Kotler has written, "It is in the neighborhood . . . that people talk to each other and amplify their feelings until they move to recover the source of value in their lives. They move towards objects that neighbors understand and share— namely, the community and its self-rule."[10] Neighborhood assemblies can probably include no fewer than five thousand citizens and certainly no more than twenty-five thousand; Wakefield, Massachu-

---

council system"; Dayton, Ohio, has six participatory planning districts; and Birmingham, Alabama, has divided its population of three hundred thousand into eighty-six neighborhoods. Los Angeles has long had branch city halls. See John Hammer, "Neighborhood Control," *Editorial Research Reports* 2, 16 (October 1975).

In what is perhaps the best-known case of decentralization, the city of New York revised its city charter in 1975 to strengthen the fifty-nine community districts (and community boards) into which the city was divided; the revision also merged and strengthened the community planning boards and "little city halls" of the 1960s. For conflicting views on how well the decentralized system works, see Maurice Carroll, "Neighborhoods Gain New Power in Political Shift," *New York Times*, 19 February 1979; and Lydia Chavez, "Decentralized City: We Don't Pick Up, We Don't Deliver," *New York Magazine*, 14 January 1980.

10. Milton Kotler, *Neighborhood Government*, p. 2. For similiar views see the works cited in note 2 and also James V. Cunningham, *The Resurgent Neighborhood* (Notre Dame, Ind.: Fides, 1965), and Douglas Yates, *Neighborhood Democracy: The Politics and Impacts of Decentralization* (Lexington, Mass.: Heath, 1973).

setts, maintains a town meeting of nearly twenty-six thousand but that is clearly the outside limit. In a densely settled urban neighborhood, a block or two can comprise the neighborhood; on a Kansas prairie, thousands of square miles may be involved.

Because the objective of a neighborhood-assembly system would initially be limited to talk and deliberation, assemblies could be founded as forums for public discussion of both local issues and regional and national referenda without encroaching on the present delegation of governmental responsibility and authority. Civic education would eventually engender civic competence, and in time the assemblies would become potential repositories of local decision-making and community action. However, the quest for neighborhood autonomy and self-rule would be separated from the quest for neighborhood consciousness, and only the latter would be on the assembly's early agenda.

The neighborhood assemblies would meet often, perhaps weekly, at times when working people and parents could attend (perhaps Saturday afternoon and Wednesday evening on a rotating basis). With the meetings conducted as an open and ongoing forum for the discussion of a flexible and citizen-generated agenda, individuals could attend at their convenience, without feeling that each and every meeting was obligatory. Free, initially, from responsibility for decision, such assemblies might be liberated from the partisan pressures of sectarian economic and social special-interest groups. In the early phase, before they assumed decision-making responsibility, their business would be threefold: to ensure local accountability, to deliberate on issues (and set agendas), and to act as ombudsman.

Ensuring the accountability of American political officials is generally the responsibility of the press, the media, and the opposition party. Neighborhood assemblies would shift some of this responsibility directly to the citizenry, permitting individuals to question their representatives on a regular basis in their own home territory and according to their own rules of procedure. A regular "question period" like that of the British Parliament would tie elected officials more closely to their constituents and act as a force of civic education for the community at large.

To deliberate on issues and form an agenda would presumably be the first priority of the neighborhood assemblies. The local assembly would provide an appropriate forum for the local discussion of regional and national issues (which might be part of an initiative and referendum process or might be on the agenda of state or national assemblies), on a scale where individuals would feel able to participate. Citizens could examine different legislative positions in detail, assess the local impact of regional and national bills, explore ideological stances in the absence of pressures from special-interest groups, and introduce new questions of interest to the neighborhood that are not on any local or regional agendas.

Finally, the neighborhood assembly would offer an accessible forum for the venting of grievances, the airing of local disputes, and the defense of neighborhood interests. It could thus serve as a kind of institutional ombudsman for individuals and the community. The art of listening praised in Chapter 8 would be given a home.

In their second phase of development, neighborhood assemblies would become voting constituencies for regional and national referenda (see below) and possibly act as community units in systems of civic telecommunications (see below). They might also come to act—town-meeting style—as local legislative assemblies for those neighborhood statutes over which the locality had jurisdictional competence.

In order that the neighborhood assembly be given permanence, it should have a physical home in the neighborhood. Initially a multiple-use building such as a school or community recreation hall could be used, but eventually it would be prudent to find a permanent civic home for the assembly where deliberation, voting, civic telecommunication hookups, and other public services could be accommodated. To talk where one votes and to vote where one debates, to debate where one learns (through television debates, for example) and to learn in a civic fashion where one talks is to integrate the several civic functions in a way that nurtures public seeing and strengthens political judgment. A physical home for the neighborhood assembly would thus become a home to citizens—a truly public space in which women and men could acknowledge their citizenship in brick and mortar. For too long citizenship has been an identity with no fixed address and no permanent residence.

To protect the rights of the quiet as well as of the aggressive, and to make the assembly an effective forum for building agendas and debating issues, an office of "facilitator" would be created to complement the assembly chairperson and secretary (record-keeper). This office would be occupied by a highly trained civil official, possibly one who had worked in the federal civil service outside the neighborhood being served. Facilitators, who would have no voting power, would be committed to the rules of fair discussion, open debate, and judicious outcomes and would not participate in any substantive fashion in discussion or debates. Like a judge in a courtroom, they would make their responsibility for the decorum of the assembly the basis for supervising and intervening in the proceedings in the name of fairness and openness. They would be allowed to overrule the chair but could in turn be overruled by the assembly, and they would clearly enjoy authority only to the extent that they earned it through their conduct of public business.

Liberal critics of participation, imbued with the priorities of privatism, will continue to believe that the neighborhood-assembly idea will falter for lack of popular response. "Voters," writes Gerald Pomper, "have too many pressing tasks, from making money to making love, to follow the arcane procedures of government."[11] If the successful and industrious will not participate because they are too busy, and the poor and victimized will not participate because they are too apathetic, who will people the assemblies and who will give to talk a new democratic life? But of course people refuse to participate only where politics does not count—or counts less than rival forms of private activity. They are apathetic because they are powerless, not powerless because they are apathetic. There is no evidence to suggest that once empowered, a people will refuse to participate. The historical evidence of New England towns, community school boards, neighborhood associations, and other local bodies is that participation fosters more participation.

The greater danger for the neighborhood-assembly idea would come from the success, not the failure, of participation: from the tendency of communes and local assemblies to fall prey to peer pressure, eloquence, social conformity, and various forms of sub-rosa manipulation and persuasion not known in larger adversary systems. Thus, in his provocatively one-sided account of prerevolutionary New England (Puritan) towns, Michael Zuckerman contended that "sociability and its attendant constraints have always governed the American character more than the individualism we vaunt."[12] And Jane J. Mansbridge found considerable evidence that

11. Gerald Pomper, "The Contribution of Political Parties to Democracy," in Pomper, ed., *Party Renewal in America* (New York: Praeger, 1980), p. 7.

12. Michael Zuckerman, *Peaceable Kingdoms: New England Towns in the Eighteenth Century* (New York: Knopf, 1970), p. vii.

justice was skewed and fairness corrupted by social coercion in the modern Vermont town meeting she studied.[13] Historical studies of communal self-government in Switzerland have uncovered evidence of the same abuses, which are peculiar to parochialized, hothouse communities governed autonomously from within.[14] But urban neighborhoods and rural regions are no longer seared by Puritan zest, and local assemblies in modern America are more likely to be troubled by mirror-image sectarianism and special-interest conflict than by uniformitarian coerciveness. In his recent study of neighborhood democracy, Douglas Yates reports that "there was almost no evidence of monopolistic control by either minorities or majorities. In fact," he concludes, "just the opposite pattern obtained. Widespread internal conflict was the dominant characteristic of neighborhood governance."[15] As one element in the American pluralist pressure system, the neighborhood assembly would be unlikely to reproduce the consensualist pressure of the villages and towns of an earlier era.

David Morris and Karl Hess have evoked how intensely "a sense of neighborhood haunts our history and our fondest memories."[16] It is time to rescue the neighborhood from nostalgia and restore it to its position as the cellular core of the democratic body politic.

2. Television Town Meetings and a Civic Communications Cooperative. Neighborhood assemblies offer vital forums for ongoing political talk, but they reach only local constituencies and can divide and parochialize both regions and the nation as a whole. Forums for regional and national talk are needed as well. Representative assemblies on the model of the representative town meetings can solve the problem of scale, particularly if their members are selected by lot (see below). But representation is always a second-order solution that (I have argued) exacts costs in civic activity and competence that its virtues fail to pay for.

What strong democracy requires is a form of town meeting in which participation is direct yet communication is regional or even national. Because scale is in part a function of communication, the

13. Jane J. Mansbridge, *Beyond Adversary Democracy* (New York: Basic Books, 1980).

14. I explored at length the history of these abuses in the traditional Republic of Raetia; see my *The Death of Communal Liberty* (Princeton: Princeton University Press, 1974).

15. Yates, *Neighborhood Democracy*, p. 160.

16. Morris and Hess, *Neighborhood Power*, p. 1.

electronic enhancement of communication offers possible solutions to the dilemmas of scale. Although it brings new kinds of risks, modern telecommunications technology can be developed as an instrument for democratic discourse at the regional and national level.[17] The wiring of homes for cable television across America (one quarter of all American homes are now wired, and another quarter will be wired by the end of the 1980s), the availability of low-frequency and satellite transmissions in areas beyond regular transmission or cable, and the interactive possibilities of video, computers, and information retrieval systems open up a new mode of human communications that can be used either in civic and constructive or in manipulative and destructive ways. The capabilities of the new technology can be used to strengthen civic education, guarantee equal access to information, and tie individuals and institutions into networks that will make real participatory discussion and debate possible across great distances. Thus for the first time we have an opportunity to create artificial town meetings among populations that could not otherwise communicate. There is little doubt that the electronic town meeting sacrifices intimacy, diminishes the sense of face-to-face confrontation, and increases the dangers of elite manipulation. Yet it would be foolish to allow these dangers to stop us from exploring television as a civic medium. Even in its rudimentary incarnation in President Carter's national town meetings, the electronic town meeting opened the president to views he might not have heard from his staff and gave a number of Americans that sense of participation that (at a minimum) the members of the White House Press Corps enjoy at a press conference.

The development of the medium to service civic participation in a strong democratic program would call for a linkage among neighborhood assemblies that permitted common discussion of shared concerns as well as national discussions among selected individuals on national initiatives and referenda. The New York–New Jersey–Connecticut Tristate League of the League of Women Voters has run

17. There is a small but growing literature on the civic uses of the new interactive television technology. My article "The Second American Revolution," *Channels* 1, 6 (February/March 1982), outlines several possible scenarios for the misuse of the new technology (which seems likely in the light of present congressional, judicial, and FCC attitudes). It also offers a constructive scenario that deals directly with the kinds of Luddite criticism being written by some liberals; see for example Jean Bethke Elshtain, "Democracy and the QUBE Tube," *The Nation*, 7–14 August 1982. A thoughtful but insufficiently cautious celebration of the civic potential of the new technology is Theodore Becker, "Teledemocracy," *The Futurist*, December 1981.

a series of television town meetings, using telephone/television interactive hookups.[18] Advocates of "teledemocracy" in California and Hawaii have developed more ambitious schemes for civic interaction via television; the University of Hawaii group designed a "televote" for New Zealand's Commission for the Future that appears to have had a considerable success.[19] A Honolulu electronic town meeting succeeded in producing a remarkably sophisticated political debate in 1982, and a similar proposal is now under consideration in Los Angeles.[20]

In other words, there is already a body of evidence that testifies to the civic utility of electronic town meetings and that answers the fears of those concerned with simplistic abuses of interactive systems. The technology exists to develop even more sophisticated uses. Warner-Amex's "QUBE" system provides subscribers with an input module with five modes that permits multichoice voting, computer information retrieval, and a variety of home shopping and security services.[21] The system has to date been used only for enter-

18. In 1979, the Tristate League of the League of Women Voters televised six "Tristate Town Meetings" in New York, New Jersey, and Connecticut. The sessions focused on interstate public transportation, taxation, housing, economic development, and the structure and function of the Tristate Regional Planning Commission. Channel 9, WOR-TV, which carried the live meetings, reported good audience ratings. The televised sessions were followed up by polls solicited from selected group audiences. For details, see *The New York Times*, 26 March 1979.

19. The University of Hawaii group, led by Ted Becker, has experimented extensively with teledemocracy and televoting in several places. A full report on their experiment in New Zealand is available as an occasional paper from Victoria University, Wellington, New Zealand; cf. Ted Becker et al., *Report on "New Zealand Televote" Conducted for the Commission for the Future* (Wellington, New Zealand: Victoria University, 1981). Dick Ryan and Ted Becker offer a critical report in "The Commission for the Future and New Zealand Televote," *World Futures* (forthcoming).

20. For the Hawaii experience, also a product of Ted Becker's team, see "Hawaii Televote: Measuring Public Opinion on Complex Policy Issues," *Political Science* 33, 1 (July 1981). Becker notes that the press covered the video experiment closely, which he feels was a crucial component of its success.

The 1982 California ballot included a proposal for televoting in that state. The system was tested in Los Angeles prior to the elections. The test included advance informational programming on selected issues, an interactive (phone-in) debate on the issues, a press-distributed ballot, and a follow-up televised program discussing the results with the audience.

Michael Malbin assails Becker's position from a Madisonian perspective in "Teledemocracy and Its Discontents," *Public Opinion*, June/July 1982.

21. The Warner-Amex QUBE system was tested in Columbus, Ohio, and is now being installed in many communities. It replaces the traditional telephone hookup with a direct-input module through which viewers can gain direct access to central computers and counters and can register votes, order services, or call up information. Warner-Amex considers that QUBE can be used for some instant polling and to allow viewers to vote inferior amateur-talent-show acts off the screen; the company seems, however, to have no real idea of how their "toy" might be put to serious civic use.

tainment purposes, but it clearly lends itself to more serious uses. Interactive systems have a great potential for equalizing access to information, stimulating participatory debate across regions, and encouraging multichoice polling and voting informed by information, discussion, and debate. It suggests ways to overcome the problem of scale and to defeat technological complexity by putting technology to work for popular democratic ends. In the 1970s a video communications network was established in Reading, Pennsylvania, among senior citizens in shut-in environments and nursing homes. The system eventually led to the political mobilization of the entire community and to the participation of elected officials and their constituents in regular town-meeting-style video sessions—results not foreseen in the original proposal to the National Science Foundation.[22]

However, despite the promise of television and in spite of the dangers it can present to privacy, to rights, and to intelligent participatory democracy when left unregulated and unplanned, there is little evidence that either the government or the private sector is disposed to intervene. The Federal Communications Commission has consistently argued that cable's multiple channels make spectrum scarcity (the availability of a limited number of wavelengths for television broadcasts)—and the justifiable regulations that issue from it—obsolete. The Supreme Court ruled in 1979 that the FCC is not justified in requiring cable companies to provide public access. And while a bill (the Cable Communications Act of 1982) that suggests some congressional activism is presently pending in Congress, the government as a whole seems content to let market forces and the logic of advertising, profits, and entertainment shape the future course of telecommunications.[23]

22. The Reading project was developed by New York University and sponsored by the National Science Foundation in 1976. It was originally intended to promote the social welfare of the elderly shut-ins. The experiment with the senior citizens has ended, but the role of cable television in Reading's political system has not. Today all budget and community development hearings are conducted by two-way cable. Citizens can participate on-camera by visiting neighborhood centers equipped with television cameras, or they can ask questions from home by telephone. Political participation in Reading has increased dramatically as a result.

23. The Cable Telecommunications Act of 1982, which amends the Communications Act of 1934, "creates a jurisdictional framework" for both the federal government and the states to regulate cable systems. Although it includes a provision that ten percent of available channels be reserved for public access, the act shows little concern for the possible civic uses of the new technology. Nonetheless, it is an important precedent in that it establishes the interest of the public sector in the new technology. For arguments for and against the bill, see Subcommittee on Communi-

For these reasons, the strong democratic program for regional and national electronic town meetings requires that a *Civic Communications Cooperative* be established. This organization would take primary responsibility both for the constructive civic uses of the new telecommunications technology and for protecting individuals against media abuse from the private and public sectors. Like the BBC, this Cooperative would be a publicly controlled but independent body. Its members would be selected by several different governmental and nongovernmental constituencies and would include delegates chosen by the neighborhood assemblies or by their regional associations. The CCC's defining mandate would be "to promote and guarantee civic and democratic uses of telecommunications, which remain a vital public resource." It would not displace but act alongside of existing private media corporations. Its aims would include: (1) pioneering and experimenting with innovative forms of civic broadcasting; (2) developing guidelines for regional and national town meetings, for tie-ins to neighborhood assemblies, for public access, for institutional ("tier II") networking, and for other interactive forms of public talk; (3) regulating and overseeing all electronic polling, voting, and other forms of public choosing; (4) setting guidelines for and where feasible originating videotext and other computer information services as a free public utility; (5) establishing or providing guidelines for video coverage of civic events, hearings, trials, and other public activities of civic interest; (6) overseeing the protection of viewers and users from possible abuses of computer data, surveillance services, polling and voting procedures, and so forth.[24]

The Civic Communications Cooperative would be expressly

---

cations of the Committee on Commerce, Science, and Transportation, United States Senate, *Cable Television Regulation: Hearings,* parts 1 and 2 (Washington, D.C.: Government Printing Office, 1982).

24. The new technology poses some considerable dangers to the Bill of Rights. Warner-Amex's QUBE system scans subscribers' homes every six seconds, recording what they are watching, their answers to poll questions, the temperature of the house (for those signed up for energy-management systems), and even the comings and goings of everyone in the house (for those signed up for home-security service). Moreover, cable systems that offer polling, banking, and shopping services as well as other interactive business transactions will accumulate detailed files on the subscribers. At present there are no safeguards to prevent the abuse of such records, other than the good will of the cable operators. John Wicklein has detailed these dangers in his *Electronic Nightmare: The New Communications and Freedom* (New York: Viking, 1981). See also David Burnham, *The Rise of the Computer State* (New York: Random House, 1983).

barred from regulating private broadcasting, which would remain under the control of the FCC, and from in any other way interfering with the rights of private broadcasters to develop and control their own programming and services. The tasks of the CCC would be affirmative rather than censorial: to provide guidelines and to develop programming that is not presently available and that the private sector is unlikely (for reasons of private interest and profitability) to make available. A prudent safeguard to ensure that the CCC would not stray from its specified functions would be the establishment of a congressional watchdog committee.

As a cooperative, the new association would be able to develop or to work with extant regional bodies that are involved in exploring the civic uses of telecommunications technology. It would thus give to the old and somewhat parochial notion of neighborhood assemblies the novel and integrating force of electronic technology.

3. *Civic Education and Equal Access to Information: A Civic Education Postal Act and a Civic Videotex Service*. Information is indispensable to the responsible exercise of citizenship and to the development of political judgment. Without civic education, democratic choice is little more than the expression and aggregation of private prejudices. In an electronically facilitated "information society," it is both easier and harder to provide wide access to pertinent economic and political information. It is harder because the quantity and specificity of data have grown to a point where the data are nearly impossssible to disseminate. The specialized character of many of the policy decisions facing citizens today seem to place them beyond the compass of mere political judgment. Yet the task is also easier because the new technologies of electronic and computer print and video systems allow almost anyone living anywhere to have access to and retrieve information.

In order to guarantee equal access to the new information technologies and to ensure an even balance between print and video information sources, the strong democratic program calls both for subsidized postal rates for civic educational publishing and for a civic videotex service under the aegis of the Civic Communications Cooperative.

The rising costs of paper and the increasing unpopularity of print in a video-oriented society each in its own way suggests the need for subsidized postal rates for newspapers, magazines, journals of opinion, and certain kinds of books. It is something of a scandal—if a fit tribute to the privatized priorities of our society—that the government subsidizes junk mail offering trivial information about consumer options and choices by delivering such mail at a second-class bulk rate, while it penalizes newspapers and journals offering significant information about political and social options and choices by saddling them with higher third-class rates. A Civic Education Postal Act would offer a subsidized rate to all legitimate publishers of newspapers, journals, magazines, and books. Smaller-circulation publications would receive larger subsidies on the principle that the less popular the point of view, the greater the need for subsidy—with a cutoff point to protect against individual eccentrics and mavericks (500 copies for a quarterly or a book, 5,000 for a monthly, and 20,000 for a weekly, for example). The free market of ideas now costs a good deal more than the free market of products; strong democratic politics cannot afford to have that market priced out of existence.

A Civic Videotex Service, coupled with the subsidization of print media, would serve the public need for equal access to civic information completely. It would offer a standard, nationwide, interactive, and free videotext service that would provide viewers with regular news, discussions of issues, and technical, political, and economic data. From the service viewers could also retrieve additional information that might affect their citizenship and their roles as participants or voters in a neighborhood assembly. Each citizen would be guaranteed the same access to vital civic information and would be linked into an information-retrieval system with vast educational and developmental potential. The citizen-service conscript (see below) might learn about alternative forms of service, the unemployed worker might learn about training programs and government job prospects, the voter might look into the background of pressing referendum issues, the teacher might develop an effective civics training kit—all through the use of a flexible videotext service.

These modest proposals would help to assure that increased participation and innovations such as the neighborhood assembly and the electronic town meeting would enhance the quality of citizenship and the prudence of popular political judgment, not create the conditions for a new plebiscitary tyranny.

4. Supplementary Institutions. Strong democracy can also be served by representative town meetings, office-holding by lot, and decriminalization and lay justice.

The representative town meeting compromises the principle that all citizens should engage fully in local deliberative processes, but it thereby rescues the town meeting from the eroding impact of scale. Thus Massachusetts has thirty-two representative town meetings in communities where full and direct participation is no longer feasible. When the representatives to the town meeting are chosen by lot and membership is rotated, over time all will be able to participate. It turns out to be easier in large-scale societies for everyone to have some participation for some of the time.

The same principle can be applied to local office-holding. The great majority of local offices in towns and municipalities can be filled by citizens chosen by lot on a rotating basis. The expertise required is not so great and the responsibility involved not so onerous that members of local boards of selectmen, of planning boards, of road, water, and conservation commissions, of zoning, housing, and education boards, and of other bodies such as library committees, the registry of voters, and cemetery commissions could not be selected by lot. The lot principle, which is discussed in detail below, is a natural extension of the democratic principle to large-scale societies.

The democratization of local offices also has a place in the criminal and civil justice system. Students of the judiciary have recently argued that a variety of small offenses should be decriminalized and have proposed alternative forums of justice for trying such cases.[25] The Europeans have successfully experimented with empowering lay juries and judges or other surrogate civic bodies to mediate, arbitrate, and settle disputes.[26] Although intended primarily to alle-

---

25. For a discussion of decriminalization, see Richard Danzig, "Toward the Creation of a Complementary Decentralized System of Criminal Justice," *26 Stanford Law Review 1*, 1973; William Felstiner, "Influences of Social Organization on Dispute Proceeding," *9 Law and Society Review 63*, 1974; and Richard Anzig and Michael J. Lowy, "Everyday Disputes and Mediation in the United States: A Reply to Professor Felstiner," *Law and Society Review 9*, Summer 1975. A complete survey of the promise and the difficulties of decriminalization and informal justice is offered by Christine Harrington in *Shadow Courts* (Ph.D. dissertation, University of Wisconsin, Madison, 1982). She has published some of her findings in "Delegalization Reform Movements: A Historical Analysis," in *The Politics of Informal Justice*, vol. 1, ed. Richard L. Apel (New York: Academic Press, 1982). The National Institute of Law Enforcement and Criminal Justice has sponsored a number of studies of model projects—for example, "Citizen Dispute Settlement: A Replication Manual," which examines the Night Prosecutor Program of Columbus, Ohio.

26. See for example William Felstiner and Ann B. Prew, *European Alternatives to Criminal Trials and Their Applicability to the United States*, U.S. Department of Justice, National Institute of Law Enforcement and Criminal Justice, 1978.

viate the courts' case load, the experiment in decriminalization has in fact engaged the larger civic community in the judicial process in a fashion that supports strong democracy. A cooperative, mediatory, participatory approach to petty misdemeanors, family quarrels, moving traffic violations, and small-sum civil disputes educates and involves the community in the justice system at the same time that it makes the judiciary more efficient. If civic participation were made a conscious goal rather than merely a side benefit of experiments in decriminalization, strong democracy would be very well served at no additional cost.

INSTITUTIONALIZING STRONG DEMOCRATIC DECISION-MAKING

5. *A National Initiative and Referendum Process.* The initiative and referendum process has been widely used in the United States at the state and local level. It also has been critical to democracy in a number of other countries, most notably in Switzerland, where it remains the preferred method of national legislation. Putting aside the "plebiscites" conducted by totalistic regimes seeking unanimous approval of national decisions that have already been taken and the constitutional referenda on the founding documents of "new" countries, the initiative and referendum continue to be used in America, Switzerland, Australia, New Zealand, France, Scandinavia, and to a lesser extent Ireland and the United Kingdom.[27]

In the United States, twenty-six states, many of them in the West, have used the initiative and referendum process. South Dakota adopted it in 1898, Utah in 1900, Oregon in 1902, and more recently Wyoming adopted it in 1968, Illinois (which has a constitutional referendum only) in 1970, and Florida in 1972.[28] But although in 1978 Senator James Abourezk proposed in Senate Joint Resolution 67 that an amendment to the Constitution establish a national initiative and

27. For a comparative survey, see David Butler and Austin Ranney, *Referendums: A Comparative Study of Practice and Theory* (Washington, D.C.: American Enterprise Institute, 1978).

28. The states that have some form of referendum are (in order of the date of introduction) South Dakota, Utah, Oregon, Oklahoma, Maine, Missouri, Arkansas, Colorado, Arizona, California, Montana, New Mexico, Idaho, Nebraska, Nevada, Ohio, Washington, Michigan, North Dakota, Kentucky, Maryland, Massachusetts, Alaska, Wyoming, Illinois, and Florida. Of these only Arizona, California, Colorado, North Dakota, Oregon, and Washington can be said to use the device with significant frequency: each has had at least one hundred statutory and constitutional referenda. For full statistics, see Austin Ranney, "The United States of America," in Butler and Ranney, *Referendums*, pp. 67–86.

referendum process, the proposal was never brought to a vote and America has never had a national referendum process. Indeed, even proposed amendments to the Constitution are voted on in the state legislatures rather than in a popular referendum.[29]

The resistance to a national referendum process derives in part from Madisonian fears of popular rule. These manifest themselves in the modern world as an anxiety about elite manipulation of public opinion, the power of image and money to influence the popular vote, the private-interest character of the balloting process, and the plebiscitary dangers of direct legislation. Now as earlier, even warm friends of democracy worry about popular obstructionism against progressive legislation and about the civic incompetence of the "sovereign" people.[30]

The dangers of elite manipulation in a mass society cannot be overestimated, but in fact the actual history of the referendum at the state level yields very little evidence of civic incompetence or obstructionism. Moreover, it is foolish to think that a nation can be rescued from the manipulation of elites by reducing the potentially manipulable public's input into the democratic process. One might as well combat crime in the subways by keeping the public at home. Indeed, it is more rather than less experience of government that will insulate voters against manipulation and prejudice. While Madisonian theorists have stood trembling at the prospects of a leviathan

29. Filtering referenda through the states and then leaving the decision to state legislatures may act as one more Madisonian filter of the popular will, but it can skew results in very nondemocratic ways. In the case of the Equal Rights Amendment, polls suggest that a large majority of Americans supported the amendment both across the nation and in the states where it was eventually defeated by legislative action. The proposal offered here is intended to remove such filters and to replace them with checks that work in concert with rather than in place of the public will.

30. The broad dimensions of the debate emerge in the proceedings of a conference on the referendum: Austin Ranney, ed., *The Referendum Device* (Washington, D.C.: American Enterprise Institute, 1981). The straightforward argument that the people would be incompetent decision-makers is based on the traditional liberal wariness about democracy. It can be found in a recent incarnation in Henry Fairlie, "The Unfiltered Voice: The Dangerous Revival of the Referendum," *The New Republic*, 24 June 1978. A more troubling form of criticism—more troubling because it comes from the democratic left—is Peter Bachrach's "Testimony to the Subcommittee on the Constitution of the Committee on the Judiciary," on S. J. Resolution 67 for a Voter Initiative Constitutional Amendment (13–14 December 1977). These hearings also include my detailed rebuttal of Bachrach's case against the referendum. Robert Michels would seem to have the last word on critics such as these when he writes:

> Where party life is concerned, the socialists for the most part reject these practical applications of democracy, using against them conservative arguments such as we are otherwise accustomed to hear only from the opponents of socialism. In articles written by socialist leaders it is ironically asked whether it would be a good thing to hand over the leadership of the party to the ignorant masses simply for love of an abstract principle. (*Political Parties* [Glencoe, Ill.: Free Press, 1915], p. 336)

public running amok in schoolrooms filled with voting machines, students of the referendum's practical effects have been offering more soothing pictures. A commentator who reviewed the experience of Michigan writes: "There is quite as likely to be a judicious and rational decision on popular votes [by referendum] as on legislative votes."[31] A student of the California referendum reports: "So far as large problems of public welfare are concerned, [the public] is markedly more likely to reach a fair and socially valuable result."[32] Of Oregon, a student writes: "The marvel is that this system of popular government, so vulnerable to apathy, indifference, and actual ignorance, has not only worked but has a considerable degree of constructive and progressive achievements to its credit."[33]

The fear of obstructionism seems no better founded than the fear of popular prejudice. Early antinuclear referenda failed in a number of states, but similar referenda have succeeded in recent years.[34] The Swiss use of the referendum has often favored tradition and opposed modernizing legislation, but in the Swiss case the "modernizing" legislation was being supported by the establishment and was defeated by a strong-willed and independently minded Swiss public that ignored pressures from big money and the media.[35] In Churchill County, Nevada, prostitution was legalized by referen-

31. Quoted from a 1940 report by James Pollock, which Ronald J. Allen cites in his superb survey and analysis, "The National Initiative Proposal: A Preliminary Analysis," *Nebraska Law Review* 58, 4 (1979): 1011.

32. Max Radin, "Popular Legislation in California," 23 *Minnesota Law Review* 559, 1939, cited in Allen, "Proposal," pp. 1011–12. Radin concludes: "One thing is clear. The vote of the people is eminently sane. The danger apprehended that quack nostrums in public policy can be forced on the voters by demagogues is demonstrably non-existent. The representative legislature is much more susceptible to such influences." Indeed, Eli M. Noam develops an efficiency criterion according to which referendum democracy can be strongly defended as efficient ("The Efficiency of Direct Democracy," *Journal of Political Economy* 88, 4 [1980]).

33. From an unpublished dissertation by Paul Culbertson, cited in Allen, "Proposal," p. 1013. See also Joseph LaPolombara, *The Initiative and Referendum in Oregon: 1938–1940* (Corvallis, Ore.: Oregon State University Press, 1950).

34. In 1976 five antinuclear petitions failed at the ballot box, but since 1978 eight have been offered in state referenda and five have succeeded. See *The San Francisco Examiner*, Section B, 3 January 1982. In the spring of 1982, a series of Vermont town meetings voted overwhelmingly to support a mutual freeze on nuclear weapons. In the November 1982 elections, freeze resolutions were approved in Massachusetts, Michigan, Montana, New Jersey, North Dakota, Oregon, Rhode Island, and even (by a narrow margin) California, despite administration intervention. Resolutions were defeated in Arizona and in two small counties in Arkansas and Colorado.

35. A relatively sympathetic and thorough survey of the Swiss experience is given by Jean-François Aubert, "Switzerland," in Butler and Ranney, *Referendums*, pp. 39–66. For some of the problems that crop up when traditionalists use the referendum as a tool against modernists, see my *The Death of Communal Liberty* (Princeton: Princeton University Press, 1974).

dum.[36] Right-to-work legislation, generally considered conservative, has been defeated by referendum in several states.[37] And Oregon led the way with progressive initiatives that abolished the poll tax and introduced female suffrage by popular ballot at the beginning of the century.[38] More recently Michigan and Maine banned disposable soft-drink containers by popular vote, Colorado voted down an Olympics proposal for the state that had been widely supported by business and political elites, New Jersey introduced casino gambling by referendum, and bond issues have continued to win popular support for selected projects despite the increasing fiscal conservatism of the electorate.[39]

In sum, the initiative and referendum can increase popular participation in and responsibility for government, provide a permanent instrument of civic education, and give popular talk the reality and discipline of power that it needs to be effective. Thus the constructive uses far outweigh the potential disadvantages—which history suggests are less alarming than critics believe in any case. It is therefore a crucial goal of the strong democratic program to institute a national initiative and referendum process as part of the effort to revitalize popular talk and public decision-making. The proposal offered here has a number of unique features, including a multichoice format and a built-in check on public mercurialness in the form of a requirement for two "readings." For purposes of discussion, we may review the proposal in terms of its chief features:

    a. a legislative initiative and referendum process;

    b. a mandatory tie-in with neighborhood assemblies and interactive-television town meetings for the purpose of civic education;

36. Churchill County approved the legalization of a brothel in 1975 after a public debate that focused on tax revenues, control of venereal disease, and the need to provide an "outlet" for the naval air-station training base. The proposal to legalize carried in every precinct.

37. Right-to-work legislation was introduced by petition during the 1970s in Montana, where progressive legislators feared a landslide antiunion vote. But following a lively public debate, the proposal was defeated, laying to rest right-to-work legislation not simply in the capital but in the state as a whole. The point is not that right-to-work legislation is necessarily unacceptable but that a referendum produced ideologically "progressive" or "liberal" results despite liberals' fears to the contrary.

38. Oregon abolished the poll tax in 1910 and introduced women's suffrage in 1912—both by referendum. Oregon regularly draws higher turnouts at referenda than at elections for representatives.

39. The Colorado vote against the proposed Winter Olympics of 1976 was a particular surprise, because the opposition based its underfunded campaign on "soft" ecological issues, while the establishment spent freely on a campaign that combined state patriotism and profit. For a full account, see L. Olson, "Power, Public Policy and the Environment: The Defeat of the 1976 Winter Olympics in Colorado" (unpublished Ph.D. dissertation, University of Iowa, 1975).

c. a multichoice format;

d. a two-stage voting process providing for two readings.

a. Initiative and Referendum Process. A national initiative and referendum act would permit Americans to petition for a legislative referendum either on popular initiatives or on laws passed by Congress. Petitioners would be allowed from twelve to eighteen months to collect signatures from registered voters in at least ten states. The number of signatures would have to equal two or three percent of the number of ballots cast in the previous presidential election. Such initiatives would then be submitted to a popular vote; if they passed, there would ensue a waiting period of six months followed by a second vote. A third vote might be required if Congress vetoed the second popular vote (or in the case of congressional laws that had been brought to the referendum by petition). The waiting period, and the resulting debate, would give the public ample opportunity to review its positions, to take into account the advice of political leaders, and to discuss the decision in the neighborhood assemblies. Since the intent of the process is to increase participation rather than to produce immediate legislative innovations, the deliberate (even ponderous) pace of a two- or three-stage procedure would be more than justified. Certainly it would help to calm any fears felt by advocates of the Madisonian representative screen.

b. Civic Education. Because civic education is an important feature of the referendum process, a national referendum and initiative act would mandate local and national discussion in the assemblies and in the print and broadcast media of the issues on the ballot. Regulations integral to the referendum bill would fund informational documents offering pro and con arguments on each issue (as is done in Massachusetts);[40] would limit the spending by interest groups on campaigns for or against bills; would organize television discussions

---

40. Massachusetts provides voters with "Voter Information Booklets" on all referenda ballot questions. The document includes the full text and summaries of each proposal, majority and minority reports from legislative committees, and a "proponents statement" and "opponents statement." A sample paper ballot is also included. The booklet also describes the national and state offices to be filled, lists the addresses of key officials, and provides a summary of relevant statutes such as the Massachusetts "Open Meeting Law," the Freedom of Information Act, and the Fair Information Practices Act. A summary Spanish version is also available.

The Swiss offer voters similar information packets on all national initiatives and referenda.

Videotex versions of such informative documents could be made available through a civic videotex service.

via the Civic Communications Cooperative and local media; and would sponsor town meetings on the air. The general aim of these regulations would be to maximize public debate and to guarantee open and fair discussion. With them, the dangers of plebiscitary abuse of the referendum would be diminished and the utility of the multichoice format discussed below would be enhanced.

c. Multichoice Format. A strong democratic referendum process would utilize a multichoice format in place of the conventional yea/nay option. Rather than being asked merely to veto or affirm a proposal, citizens would be offered a more varied and searching set of choices capable of eliciting more nuanced and thoughtful responses.[41] The range of options would include: yes in principle—strongly for the proposal; yes in principle—but not a first priority; no in principle—strongly against the proposal; no with respect to this formulation—but not against the proposal in principle, suggest reformulation and resubmission; and no for the time being—although not necessarily opposed in principle, suggest postponement. A ballot on a concrete proposition would look like this:

A PROPOSAL TO CREATE AND MAINTAIN ABORTION CLINICS
WITH PUBLIC FUNDS:

(1) YES: I strongly support the public funding of abortion clinics.

(2) YES: I support the principle of public funding of abortion clinics, but I am concerned with the character and intensity of arguments against the proposal, and suggest proceeding with caution.

(3) NO: I am strongly opposed to abortion clinics on principle and equally opposed to public funding of such clinics.

(4) NO: I am opposed to the proposal to support abortion clinics from public funds in the way it is formulated here, but I am not necessarily against abortion clinics in principle. I suggest the proponents reformulate and resubmit their proposal.

(5) NO: I am opposed to the proposal because, although I am not personally against the public funding of abortion clinics, I do not believe the community can afford to take a decision until there is more debate and deliberation and until the two sides understand one another better. I therefore suggest postponement.

41. The device described here is not a product of the imagination but is drawn from the experience of the Republic of Raetia (Eastern Switzerland), which used the multichoice format for centuries to register the votes of its constituent communes. The system, although it was aimed at registering group rather than individual preferences, worked exceedingly well, although it created some novel problems. For a full discussion see my *The Death of Communal Liberty*, chap. 7.

Now the yeas and the nays on such a ballot would be counted in the aggregate, and the proposal would pass or fail as legislation in the usual majoritarian manner—if, as a first reading (see below), only provisionally. Nevertheless, the insistence on reasoned and shaded responses would serve important aims. It would enable the proponents of a referendum to glean significant information about why their proposal won or lost and to evaluate (along with the community generally) what effects the outcome might have on their own objectives and on the political system at large. A bill that passed by a small majority of votes in the 2 column and was vigorously opposed by a large minority of votes in the 3 column would suggest the dangers of what social scientists call asymmetrical intensity, where a passive, unconcerned majority overrules an impassioned minority and thereby risks destabilizing the community. Under these circumstances, those responsible for implementation would presumably proceed with utmost caution—which is the strategy suggested by the mandate under YES–2 to begin with. It might also persuade cautious voters to switch from a YES–2 to a NO–5 (more debate needed) on the second reading of the proposal.

On the other hand, the defeat of a bill by a narrow margin of NO–4 voters over YES–1 voters would argue strongly that the proposal should be reformulated and resubmitted, since the yeas were deeply committed advocates and the nays primarily objected to the particular formulation at issue. Yeas in the 1 column countered by nays in the 3 column draw a political picture of intense symmetrical disagreement—of principled polarization, in other words—and call for caution on both sides.

At the same time that it yielded this vital political information, the multichoice vote would compel citizens to examine their own electoral opinions. Forced to attach each yea and nay to an explanation, they would have to start making the kinds of distinctions familiar to "professional legislators." How strongly do I feel? Is the achievement of my goal worth destabilizing the community? If I support something only weakly, is it fair to overrule a minority that strongly opposes it? Might it not be better to wait until the opposition understands me better or can be offered a version of the bill that is less offensive to their convictions (e.g., the *indirect* public funding of semiprivate abortion clinics)? By building nuanced consideration of issues into the ballot, the multichoice format discourages purely private choices and encourages voters to have public reasons for what

are after all public acts. Yea/nay choices are typical of market interactions, which assume fixed interests founded on private needs; the
multichoice format is typical of political interactions, which assume
that interests are flexible and can be transformed by political judgment and public seeing. The multichoice format solicits a judgment
about the public good rather than a registering of private preferences. It is thus a form of civic education even as it is a form of balloting, and it strengthens democracy not simply by allowing citizens
to choose alternative futures but by compelling them to think like
public beings.

d. Two Readings. To take full advantage of the educational benefits
of the multichoice referendum, and at the same time to guard
against a too-impetuous citizenry or a too-powerful elite gaining
temporary control of public opinion, the referendum process would
unfold in two voting stages, separated by six months of deliberation
and debate. The second vote ("second reading") would in effect
reevaluate the results of the first vote. A public unwilling to reaffirm
a yea vote after a period of six months is issuing itself a warning.
Indeed, until it speaks in a clear, consistent voice, a voting citizenry
does not become a public with a will worth trusting. A no on the first
round would defeat a bill; a yes would not yet enact a bill but rather
would necessitate a second round. This check against whimsical
majorities could be further strengthened by permitting Congress or
the president to veto a measure following a second vote and then
requiring a third reading for an override of the veto and final passage.[42] Checks such as these would certainly obstruct rapid legislation, and would prevent majorities from working their will without
prolonged debate and deliberation. But for strong democracy,
public talk and political judgment are the goal, not plebiscitary
willfulness.

Skeptics and defenders of the rule of expertise will continue to
distrust legislation by referendum, arguing that in an age as complex and technical as ours, no public can ever govern both judiciously and directly. However, this is to misunderstand the legislative function itself, which is not to institutionalize science or truth
but to judge the public effects of what passes for science or truth.
Citizens are not different from elected legislators in this regard: their

---

42. The aim is not to make it *easy* for the public to self-legislate but to make it
possible and feasible for them to do so. Thus congressional checks would function as
a prudent safeguard on a referendum system.

task is to judge, evaluate, and assess—to employ judgment rather than expertise. The average voter can no more penetrate the secrets of monetarism than can the average Congress member rate the cost-efficiency of the M-1 tank. But both are capable of judging whether high unemployment is an acceptable price to pay for lowered inflation, and each has his convictions about the ratio of public monies to be spent on guns and on butter. Political judgment above all involves evaluating options in terms of value priorities, and as such it is available to every woman and man willing to submit their personal opinions and private interests to the test of public debate and political deliberation. A properly thought-out system of initiative and referendum actually enhances the public's capacity to reach wise political judgments: as such, it is a crucial component of a strong democratic program.

6. Electronic Balloting. Interactive video communications make possible new forms of balloting that, carefully used, can enhance democracy.[43] The use of feedback polls in public debates on neighborhood-assembly issues or on national referenda can be a valuable instrument of civic education. As an example, let us return to the abortion-clinic proposal used as an illustration above. A video town meeting might ask viewers: "If you oppose abortion on principle, how do you think the community should deal with the reality that illegal abortions are available to the wealthy? Or with the fact that poor women often attempt to abort themselves at grave medical risk to themselves and to the fetuses?" Or: "If you support the right of women to choose abortion, how do you think the community ought to deal with its legitimate concern with the rights of babies—including the 'rights' of fetuses?" Or: "How should a democratic community deal with disagreements as fundamental as those separating the 'prochoice' and the 'right-to-life' movements?" The objective is not to canvass opinion or to take a straw poll, but to catalyze discussion and to nurture empathetic forms of reasoning. The capacity of interactive television for instant polling is a great advantage here, for it permits regionwide or even nationwide responses to be tapped and used in a live debate on the issues.

Instant votes of the kind envisioned by certain mindless plebiscitary democrats are as insidious as interactive discussion questions

43. Ted Becker and his colleagues have made extensive use of video balloting as an element in public political debate. Their findings are encouraging—see above, notes 19 and 20.

are useful. Soliciting instant votes on every conceivable issue from an otherwise uninformed audience that has neither deliberated nor debated an issue would be the death of democracy—which is concerned with public seeing rather than with the expression of preferences and which aspires to achieve common judgment rather than to aggregate private opinions.

For the same reasons, the strong democrat will approach the idea of home voting with great caution. Home voting, like the mail ballot, has the great advantage of making citizenship convenient. The five-position QUBE module offers a perfect technological replication of the multichoice ballot and makes voting at home feasible. For the elderly, for shut-ins, for mothers of young children, or for others unable to leave home, it makes the possibilities of citizenship available as never before. The excuses for neglecting to vote, from "too little free time" to "too much laziness," all vanish. Yet as with the secret ballot and the mail ballot, the home vote via video takes voting one step farther away from its public habitation. Home voting inevitably means privatistic voting; it means public preferences will be expressed from the inner sanctum of private existence; it means the voter choosing without thinking of his fellow citizens since he is away from the halls and assemblies in which he normally meets with them.

If we are to utilize the electronic efficiency of the new video technologies to electoral advantage, we would do better to bring interactive sets into the neighborhood assembly halls or into the schoolrooms where so much voting takes place—and to reserve the right of home voting to those with physical disabilities. Of course all of the advantages of videotex and computer information-retrieval services would be available to voters at home. But voting itself, as the most public of all acts, should be true to its symbolism and allow itself to be celebrated in the most public of places—town halls, neighborhood schools, district assemblies. A man's home is his castle, a citizen's home is his neighborhood; he can eat, sleep, and pray in the first, but he ought to vote only in the second. A suitable technology, if it is democracy's servant rather than its guide, will assist the citizen in doing so.

7. Election by Lot: Sortition, Rotation, and Pay. There was a time when Montesquieu could note, as if it were a cliché, that "the suffrage by lot is natural to democracy, as that by choice is to aristocracy."[44] And the *Cambridge Ancient History* informs us that "all our ancient authorities are agreed in regarding sortition as a democratic device for equalizing the chances of rich and poor"—a position that Aristotle fully supports in *The Constitution of Athens*.[45]

Yet despite the ancient popularity of sortition, and its fleeting existence in the republican constitutions of Venice, Florence, and Raetia in the early modern period, it has all but disappeared from modern democratic practice. It persists only in the Anglo-American jury, where it continues to exercise a beneficent democratic influence on the judicial system. Robert Michels raised the dilemma that the principle of representation that rescues democracy from the problems of scale is itself inherently oligarchical and so destroys what it saves. The reintroduction of election by lot on a limited basis might act to save representation from itself, by permitting some citizens to act on behalf of others (thus dealing with the problems of scale) while making their service a function of lot (thus preserving the democratic nature of public service). Election by lot would also neutralize the skewing effect of wealth on public service, spread public responsibilities more equitably across the entire population, and engage a great many more citizens in making and administering policy as office-holders than generally have that opportunity in a representative system. Since the nurturing of political judgment does not require that every citizen be involved in all decisions, the lot is a way of maximizing meaningful engagement in large-scale societies.

There are two arenas in which election by lot might be appropriate in modern representative systems. The first is the local assembly, where the lot system could select delegates to regional representative assemblies such as representative town meetings or neighborhood assembly congresses at the district or state level. Where the intent is to maintain direct participation but the number of citizens is too great to permit everyone to assemble, lot selection guarantees equal access and fair representation. It might even be worth experimenting with election by lot of a limited number of statewide delegates to state legislative assemblies: say five members-at-large, chosen by lot from five different neighborhood assemblies each year.

The second arena in which the lot principle would work, and the

---

44. Montesquieu, *Spirit of the Laws*, trans. T. Nugent (New York: Hafner, 1966), p. 11.

45. J. B. Bury et al., *The Cambridge Ancient History*, vol. 4: *The Persian Empire and the West* (New York: Macmillan, 1926), p. 156.

one in which it would work best, would be the filling of local offices where special knowledge or expertise is not required. The Greeks left military offices and the ruling archons out of the sortition process, although they did include their boards of finance.[46] In a typical municipality such as North Adams, Massachusetts, it would seem reasonable to choose by lot some or even all members of the board of assessors, the school committee, the registry of voters, the planning board, the zoning board, the conservation commission, the housing authority, and the licensing board. Following some initial training of the new members in the substantive matters of relevance, and with the help of permanent staff people, such boards and committees would simultaneously function as genuinely representative civic institutions of the town and as schools of citizenship and statesmanship (which, in a strong democracy, are one and the same thing).

The Greeks employed safeguards that could be emulated as well. Candidates for selection by lot might undergo some minimal training in community offices and responsibilities; towns and municipalities—or even the neighborhood assemblies—could review the conduct of administrators and office-holders and recall those derelict in their responsibilities. The pool from which delegates are chosen could be made voluntary, thus institutionalizing the principle of self-selection and preventing those without any interest or concern from occupying public offices—although this provision runs the risk of disenfranchising the victims of apathy and powerlessness from a vital civic opportunity and thereby increasing the power of those already advantaged by education and income.[47]

To be democratically efficacious, the lot idea would have to be coupled with some system of regular rotation. In order that as many citizens as possible could experience holding office, individual citizens would be limited to one period of tenure in one office for a

46. After the time of Cleisthenes, even the archons were elected by lot. However, it seems likely that this change was part of a strategy to diminish the archons' importance and to enhance the prestige of the Board of Generals. For a complete discussion of the lot and its political ramifications, see E. S. Staveley, *Greek and Roman Voting and Elections* (Ithaca: Cornell University Press, 1972). On the election by lot of the archons, see pp. 40–42.

47. Hannah Arendt has argued strenuously for the principle of self-selection. This system would clearly guarantee a committed citizenry, but it raises serious questions about the causes of nonparticipation and would risk institutionalizing the nonpolitical status of the disadvantaged, the ignorant, the poor, and other victims of a representative system.

limited time and would then be removed from the pool until some specified percentage of their fellow citizens had been able to serve.

The payment of a per diem for these minor office-holders would both provide an incentive to serve and compensate for private time spent for the public weal. It would not be unthinkable to permit those who did not wish to serve to buy off their debt to the community. Permitting the wealthy to disenfranchise themselves might be less troubling to a democracy than making poverty an obstacle to citizenship, as happens too often in the current political system.[48]

A lottery principle applied in modern democratic settings would obviously have to be treated with great caution.[49] But given the safeguards built into the pluralism, the liberalism, and the apathy of our representative regime, selection by lot could mitigate the oligarchical tendencies of representation and could guarantee a fundamental fairness in such selection of local delegates and officers as might be required by scale. Where every citizen is equally capable of political judgment and equally responsible for the public good, the rotation of reponsibilities among citizens chosen by lot becomes a powerful symbol of genuine democracy. It is the simplest, but by no means the least potent, tool of strong democracy.

8. Vouchers and the Market Approach to Public Choice. The primary instrument of political judgment in democracy is voting. We either vote directly for laws or for representatives responsible for the laws. In recent decades, however, a decentralized or market approach to public choice has found advocates on both the right and the left. This market or voucher approach aspires to vest individuals directly with the power to make "public" choices. It would thus replace the public mechanisms for determining what is in the public interest with market mechanisms. Citizens armed with government-issued

48. The Swiss permit the wealthy to buy off military service under certain circumstances. The policy seems unwise, since military service is an obligation as well as a right. But the right to self-government would seem to be more significant than the obligation to serve in the case of local and regional offices, so that permitting the rich to buy out of their rights would not necessarily offend the idea of universal obligations.

49. As A. H. M. Jones has warned:

it was not "the rulers of the city" who were chosen by lot, but officials charged with limited routine duties, for which little more than a "sense of decency" was required. Furthermore, it must be remembered that a magistrate had to pass a preliminary examination; . . . was liable to be deposed by vote of the assembly taken ten times a year; and after his year, was subject to a scrutiny in which his accounts were audited and any citizen could charge him with inefficiency or abuse of authority. (*Athenian Democracy* [Oxford: Blackwell, 1957], p. 48)

vouchers would be endowed with the economic power to buy housing or education or transportation of their own choosing, while the creation and sustaining of housing, education, and transportation services would be left to private vendors who would compete in a free market for these consumer vouchers.

The idea is as old as the free market itself, and was in fact first postulated by Adam Smith and then reformulated for an American audience by Tom Paine. The G.I. Bill, which permitted veterans of World War II to attend colleges of their choice, can be seen as an implicit voucher scheme. In the 1950s Milton Friedman revitalized Adam Smith's idea, and libertarians have given it their ardent support since then.[50] If it were only a libertarian idea, it would have no place in a strong democratic program. But during the 1960s social critics such as Christopher Jencks and progressive school reformers such as John E. Coons and Stephen D. Sugarman in California took up the voucher idea as a progressive alternative to the expiring public school system and to the seeming disaster of forced busing that was polarizing communities without markedly improving schools.[51] They claimed that such a system would increase parent activism, equalize choice, and help improve the deeply faulty public school system. These arguments started a controversy that is directly relevant to strong democracy and suggested virtues at least worth considering in developing its program.

Jencks, Coons, and Sugarman argue that the "public" character of state schools is corrupted by the segregation by income and race of the school districts into which neighborhoods are divided. Neither parents nor children have any real choice; they are forced to participate in a segmented, segregated system that discriminates

50. Milton Friedman, *Capitalism and Freedom* (Chicago: University of Chicago Press, 1962), pp. 85–107. I have benefited greatly in this section from the research of Richard M. Battistoni, who offers an excellent discussion of the voucher idea in the context of civic education in his "Public Schooling and the Education of Democratic Citizens" (unpublished Ph.D. thesis, Rutgers University, 1982). He finally dismisses the market approach while I remain more ambivalent, but his assessment of its defects is very persuasive.

51. Christopher Jencks's essay "Is the Public School Obsolete?", which appeared in *The Public Interest* in the winter of 1966, set the terms for a progressive, left-leaning adaptation of Friedman's libertarian idea. The Center for the Study of Public Policy published the lengthy study that Jencks undertook with Judith Areen under the title *Vouchers: A Report on Financing Education by Payments to Parents* (Cambridge, Mass.: Center for the Study of Public Policy, December 1970). A useful summary is found in "Education Vouchers: A Proposal for Diversity and Choice," *Teachers College Record* no. 72 (February 1971). The Coons and Sugarman proposals are found in their *Education by Choice: The Case for Family Control* (Berkeley: University of California Press, 1978).

against the least advantaged, who receive only that education which the tax base of their community will support—poor for the poor, worthwhile for the rich. Coons and Sugarman's proposals, which appeared on the California ballot in November 1982, call for a voucher system, for the termination of public certification of and tenure for teachers, and for the continuation of extant public schools—which, however, would have to compete for parental vouchers with a new tier of "private" schools.[52]

Housing vouchers are designed along comparable lines. In place of public housing capitalized by public funds, private builders would compete for the housing vouchers issued to all citizens qualifying for "public" housing. Not only would the market produce housing more efficiently, argue proponents, but individuals would be making their own choices and controlling their own destinies. Transportation vouchers would permit private companies to serve in public communities by competing for the patronage of travelers. In each case, publicly funded capital construction would give way to privately funded construction, central planning would give way to private choice, and a top-heavy bureaucracy would give way to efficiency-conscious (i.e., cost-conscious) private purveyors. In the school area, it has been estimated that the private-market costs of educating a child are about one-half of the state costs.

The strong democrat must feel considerable ambivalence about voucher schemes. Their great virtue is that they are intolerant of state bureaucracies and that they mobilize parent/student constituencies in a fashion that also serves to mobilize citizenship. Parents engaged in their children's education become citizens engaged in their neighborhoods: to care for and to act on behalf of one's own interests is the first step toward civic activity in a lethargic representative system where individuals are accustomed to deferring to politicians, bureaucrats, experts, and managers.[53] Vouchers are a form

52. The California initiative, entitled "An Initiative for Education by Choice," calls for voucher payments to parents and for the creation of a new tier of schools—public and private—that will coexist with the public and private schools already in operation.

53. Some critics of vouchers dispute the prediction that parents will be galvanized into action by the power of choice. They cite the Rand Corporation's report on an experiment with vouchers in the Alum Rock school district of San Jose, California. In this heavily Mexican-American district, parents remained passive, and lethargy was as widespread after as before the introduction of vouchers. See Daniel Weiler, *A Public School Voucher Demonstration: The First Year at Alum Rock* (Santa Monica, Cal.: Rand Corporation, 1974). But even those sympathetic with the criticism acknowledge that one year is hardly a sufficient period within which to introduce a new system—particularly in a district like Alum Rock. See D. Stern, R. H. deLone, and R. J. Murname, "Evolution at Alum Rock," *Review of Education* 1 (August 1975): 309–18.

of power, and power is the most effective catalyst citizenship can have. In any case, there seems little doubt that public schools, like the public welfare bureaucracy, are run by a routinized union of educational bureaucrats whose certification and tenure rules give them a greater interest in security and tranquility than in education; moreover, public schools are themselves little more than the compulsory private domain of those trapped in poverty.[54]

If strong democracy means autonomous activity by mobilized individuals who aspire to control their own lives and to affect the character of the communities in which they live, then a voucher system that substitutes the active will of parents for the paternalistic will of state bureaucracies is surely a reform worth considering. When the idea is coupled with the elimination of local school districts, with a clause barring add-on tuitions over and above the voucher amount (which would prevent elite schools from discriminating against those parents who offered only vouchers), with a subsidized transportation system that guarantees all children access to schools within an extended region, and with a voice for children as well as for parents in selection, it would seem to be worth adopting.

Yet the strong democrat remains ambivalent, and with excellent reason. There are great dangers in the libertarian spirit of the voucher scheme, which is inimical to the very idea of a public good and of public judgments politically generated. The voucher system would mobilize individuals, but it would mobilize them via private incentives; it speaks exclusively to their private interests as parents and thus as consumers of parental goods (such as education). The origins of the idea in laissez-faire liberalism and Friedmanite libertarianism cannot ultimately be disguised by the egalitarian and integrationist use to which reformers aspire to put it. Incentives privatize: vouchers transform what ought to be a public question ("What is a good system of public education for *our* children?") into a personal question ("What kind of school do I want for *my* children?"). It permits citizens to think of education as a matter of private preference and encourages them to dissociate the generational ties that bind them to their own children from the lateral ties that

54. "We call neighborhood schools 'public,' despite the fact that nobody outside the neighborhood can attend them, and nobody can move into the neighborhood unless he has white skin and a down-payment on a $30,000 home. And we call whole school systems 'public,' even though they refuse to give anyone information about what they are doing, how well they are doing it, and whether children are getting what their parents want" (Areen and Jencks, "Education Vouchers," p. 330).

bind them (and their children) to other parents and children. One prominent critic of vouchers thus contends that a voucher system can only damage the "overall sense of political community needed for a viable public life."[55] And even proponents of vouchers tend to call educators "managers," students and parents "clients," and education itself a "product"—a rhetoric that is harmful not only to education but to politics and the civic community.[56]

Politics suffers because the invisible hand is no substitute for public deliberation and decision either in economics or in education. What individuals choose for their children and what they choose for the community will very often differ: like free-riders everywhere, they may envision an ideal educational environment in theory that they will refuse to honor in practice. If decisions about schools are kept in the political domain, free-riders are compelled to live with their political decisions and are thus forced to bring their private views into line with their public beliefs. Vouchers do not stimulate political judgment, they bypass it, and thus contribute to its atrophy.

Vouchers also have the defect of being incompatible with the idea of the neighborhood, which is the necessary home of the civic community. Neighborhood schools are prisons from the point of view of libertarians: parents must be free, they say, to buy education from purveyors throughout an extended region.[57] The abstract market displaces the concrete neighborhood, just as the self-interested client displaces the community-minded neighbor. The neighborhood bigot trying to keep blacks from moving onto his block and into his schools at least has a concept of a neighborhood and an attachment to his neighbors by which he rationalizes his prejudice. The strong democrat would prefer to try to educate the bigot and to enlarge his notion of what a neighborhood means, instead of destroying his neighborhood and getting him to think in regional but wholly privatistic terms.

Vouchers would seem then to serve activity but to corrupt community. They mobilize individuals but only by privatizing their interests. Nonetheless, these partial virtues are not inconsiderable

---

55. F. R. Butts, "Educational Vouchers: The Public Pursuit of the Private Purse," *Phi Delta Kappa*, September 1979, pp. 7–9.

56. In a popular essay on his ideas, John Coons uses this market language with gusto: "The Public-School Monopoly," *Newsweek*, 9 June 1980.

57. Thus Christopher Jencks makes "getting rid of the neighborhood school" the linchpin of his proposal for vouchers. See "Is the Public School Obsolete?", p. 26.

when measured against the actual failure of the public school system either to provide education or to symbolize common values and
community spirit. The comparison encourages some modest experimentation with vouchers. With appropriate checks, and in the
framework of what a third-stream alternative-education pioneer
calls an "internal voucher system" (i.e., one that offers choice
among public but not private schools), a voucher plan certainly belongs on the strong democratic agenda—where it might be introduced in selected neighborhoods on an experimental basis.[58] It also
deserves more of a chance in transportation and in housing than it
has received to date.

The strong democrat cannot endorse the voucher idea with en-
thusiasm, but he may nonetheless feel persuaded to agree with a
dean of the Harvard School of Education, who has written: "Given
the condition of the schools that serve poor youngsters, it takes a
depressing amount of paranoia to suggest that we should not even
give the voucher plan a reasonable trial."[59]

INSTITUTIONALIZING STRONG DEMOCRATIC ACTION

*9. National Citizenship and Common Action: Universal Citizen Service
and Related Training and Employment Opportunities.* National service is
a vital constituent in the relationship between rights and duties under a strong democratic regime. The moral force of rights often suggests something God-given and natural, but in practice rights no
less than duties are the creation of constitutional systems and depend for their survival on a healthy citizenship. A people that will

---

58. The educator who seems most aware of the limits of vouchers, although he is
still committed to change, is Mario Fantini; see his *Alternative Education: A Sourcebook
for Parents, Teachers, Students, and Administrators* (New York: Anchor Doubleday,
1976), and his *The People and Their Schools: Community Participation* (Bloomington, Ind.:
Phi Delta Kappa Foundation, 1975). Fantini is the primary author of the "internal
voucher system."

The adaptability of the voucher scheme is not necessarily a virtue. As a critic notes,
"Since the voucher scheme is so malleable in its basic design, it is possible that the
result of adopting it, if it were fashioned by the wrong political motives, would be to
aggravate each of the problems it wants to solve" (Stephen Arons, "Equity, Option,
and Vouchers," *Teachers College Record* no. 72 [February 1971]: 361). Of course this
comment also suggests that when fashioned with the "right" political motives—say
as part of a strong democratic program—a voucher system might not only solve certain problems but also be less subject to the abuses of privatization noted in the text.

59. Theodor Sitzer, cited by Robert Lekachman in his testimony before the Select
Committee on Equal Educational Opportunity, United States Senate, 92nd Congress,
First Session, Part 22—Educational Information, 1–3 December 1971, p. 1116.

celebrate its rights but is not willing to defend them directly will soon be without a cause for celebration.

Neither a professional nor a "volunteeer" army is compatible with democratic citizenship: the former separates national defense from democratic responsibility and the latter makes service a function of economic need—in reality the poor, the undereducated, and the ill-trained volunteer, certainly not freely but because they have no alternatives.[60] Both armies are mercenary in character and contribute to the privatization of social life that has been corrosive to citizenship in other realms.[61] A professional or volunteer force can be used abroad for purposes that a conscript army might not brook (the American experience in Vietnam and the Israeli experience in Lebanon in 1982 are illustrations of conscript armies resisting unpopular wars), and it can be used domestically to subvert civilian rule and the Constitution.[62]

Some form of general national service would seem to be warranted, then, for both military and civic purposes. When the problem is reviewed in light of the strong democratic commitment to civic education, to national (as against merely local) citizenship, and to an engaged citizenry, then the argument for strong democracy

60. The military itself is split over the virtues and deficiencies of the voluntary army. But it is widely conceded that in the voluntary army the level of education is lower and the percentage of minorities higher than in the population at large. The idea of universal (or national) service has attracted increasing political support, however. In 1983 it won the support of Mayor Ed Koch of New York and of his City Planning Commission chair, Herbert Sturz. Franklin A. Thomas, president of the Ford Foundation, has also endorsed the idea. Nonetheless, these questions continue to arouse extensive public debate, to which I have contributed in several places in greater detail than I can employ here. See my "Rights without Duties," *Worldview* 23, 10 (October 1980); "A Democratic Alternative to the Draft," *Newsday*, Sunday Supplement Ideas Section, 14 September 1980; and "A Case for Universal Citizen Service," *Dissent*, Summer 1981. For an example of the debate in the popular press, see the *Time Magazine* cover story "Who'll Fight for America? The Manpower Crisis," 9 June 1980.

61. As with vouchers, reliance on pay incentives to draw "volunteers" into the military has a privatizing impact on citizenship even as it gives to military duty a mercenary air. While it may be true, as some military experts say, that higher wages are the key to a better-quality volunteer, there seems little doubt that citizenship cannot be purchased. Moreover, needy minorities with a depreciated view of what constitutes a good wage may respond to "volunteer" programs more readily than whites.

62. It is an irony of the current opposition to the draft in the name of the anti–Vietnam War movement that the original movement came about precisely because there was a draft and because the middle class found its own interests threatened by the war. An all-volunteer army would have complained far less, and the war might have lasted much longer. Similarly, a volunteer army of well-paid mercenaries or of nationalistic zealots would probably not have raised its voice against Israel's Lebanese strategy. The only assurance we can have that our army will fight only for just and civic causes is to fill it with citizens.

necessarily becomes an argument for universal citizen service. This form of service, in turn, provides a setting for the development of manpower-training programs and of government employment opportunities that further reenforce democracy.

A program of universal citizen service would enlist every American citizen—male and female alike—in a service corps for one to two years of either military or nonmilitary training and service. Service in the corps would be a concomitant of citizenship itself and would last at least twelve (perhaps up to eighteen or twenty-four) months, with the possibility of reenlistment available to those in specified training and work areas.[63] The corps would comprise five branches, including an armed-forces option. Except in time of congressionally declared wars, citizens could choose freely among the branches. In addition to the armed forces, which would continue (following an initial basic-training period shared by all service personnel) under the direct supervision of the Department of Defense, the services would include an Urban Projects Corps, a Rural Projects Corps, an International (Peace) Corps, and a Special Services Corps.

Before entering the corps of their choice (including the military), individuals would undergo a rigorous three-month training period in physical fitness, in applied skills of general utility such as mechanics, agriculture, tools, and ecology, and in civic education, including parliamentary and electoral skills, community structure and organization, some elementary social science, and perhaps American history. Final choice of a service corps specialty might be reserved until completion of the introductory training.

Initiation into the chosen corps would entail a shorter period of more specialized training related to that corps's particular projects and social tasks. Finally, groups of about a hundred corps members each would be designated as "communities," which would be divided into "community teams" of twenty-five. These teams would be deployed in appropriate urban, rural, or international settings. Their activities would focus on projects that the tax-supported structure could not itself afford and in which the private sector finds no profit. The projects would be conceived and carried out with the

63. To minimize career disruption and maximize flexibility, individuals might be permitted to choose a service period at any time between their eighteenth and twenty-fifth birthdays—before or after college, before or during their early job careers.

The question of reenlistment would have to be examined in light of the public-works and job-training programs discussed below.

cooperation and guidance of responsible local authorities: the neighborhood assembly or the host town, city, county, or nation. A special goal of corps efforts might be to repair the national infrastructure of roadways, bridges, tunnels, viaducts, sewer systems, and waterways. These systems have fallen into a state of critical disrepair over the last decades yet seem at present to be beyond the ministrations of either the public or the private sector.

Urban projects might include helping homesteaders and sweat-equity efforts, restoring parks and recreational grounds, removing graffiti, assisting shut-ins and the elderly, traffic control, day-care and remedial education, paraprofessional services, and infrastructure repairs of the kind suggested above.

Rural projects could include conservation and ecological programs, flood and water control, rural road repair and maintenance, town and village construction and restoration projects, reforestation and irrigation programs, and forest-fire control and other disaster relief.

The International Corps would be patterned after and incorporate the Peace Corps (presently under the federal government's ACTION program). It would work in close consultation with and under the supervision of the host countries and of the relevant international agencies.

The Special Services Corps would provide all branches with vital special skills (medical, communication, transportation, housing, construction, training, and administration). It would also act as a secretariat for the Citizen Corps, with responsibility for introductory training and education, organizational structure, project planning, Pentagon liaison, budgeting and accounting, and corps deployment.

Universal citizen service would answer a number of problems that plague the current programs of military conscription, manpower-training, and public works. It would enable women to serve equally with men, without forcing them directly into military duty (although the military would remain an option for them). It would distribute the burden of responsibility for service equally over all citizens and thereby help to overcome divisions of class, wealth, and race. Critics of peacetime conscription would be mollified while alienated liberals would be given a chance to put their principles into practice. At the same time, the military would have the chance to build an army that was more efficient and more democratic. Universal citizen service could not guarantee the Pentagon a force that met the standards set in straightforward military conscription, but it would be an improvement over the volunteer army while preserving choice for all citizens—particularly for those prepared to serve but reluctant to soldier in peacetime. The recruits whom the army did draw would have already undergone useful introductory training, and they would be young men and women attracted to military service rather than those fleeing from hopeless civilian lives. Given the obligation to serve in one of the corps, and the size of the annual pool (about four million women and men), considerable numbers of able, educated Americans could be expected to select the military option. If necessary, a somewhat shorter military service period or other incentives could be experimented with.

The greatest advantages of universal citizen service would be civic, however. It could offer many of the undisputed virtues of military service: fellowship and camaraderie, common activity, teamwork, service for and with others, and a sense of community. Yet in place of military hierarchy, it could offer equality; in place of obedience, cooperation; and in place of us/them conflict of the kind generated by parochial participation, a sense of mutuality and national interdependence.

Almost all of the proposals examined in this chapter focus on local citizenship and therefore have the defects of parochialism. Universal citizen service thus becomes a crucial instrument of national citizenship and the instrument of choice for opening up neighborhoods and overcoming localism.

Citizen service could also play a role in public efforts to deal with the economy under strong democracy. Although Roosevelt's TVA, his Civilian Conservation Corps, and the Works Projects Administration were models of both democracy and economic efficiency, and although the federal government has taken a certain responsibility for job training and public employment since the Manpower Training Act of 1963 helped to usher in the Great Society, there has been no single governmental source of training and jobs. Because citizen service incorporates elements of job training and public-works programs, it would help to legitimize the idea of "public goods" such as the nation's infrastructure and would offer a way to involve government in the economy without directly challenging the role of the private sector. Citizens serving their country become a true "public." Public works take on a new meaning when they are the province of a genuine public. The disintegrating infrastructure has had no constituency up until now, which may be why neither private interests nor governmental authorities have taken steps to repair it. A universal citizen service would be in a position to treat with such a problem, and it would become a model of government activity that could encourage further public engagement in the economic realm, beyond the resources and scope of the corps. Youth unemployment—perhaps the severest problem in the American economy—would be mitigated directly by service in the corps, and the training the young people received would improve their chances at private sector jobs. A healthy civic community contributes to, if it does not guarantee, a healthy economy.

10. *Neighborhood Citizenship and Common Action: Local Options.* Political participation in common action is more easily achieved at the neighborhood level, where there is a variety of opportunities for engagement. We have already noted under the section on decision-making institutions the potential role that selection by lot could play in bringing citizens more directly into the governing process. The several federal volunteer programs originally conceived as part of President Johnson's Great Society and in 1971 (under President Nixon) combined under a single agency (ACTION) continue to operate in neighborhoods throughout America.[64] They stand as a model for local self-help and self-rule programs. Foster Grandparents, Retired Senior Volunteers, Senior Companions, and VISTA (Volunteers In Service To America) are the best known among these programs, which have survived several changes of party, administration, and political philosophy in Washington (although it is not clear that they will survive the Reagan era).

A strong democratic program would encourage ACTION to develop and nurture a variety of other local programs. Several promising programs are already in place in certain localities. For example, retired persons and shut-ins act as "blockwatchers" in crime-watch organizations, a task that gives the elderly a civic role and improves neighborhood security at the same time.[65] Sweat-equity programs

64. ACTION agencies were particularly active in the Carter years, when Sam Brown was ACTION director. A clear picture of the content and the spirit of its programs can be gleaned from its annual reports, available from the Government Printing Office.

65. As with a number of the other proposals offered here, crime-watch and blockwatcher organizations already exist in a great number of cities and have demonstrated their worth both to community safety and security and to the civic health of those who participate.

enable tenants of deteriorating buildings that the proprietors have abandoned to take over ownership of their apartments in return for the labor they expend in improving them and bringing them back on the tax rolls.[66] Urban parks and farms have been developed in unused lots or parks that have fallen into desuetude.[67] Cleaning up and developing unused space improves the character and physical definition of a neighborhood and brings neighbors who might otherwise remain apathetic into activities that have a local payoff. Local security operations can help to unite a neighborhood when they are guided by local police and prevented from slipping into vigilantism.[68]

These options are, however, all voluntary in nature, and they share the defects of volunteerism in general: they encourage self-interestedness and place barriers between neighborhoods even as they unite blocks internally.[69] The more challenging project is to find ways for citizens to participate in the execution of common decisions taken by neighborhood assemblies or local governments. Responsibility for the realization of goals decided upon in common both disciplines the decision process and gives spirited confirmation to political judgment. Sweat-equity projects pursued in isolation serve the community less than do projects in which the entire community takes some part—even if only on a nominal basis. Crime-watch programs coordinated by public officials and participated in by every citizen in the relevant class (e.g., shut-ins or the retired) are more likely to foster public-spiritedness than is the zealotry of a few individuals who have been touched personally by crime.

66. Extensive programs of sweat equity can be found in the Northeast—in Washington, Baltimore, Philadelphia, and New York, for example. The Manhattan Valley program on New York's Upper West Side is a typical example: it has sponsored tenant takeover and rehabilitation of a number of brownstones in the area.

67. Cornell University sponsored an urban farm program for several years in the 1970s as part of its experimentation with urban soil, plant pollution, and related horticultural themes. But the communities that benefited from Cornell's project found the civic benefits far greater than the agricultural benefits.

68. The Guardian Angels, a New York citizen crime-patrol group made up primarily of ghetto youths under the leadership of Curtis Sliwa, has spread across the country. New York officials acknowledge that the group has deterred crime, and they are now working with Sliwa on training and liaison. The line between civic action and vigilantism is a slender one, but it seems foolhardy to resist the public-spirited impulse to serve of some of society's least-advantaged young people. Their commitment is further evidence of Titmuss's case for the will to give and for this book's insistence on the need to serve.

69. The Reagan administration has encouraged volunteerism as part of its program to disengage government from civic life. But of course it is *public* volunteer activity that is valuable to democracy, not private volunteer activity, which gives privatization still one more boost.

Ultimately it is neither volunteerism—with its concomitant privatism and its neglect of the apathetic, the victimized, and the self-preoccupied—nor civic compulsion—with its reliance on sanctions and its conflation of citizenship and pure duty—that serves democracy. Citizenship will remain voluntary, for it is as much a right as a duty, and to coerce it is to destroy it. This means that local programs of common action will have to develop alongside of a generalized spirit of civic responsibility.

11. Democracy in the Workplace. Our fundamental argument for strong democracy places politics before economics and suggests that only through civic revitalization can we hope, eventually, for greater economic democracy. Nonetheless, there are a great number of proposals for democratization of the workplace that are in tune with strong democracy. The possibility of using government-sponsored projects as models of humane management and egalitarianism has been underexplored, despite the stunning success of certain experiments—among which the Tennessee Valley Authority is perhaps best known. Government economic activity, when it competes with rather than replaces activity in the private sector, will seem less intrusive and so more likely to succeed in altering economic attitudes.

Similarly, worker-owned operations on the model of the cooperative movement do more for citizenship than does the regulation of industry, however necessary such regulation may be. The sharing of decision-making by workers and management, experiments on the German model in codetermination (*Mitbestimmung*), profit-sharing schemes, and stock-ownership options all not only serve economic egalitarianism but foster civic spirit. The elaboration of these options can best be left to those who have been advocating them for a number of years in such journals as *Working Papers*, *Dissent*, and *Democracy*, but they clearly would occupy an important place in the strong democratic program.[70]

12. Recreating the Neighborhood as a Physical Public Space. A number of recent students of community, architecture, and physical space, from Paul Goodman to Jane Jacobs, have been able to show us how

70. The best survey of experiments in alternative economic forms is Martin Carnoy and Derek Shearer, *Economic Democracy: The Challenge of the 1980's* (Armonk, N.Y.: Sharpe, 1980). The National Conference on Alternative State and Local Policy publishes a newsletter, develops model legislation, and sponsors gatherings on economic alternatives.

intimate the linkage is between the physical design of neighborhoods and their political and social character.[71] Among these, Oscar
Newman has become particularly well known for his attempts to
improve crime prevention through urban design. But his idea of
"defensible space" is hostile to the idea of an expanding circle of
neighborhoods, participation in the core of which leads on to participation on the moving peripheries.[72]

A strong democratic program requires an architecture and design
that can respond to the demands of talk and give to citizenship a
physical habitation. Civic arenas should also be places of pleasure
and camaraderie—of discourse and activity as well as of hard-
headed decision-making. Neighborhood assemblies need homes
that will support their mission of bringing strangers together and of
recreating them as neighbors. Neighborhood must be divided from
neighborhood so that each has its own identity, and yet each should
open up to the other; thus parochialism would be given no reenforcing physical momentum. High-rise apartment buildings with built-
in shopping malls, suburban shopping plazas, and transportation
corridors constructed solely for automobiles have a devastating effect on community and underscore the privatism of our social lives.
We have learned from Jane Jacobs not only that traditional neighborhoods were safer but that they were far more social, conversa-
tional, and thus public in character (compare Hester Street in 1910
to a shopping mall in 1980). The neighborhood school may harbor
racism and be a monument to parochialism—which is why voucher
advocates oppose it—but it also endows a community with a heart
and gives youngsters their first inkling of what it means to be a
neighbor and a citizen.

The strong democratic community will have to find new forms of
physical dwelling if it is to thrive in large cities or suburban landscapes, and to do this it will need architects who share the democratic vision.

71. See Jane Jacobs, *The Death and Life of American Cities* (New York: Random
House, 1965); Paul Goodman and Percival Goodman, *Communitas: Means of Livelihood
and Ways of Life*, rev. ed. (New York: Random House, 1960).

72. Oscar Newman, *Defensible Space: Crime Prevention through Urban Design* (New
York: Macmillan, 1972). Newman's basic solution to the deterioration of public space
is to recreate it as private space and thus to enlist private-interest incentives in the
war on urban breakdown. But as with vouchers and volunteerism, the solution
solves the problem only by reenforcing its root cause: privatism. For a discussion of
Newman's recent work, see "Planner Urges a New Community Concept," *The New
York Times*, Sunday edition, Real Estate Section, 1 June 1980.

The strong democratic agenda is then an extended and varied one. It does not depend on any single reform, but it does require a critical mass if its impact is to be noticeable and if its innovations are not to be swallowed up by the thin democratic system already in place. It might therefore be useful here to recapitulate the program in the form of a unified agenda. That agenda would read:

A STRONG DEMOCRATIC PROGRAM
FOR THE REVITALIZATION OF CITIZENSHIP:

1. A national system of NEIGHBORHOOD ASSEMBLIES of from one to five thousand citizens; these would initially have only deliberative functions but would eventually have local legislative competence as well.

2. A national CIVIC COMMUNICATIONS COOPERATIVE to regulate and oversee the civic use of new telecommunications technology and to supervise debate and discussion of referendum issues.

3. A CIVIC VIDEOTEX SERVICE and a CIVIC EDUCATION POSTAL ACT to equalize access to information and promote the full civic education of all citizens.

4. Experiments in DECRIMINALIZATION and INFORMAL LAY JUSTICE by an engaged local citizenry.

5. A national INITIATIVE AND REFERENDUM PROCESS permitting popular initiatives and referenda on congressional legislation, with a multichoice format and a two-stage voting plan.

6. Experimental ELECTRONIC BALLOTING, initially for educational and polling purposes only, under the supervision of the Civic Communications Cooperative.

7. Selective local elections to local office by LOTTERY, with pay incentives.

8. Experiments with an INTERNAL VOUCHER SYSTEM for selected schools, public housing projects, and transportation systems.

9. A program of UNIVERSAL CITIZEN SERVICE, including a military-service option for all citizens.

10. Public sponsorship of LOCAL VOLUNTEER PROGRAMS in "common work" and "common action."

11. Public support of experiments in WORKPLACE DEMOCRACY, with public institutions as models for economic alternatives.

12. A new ARCHITECTURE OF CIVIC AND PUBLIC SPACE.

This program does not illustrate strong democracy; it *is* strong democracy. Implemented, it will give to the theory developed above the life and breath of a genuine practice.

INSTITUTIONALIZING REGRET

Even the most sympathetic reader may scan this panoply of novel institutions and procedural innovations and conclude that proposals so varied, novel, and uncertain pose too many risks. More democracy, even if achieved, will surely mean more legislation, more interference, more encroachment, and thus less liberty. A more competent citizenry may feel impelled to do more and so grow in time to be less tolerant of resistance to its wisdom and of deviation from its common judgments. Democratic tinkerers may start by making minor changes and end by scrapping the Constitution. Such a reader, like so many democratic liberals, will finally come to see Burke as the ally of Locke—to think it more prudent to keep what we have, however incomplete it is, than to gamble it away for what we might have, however attractive.

The uncertainty of all knowledge and the foibles of women and men—which may but do not necessarily lessen with their transformation into citizens—impose on the strong democrat a responsibility to institutionalize regret: to build into his reforms limits on the will to change and to build into mechanisms of public choice limits on all political will.

One tactical choice that conditions all the reforms offered here is the favoring of complementary over substitute institutions. We might more quickly realize the strong democratic program by first removing certain liberal obstacles; representation, the party system, single-member legislative districts, and the separation of powers come immediately to mind. But the prudent democrat reforms by adding participatory ingredients to the constitutional formula, not by removing representative ingredients. The objective is to reorient liberal democracy toward civic engagement and political community, not to raze it—destroying its virtues along with its defects. To call for the abolition of parties is to call for utopia. To call for a constitutional convention is to invite disaster. The American system (like entrenched democratic constitutions everywhere) survives by evolving and evolves by accreting new institutional layers that conform to the contours of a historically tested practice even as they alter the system's dimensions and center of gravity.

The best check that strong democracy has is the inertial force of the American Constitution. Federalism divides power vertically while the separation of powers and the independent judiciary divide it horizontally, and no popular will—however successful the magic of strong democratic community—is likely to fall prey to unitary totalism as long as these checks are in place. Indeed, we have noticed with sorrow that strong democracy is itself divided from within: its tendency to local participation engenders parochialism and a spirit of partisan localism even as its consensus-seeking procedures engender a will to commonality and a disposition to use power in the name of public goods. The strong democrat who says, "Let us experiment with neighborhood assemblies, with an initiative and referendum process, with television debates, with citizen service, with local participation in neighborhood common work, and with national participation in legislative decision-making," speaks a language liberal democrats can respect even when they disagree with its recommendations. The strong democrat who says, "Let us tear down our oligarchic representative institutions and shove aside the plodding constitutional safeguards that mire the sovereign people in a swamp of checks and balances from which no common action can ever emerge," subverts his democratic faith in the rush to achieve his democratic goals. He is not to be trusted. Strong democracy is a complementary strategy that adds without removing and that reorients without distorting. There is no other way.

In order that the commitment to limits be more than a matter of good faith, however, strong democratic institutions should themselves be equipped with fail-safe checks and self-regulating balances that do not depend on the intentions of an engaged citizenry. In fact, the proposals introduced earlier are surrounded by checks designed to curb the potential for excess of zealous communities in possession of what they take to be a collective vision. From a purely practical political viewpoint, the checks on the referendum process are paramount. The requirement for two readings, the possibility of a congressional veto, and the commitment to full and informed debate on a network supervised by a Civic Communications Cooperative all hem in possibly impulsive publics with obstacles and put a premium on prudent and carefully thought-out legislation.

Our discussion of listening in Chapter 8, and the role assigned neighborhood assemblies and the assembly facilitators, suggest an approach to public discourse that if it does not embody an actual *veto liberum* on legislation, does give special weight to minority expressions of dissent and indignation. Majorities ride roughshod over dissenters in their pursuit of majority interests—which turn out to be private interests that have a numerically large following. Civic communities act with the greatest caution in the face of dissent because dissent is a signal that community itself may be in jeopardy, while the presence of majorities and minorities is a symbol of the disintegration of community altogether. In this spirit, neighborhood assemblies might want to experiment with requiring near-unanimous consensus in matters of local jurisdiction, and even the national referendum process could recognize the right of a large, intense minority, defeated in a second reading, to call for one final (third) reading of a major legislative initiative.

An office that has played only a small role in America, where the adversary system and the constitutional guarantees of rights perhaps obviate the need for it, is the ombudsman. Perhaps, however, if our system were reoriented toward greater participation, if citizens were to gain more legislative power and thus to require fewer rights, then "the availability of channels through which Americans can express their frustrations with public bureaucracies and seek redress of grievances" would have a crucial restraining role to play.[73] Dissenters, forced to live with new consensual communities whose will is all the more irresistible because it is more legitimate, could find in a neighborhood ombudsman a consolation to their integrity if not a support for their dissent. To some extent the facilitators would play this part, but their loyalty would be to the community of citizens rather than to individual citizens. It would pay tribute to the mutual respect of citizens to create a public officer whose single duty would be to serve those aggrieved by the community, even when— especially when—it acts legitimately in the full grandeur of its communal responsibility for public goods. We permit and encourage public defenders because we believe that those accused of the more dastardly felonies are innocent until proven otherwise. Surely we can afford to encourage ombudsmen because we believe that the outtalked or outvoted are innocent of immorality or wrong-headedness despite their dissent.

Above all, strong democracy needs to advance its program in a temperate spirit. If final solutions could be discerned, what need would we have to deliberate and debate or to rely on the artifice of a changing public will? If truth is the object, philosophers will do for kings. But democracy begins where truth and certitude and final solutions disappear into the murky uncertainties of the human con-

73. Alan J. Wyner, ed., *Executive Ombudsmen in the United States* (Berkeley: Institute of Governmental Studies, 1973), p. 3. For a full discussion of the experience with and promise of the ombudsman office in America, see Stanley V. Anderson, *Ombudsman Papers: American Experience and Proposals* (Berkeley: Institute of Governmental Studies, 1969).

dition, and its temper is thus necessarily judicious. Plato was right in insisting on the need for temperateness and moderation in a well-governed people, but he was wrong in thinking that moderation takes the form of deference to truth or to its putative proprietors. It is the self-governing people who most need moderation, for they have nothing but moderation to remind them of the weakness and infirmities on which their self-government relies, and by which it is justified.

The case for democracy has two advocates: one speaks from human weakness and, pointing to the sand on which every claim to knowledge finally must rest, says with regret, "We must govern ourselves together; there is no one else who can govern for us." It is that voice to which the call for limits responds.

But there is another, more affirmative advocate—one who perceives in speech itself, in the Greek faculty of reason called *logos*, the distinctive feature that sets humankind off from the animal kingdom and bestows the twin gifts of self-consciousness and other-consciousness. To this advocate the right of every individual to speak to others, to assert his being through the act of communication, is identified with the precious wellspring of human autonomy and dignity. Thus it was that in Greece *Isegoria*—the universal right to speak in the assembly—came to be a synonym not merely for democratic participation but for democracy itself. Thus it is that democracy, if it is to survive the shrinking of the world and the assaults of a hostile modernity, will have to rediscover its multiple voices and give to citizens once again the power to speak, to decide, and to act; for in the end human freedom will be found not in caverns of private solitude but in the noisy assemblies where women and men meet daily as citizens and discover in each other's talk the consolation of a common humanity.

Index

Bill of Rights, 158, 160, 234
Black, Duncan, 204, 204n
Bosanquet, Bernard, freedom defined
    by, 35n
Boyte, Harry C., 265n
Brecht, Bertolt, 238; and necessity, 125
Buchanan, James, 204, 224, 231
Burke, Edmund, 12, 194; against ab-
    straction, 130–31; against rational phi-
    losophy, 22–23; on deduction, 31–32;
    localism and scale in, 248–49; on meta-
    physical madness, 165; on reduction-
    ism, 32n
Busing, 157, 196; and justice, 146n

Cable Communications Act, 276
Caesar, Julius, 241
Capitalism, 251–57
Carlyle, Thomas, 7
Carter, James, national town meeting
    under, 274
Cartesianism, reductionism as, 51–57
Cassirer, Ernst, 83
Castille, Hippolyte, as unitary demo-
    crat, 149
Categorical Imperative, 201
Citizen service (military conscription),
    in strong democracy, 298–303
Citizenship, 127; Aryan, 226; bounda-
    ries of, 225–29; and education, 270;
    forms of, 219 (figure 3); grounds of,
    218–20; under strong democracy, 153–
    55
Civic bond, 220
Civic Communication Cooperative, de-
    fined, 277–78
Civic education, 270; as condition of citi-
    zenship, 233–37; in referendum pro-
    cess, 285–86
Civic Education Postal Act, 279
Civility, and citizenship, 223
Civil religion, 243
Choice: as a formal condition of politics,
    126; in strong democracy, 134
Churchill, Winston, 4, 238, 241; on de-
    mocracy, 21
Clarion, of Great Britain, 257
Cleasthenes, in Hume's *Dialogues Con-
    cerning Natural Religion*, 164
Clemenceau, Georges, 87
"Climate of opinion," Carl Becker on,
    28n
Codetermination (*Mitbestimmung*), 305
Commensurability, corollary of, de-
    fined, 33
Common Cause, 63, 243
Common Consciousness, in T. H.
    Green, 173

Commoner, Barry, 13
Common work, 209
"Communicative rationality," in works
    of J. Habermas, 130
Communitarian, 120; activities, 243–44
Community: Aryan, 221; as an instru-
    mental good, 7–8; strong democratic,
    229–37
Community Action Organization, 264n
Conflict: as condition of politics, 5–6; as
    a formal condition of politics, 128; in
    strong democracy, 135; transforming,
    151
Connally, William, 147n
Conrad, Joseph, 103
Conscription, military. *See* Citizen
    service
Consensus, 128–29; in strong democ-
    racy, 149; varieties of, 224
Consent, 137
Consequentialism, 124–25
Conservatism, 248
Considérant, Victor, 146n
Consociationism, 199n
Constantinople, 165
Constituent, as citizen, 221
Consumer, as model of liberal individ-
    ual, 22
Contextualism, 195
Conversation, and politics, 183–85
Coons, John E., 294
Corporation, and democracy, 256n. *See
    also* Multinational corporation
Crime-watch, 303–4

Dahl, Robert, 7, 143, 144n, 207n
Debs, Eugene, against leadership, 242
Decentralization, 268–69, 268n
Decision-making, 198; under strong de-
    mocracy, 198–203
Declaration of Independence, 7; as ex-
    ample of individualism, 38
Decriminalization, and informal justice,
    280–81, 280n
Deduction, 29
"Defensible space," 306n
DeGaulle, Charles, 191
Democracy: adversary, in works of J. J.
    Mansbridge, 96n; authoritative, de-
    fined, 140–42; defects of, 24–25; dis-
    temper of, 93–94; juridical, defined,
    142; juridical, T. Lowi on, 142n; liberal
    critique of, defects in the, 95–97; plu-
    ralist, defined, 143; strong, defined
    formally, 131–32, 151; strong, defined
    generally, 117–20; "thin" theory of, 4;
    "thin" theory of as pathological, 93–